IRELAND & THE ENGLISH CRISIS

Also by Tom Paulin

Thomas Hardy: the Poetry of Perception (Macmillan, 1975)
A State of Justice (Faber, 1977)
The Strange Museum (Faber, 1980)
The Book of Juniper [with Noel Connor] (Bloodaxe Books, 1981)
Liberty Tree (Faber, 1983)

IRELAND
& THE ENGLISH
CRISIS

TOM PAULIN

BLOODAXE BOOKS

ISBN: 0 906427 63 0 hardback
       0 906427 64 9 paperback

First published 1984 by
Bloodaxe Books Ltd,
P.O. Box 1SN,
Newcastle upon Tyne NE99 1SN.

Bloodaxe Books Ltd acknowledges the financial assistance
of the Arts Council of Northern Ireland in the publication
of this volume.

Bloodaxe Books Ltd also acknowledges
the financial assistance of Northern Arts.

Typesetting by
Tyneside Free Press Workshop Ltd, Newcastle upon Tyne.

Printed in Great Britain by
Unwin Brothers Ltd, Old Woking, Surrey.

*For Brian Friel and Stephen Rea,
founders of Field Day.*

Contents

Acknowledgements

Acknowledgements are due to the editors of the following publications in which some of these essays first appeared:

ENCOUNTER: 'The Cruelty That Is Natural' (January 1979); 'The French Are on the Sea' (January 1980); 'National Myths' (June 1980).

THE HONEST ULSTERMAN: 'A Terminal Ironist' (June 1980); 'Nineteen Twelve' (June/October 1981).

LONDON REVIEW OF BOOKS: 'Britishmen' (5-18 November 1981); 'Paisley's Progress' (1-14 April 1982); 'English Now' (17-30 June 1982); 'A New England' (3-16 March 1983); 'The Aesthetic Fenian: Oscar Wilde' (17-30 November 1983); 'In the Beginning Was the Aeneid: On Translation' (17 May-6 June 1984).

NEW STATESMAN: 'A Professional Irishman' (12 August 1977); 'Those Foul Ulster Tories' (3 July 1981); 'The Earnest Puppet: Edward Carson' (30 October 1981); 'James Joyce: A Centenary Celebration' (5 February 1982); 'The Disloyalist' (12 February 1982).

OBSERVER: 'Shadow of the Gunmen' (10 June 1984).

POETRY REVIEW: 'The Man from No Part: Louis MacNeice' (March 1980).

QUARTO: 'In Golden Mentmore: Henry James' (March 1980); 'The Writer Underground' (September 1980).

SEWANEE REVIEW: 'Disaffection and Defection: W.H. Auden' (Winter 1982).

SUNDAY TIMES: 'Life Sculpture: Patrick Kavanagh' (10 February 1980); 'For the Ancient Britons: Edward Thomas' (13 September 1981).

TIMES LITERARY SUPPLEMENT: 'In the Salt Mines' (16 May 1980); 'The Making of a Loyalist' (14 November 1980); 'Formal Pleasure: The Short Story (24 April 1981).

The essay 'Nineteen Twelve' was originally a BBC Radio 3 talk entitled 'The Red Hand of Ulster'; 'Lawrence after Fifty Years' was an anniversary lecture commissioned by Nottingham Central Library; 'Paisley's Progress', originally a paper entitled 'Imagining History: Ian Paisley and the Historians', was presented to the third conference of Irish historians in Britain.

'A New Look at the Language Question' appeared in 1983 with Seamus Heaney's 'An Open Letter' and Seamus Deane's 'Civilians and Barbarians' in the first series of Field Day pamphlets.

The poem 'House on a Cliff' and extracts from other poems from *The Collected Poems of Louis MacNeice* are reprinted by permission of Faber and Faber Ltd; extracts from Derek Mahon's *Poems 1962-1978* are reprinted by permission of Oxford University Press.

Inevitably, some changes have been made to the original texts—dropping nonce place-name derivations, for example. I am variously and deeply grateful to the literary editors who commissioned me to write for them. Their encouragement and ruthless editing have helped me to appreciate just how completely the letter giveth life.

T.P.

Introduction

'Nothing happens, nobody comes, nobody goes, it's awful!'

Anyone who writes to the moment must be deaf to Estragon's exclamation. As he waits for Godot's non-arrival, Estragon's quietism offers a passive challenge to the puritan journalist's view that history is spirit and reality a seethe of ideas and opinions, always forming, always in process. Beckett's displaced voices contradict the Whig idea of history and the concept of progress it shares with Marxism. With the prophets of deindustrialisation and permanently high unemployment, Estragon is saying 'forget the work ethic, forget the future, there is no point in saying anything'. He is telling the critic to lay by his forceps.

All literary criticism is a form of journalism, though at present many "professional" critics and theorists regard literary journalists and most other critics as merely amateurish devotees of *belles lettres*. The long-standing hostility between Grub Street and the Academy has given way to an argument between a loose coalition composed of writers, scholars, journalists and traditional literary critics, and a party of theoretical critics and semiotic pedagogues whose manifesto is a book of essays called *Re-Reading English*. Literary works continue to be reviewed in newspapers and magazines, but elsewhere—in certain journals, students' handbooks, seminars—literary criticism has become either Theory or a form of anti-Art which believes itself superior to what was once accepted as Art. Put simply, the Reader has taken power and liquidated the Author. Or as a teacher of English states: 'What is most exciting about Barthes is the feeling of power he gives to the reader. Criticism has become a creative activity.'* In truth, criticism has always been one of the fine arts, as Oscar Wilde argued long ago in *The Critic As Artist*.

Sadly, there is nothing Wildean about the contemporary creative reader. S/he is a kind of freewheeling nihilist with a

*Richard Exton, 'The Post-Structuralist Always Reads Twice', in the *English Magazine*, 10 (Autumn 1982). This magazine is published by the ILEA English Centre and shows how influential current literary theory is in the classroom.

taste for sociology and anthropology and a disquieting resemblance to a character from a Glen Baxter cartoon. This new reader represents a recent attitude of mind which aspires to the condition of Beckett's drama or of Tadeusz Różewicz's poetry. But such an attitude ignores the historical reality which Beckett and Różewicz are reflecting and accepts itself, comfortably, as a symptom of extreme leisure or advanced boredom. The creative reader tends in the United States to be an academic Undershaft who writes essays with subtitles like 'Towards a Generative Typology of the Text', and sometimes that reader writes like this:

> It would hardly be an exaggeration to say that the line unit's segmentation of syntagmaticity in poetry cuts across the signifier continuum so as to achieve an interpenetration of sense between signifiers in different lines, whereas narrative discourse's "spread-eagling" of paradigmaticity reinforces the signifier continuum so strongly as to allow linkups even at a distance, and this favors the production of a sustained differentiation and evolution of sense between signifiers in different word sequences.*

At international conferences papers are offered on 'Barbara Johnson's reading of Derrida's reading of Lacan's reading of Poe's *The Purloined Letter*'. Poor Poe, crushed underfoot by his sophisticated readership.

In England, this novel jargon is often bound in with a debased form of Marxist literary criticism and with that belief in creative expression which developed during the 1960s. There is now a generation of teachers and critics who believe that literary culture is no more than élitist bullshit. Confronted with pupils who have been encouraged to reject a knowledge of history, these teachers believe that the best method of educating a "post-literate generation" is to make English into the softest of soft subjects. After English Studies, after American Studies, there are Communications Studies, Contemporary Cultural Studies and other forms of facile sociology.

Colin McCabe has accurately described the problem:

> Literature is now taught in the universities to students who have read almost none of the English classics, who have none of the grounding in prosody, grammar or classical themes which the courses assume, and whose own major aesthetic experiences remain unacknowledged. The situation would be tragic if it were

New Literary History, 1982-83.

only the pupils who were thus unfitted to the courses they take. When one adds a substantial proportion of the teachers the whole affair becomes ludicrous.

Unfortunately, McCabe's answer to the problem is not to draw up courses which insist on reading classical texts and on learning prosody and grammar. Instead he wants to:

> break open the very category of literature—allowing in forms of writing such as science fiction and the thriller in which many of the most exciting experiments in language and narration now take place. The first necessity for any course in English literature is to come to terms with that fragmentation of tradition and language which T.S. Eliot did so much both to recognise and oppose, nailing us all to the cross of his own cruel fiction.

Although Eliot's *Notes Towards the Definition of Culture* needs to be recognised as an elegantly reactionary challenge to the current of opinion which led to Butler's 1944 Education Act,* it is both damaging and irresponsible to concede Eliot's arguments against democratic education by adopting an alternative form of populism to that of the *Daily Express.*

Like many of his party, McCabe seems to harbour guilt-feelings about being English and middle-class:

> It is only when we come to read the broken English of the twentieth century in the tongues of many races that we can then come to terms with the more measured tones of our imperialist ancestors. †

On the one hand, McCabe acknowledges the existence of a multi-racial society; on the other, his use of 'our' excludes everyone who has colonised ancestors, rather than 'imperialist' ones. In a reflex and unthinking manner, he appears to identify himself with a thin white band of pith helmets and ruling accents—those 'more measured tones' with which 'we' must come to terms. There is in his analysis an agonized or embarrassed sense of superiority which is deeply condescending.

Although McCabe appears to hold anti-establishment views, and although he is attractively concerned to expiate

---

*See chapter VI, 'Notes on Education and Culture'. In the preface to the 1962 edition Eliot says that his 'Notes' began to take shape towards the end of the Second World War.

† 'The Sunset of the English Empire', *Guardian*, 28 January 1983.

some form of post-imperial guilt, his exclusive use of 'we' is curiously old-fashioned and nationalistic. Certain ancestral voices muddle his argument and prevent him from recognising the educational needs of minorities within a pluralistic society. Anyone whose first language is not English needs to be given access to the forms and coherent shapes of the language and the culture. This need not, and should not, involve a repudiation of the student's first language or dialect. Tragically, many English teachers are now so dedicated to superficial notions of creativity—and so hostile to ideas of linguistic correctness—that they put both their native working-class and their non-English pupils at an even greater social disadvantage. By insisting on a formless creativity, a naive antinomianism, they hand over powerful arguments to those influential reactionaries who are opposed to comprehensive education and in favour of refloating Victorian Britain.

While McCabe and his followers are making a confused adjustment to the waning of imperial power, there are others who wish to revive a Victorian concept of national destiny. This wish finds its most rabid expression in the *Salisbury Review*, a conservative "intellectual" quarterly which has a limited but influential circulation. A recent issue contained this prefatory survey of its contents:

> As Sisson demonstrates, the search for a national Church need not constitute a falling away from the Church's universal meaning. It may be part of the attempt to build in history, the enduring edifice which is the visible reminder of eternal truths. The Christian belief in the Incarnation is already a recognition that the universality of the Church may, without detriment to its mission, be localised in events and sympathies that are not detachable from history. And history is undoubtedly the history of nations. At the same time, national consciousness, while bound by the circumstances of those who possess it, contains, as Clive Ashworth argues, a transcendent dimension, a reaching out towards the mystical and the timeless.
>
> National consciousness provides, therefore, one of the strongest experiences of the immanence of God. Our nation was outraged by the ludicrous service held to commemorate the victory in the Falklands. This outrage stemmed, not from war-mongering sentiments or vain triumphalism, but from the sense that a religious experience had been denied its true expression. We were being asked to come before God denuded of those very feelings which made worship necessary. Life which willingly sacrifices itself for

the sake of country inspires awe and admiration. It also presents the most vivid human example of the sacred, of the temporal order overcome by a transcendent meaning. The nation may not be a necessary idea: but it is undeniably a beneficial idea for it enables us to enact, in time, the eternal destiny of man. And it is this destiny which justifies Europe's struggle to survive.*

This fatuously exclusive statement was penned by a professed atheist, and it shows with what cynical firmness the present generation of conservative intellectuals believes in the social utility of religion. Like the ideologues of the old Provisional IRA, these thinkers have a cyclopean vision of an island inhabited entirely by people of the same religious creed and ethnic origins.

The war in the South Atlantic caused a renewal of national consciousness in England and at the end of 1982 the *Daily Express* cheered its readers with this facetious version of the *Salisbury Review*'s message:

England expects!

What have our sailors, soldiers and airmen been up to now. The latest news is that there is a boom in babies among wives of the men who served in the Falklands. It has been said by many economists and specialists in these matters that a boom in babies is an index of national prosperity. Indeed, the boom in babies was a mark of the western world's economic success.

It is now clear that the Services, having commanded so admirably the battle for the Falklands, were doing their bit at home as well. It now falls to the rest of us to do our bit also. The year 1982 has been in some ways dark as well as triumphant for Britain. Among the good things is the boom in post-Falklands babies.

Perhaps 1983 will see a boom for Britain. In that case the Services will have shown us all the way.

In England, now, the argument would appear to be polarised between those who still thrill to Nelson's words and those who wish to see a country which is fully multi-racial, nuclear-free and more socially just. Those English people who wish to forget Nelson's words imagine a country which is close to the mystical idea of Albion. It does not rule over Scotland, Wales and Northern Ireland, and although it rejects the EEC—wrongly, in my

*'Peace on Earth', *Salisbury Review* (Winter 1983). This unsigned article was written by Roger Scruton. The *Salisbury Review* has strong connections with the Anglican nationalism of *Poetry Nation Review*.

view—it has drawn closer to Europe by modelling itself on Holland and Sweden. Like the new Tory definition of the nation, this peaceable concept may never gain power; indeed, it is the very idealistic gentleness of its adherents which may leave the Labour Party stranded in permanent opposition. Although English deconstructionism appears to issue in part from a healthy desire to overthrow the assumptions which underlie Geoffrey Thurley's "traditionalist" and unexamined remark that literary criticism is 'important in our kind of society',* its ironies and subversions are often gracelessly simple-minded. Thus the naive deconstructionist argues like this:

If you believe that some works of art are better than others, then you must condone social inequality. This is because aesthetic judgments assume a hierarchy of values and therefore anyone who makes a value judgment is consciously or unconsciously upholding an unjust social hierarchy. Come to think of it, isn't that phrase "work of art" really a mystical term shot through with bourgeois value judgments? Better replace it with a neutral and descriptive term like "cultural artefact". The way is then clear for a systematic and committed "egalitarian" form of criticism.

This brand of criticism—strong on issues and weak on the formal properties of texts—is now being purveyed in many educational institutions (at Lewes Technical College, for example, some teachers insist that *Crossroads* is 'part of modern literature'). Elsewhere academics remark that 'quite a large number of students now prefer *Dallas* to *Daniel Deronda*' and the consensus seems to be that this democratic preference ought to be respected and catered for.

Although the debate about what constitutes the "canon" of English literature challenges the view that art is sacred and supranational, the argument's more extreme lunacies sometimes remind me of that sinister phrase, 'England's difficulty is

*In *Counter-Modernism in Current Critical Theory* (1983), Geoffrey Thurley mounted a spectacularly ineffective polemic against current deconstructionism. A similarly ineffective contribution is *Reconstructing Literature*, edited by Laurence Lerner (1983). Both works are remarkable for their espousal of an aggressive, bullish nationalism, and for their dedication to an unexamined concept called the "Anglo-Saxon" mind.

14

Ireland's opportunity'. In moments of aggravation it seems to me that if England no longer wants both the canon of English literature *and* the desperate, wrecked state of Northern Ireland, then perhaps something could be created out of this double rejection? A united Irish Arts Council could buy up all those remaindered copies of *Hamlet* and *Macbeth* and use them to construct a new culture. MacMorris in *Henry V* could ask 'what ish my nation?' and his *auteur* could reply, 'same as mine ould boy'.

Of course, those texts already form part of anglophone culture in Ireland, and like the United States, Ireland is nourished by English literature. Perhaps, then, the day is not far off when a conference of Irish structuralists will meet in Belfast to discuss the latest reading of Barbara Johnson's reading of Derrida's reading of Lacan's reading of Poe's *The Purloined Letter?*

The idea is hopelessly utopian. Deconstruction is the cry of a culture cracking under the weight of its achievements. In Ireland, though, there is as yet no ratified idea of a culture which literary theorists could begin to undermine. However, many years after the establishment of an all-Ireland examination system, boredom and doubt may become so strong that teachers will begin introducing their pupils to semiotic accounts of soap operas. Instead of studying *Wuthering Heights*, they will follow the current English pedagogic fashion and deconstruct video cassettes of the film of *Wuthering Heights.*

Such an approach is both arid and self-conscious, but there is much to be said for a type of deconstructionist argument which would begin by splitting the concept, "English literature", into some of its component parts—i.e. Scottish, Irish, Welsh, American and what used to be quaintly termed "Commonwealth" literature. This would have the effect of Balkanizing an unwieldy subject and it would redistribute some of the power which had previously been centred in the term "English"—a term which very often imposes British nationality on writers such as Joyce and Yeats who were deeply hostile to that identity. Although most radical critics and educationalists are more interested in texts which enforce a type of class-consciousness, it seems to me that it is the term "English" which needs to be first deconstructed and then redefined. This involves arguing from and for a specifically

15

post-colonial or post-imperial idea—it means that the critic must come out into the open and say *'credo'*.

First and foremost I believe in the existence of literature rather than *écriture* and so find it hard to comprehend a critical attitude which wants to abolish the distinction between, say, a newspaper editorial and a poem by Burns, Clare or Elizabeth Bishop. And yet politics—that rhetoric of the will which rasps like claggy velvet in *Times* leaders—does affect one's admiration of art. So is it really possible, I wonder, to admire platonic England and detach that concept from the vicious and demoralised atmosphere on board *Battleship Britain?* Now and then I doubt it, but for the most part I see no contradiction in revering that idea of England and at the same time hoping that Ireland will eventually be a united and separate country with strong cultural institutions of its own.

Until about 1980 I took a different view and believed what most Ulster Protestants still believe—that Northern Ireland was, and ought to remain, permanently wedded to Great Britain. Although I had always hated Ulster Unionism very bitterly and supported the Civil Rights movement from the beginning, I believed that civil rights and greater social justice in Northern Ireland could be achieved within the context of the United Kingdom. I rejoiced, therefore, at the fall of Stormont and the same week attacked a Provo supporter who was selling nationalist newspapers. As the situation hardened, I reacted like most members of the Unionist middle class and believed that Conor Cruise O'Brien was putting 'our case'. But there was something different in the air as the decade ended. I started reading Irish history again and found myself drawn to John Hume's eloquence, his humane and constitutional politics. As a result, O'Brien's articles in the *Observer* began to seem sloppy and unconvincing and I felt angered by them. With this change of mood went a rejection of that attitude held by many people—men mostly—who belong to the sixties generation. It is a deeply earnest attitude which identifies with a form of hyperborean and Lawrentian provincialism, and it is hostile to the idea of institutions, formality, opera, educated southern accents, the necessary insincerities of good manners. Although I shall always remain what Henry Joy McCracken termed 'a northern', I no longer feel, either in Ireland or England, any hostility towards a southern insouciance. It seems wrong to hug too closely that 'provincialism of feeling' which Hardy recommended. Hardy opposed this regional idea to Arnold's metropolitan ideal of cultivation and it anticipates Lawrence's ethic of authenticity. I used to accept this idea, but then I believed that the writer from Northern Ireland was in the same position as a Welsh, Scottish or northern English writer. I believed that to oppose the partition of Ireland was necessarily to espouse a violent and simplistic nationalism.

This belief was shaped by the experience of growing up inside an Ulster Protestant community. That community possesses very little in the way of an indigenous cultural tradition of its own and in its more reflective moments tends to identify with "the British way of life". Although the dissenting tradition in Ulster created a distinctive and notable culture in the closing decades of the eighteenth century, that tradition went underground after the Act of Union and has still not been given the attention it deserves. This is largely because most Unionists have a highly selective historical memory and cling desperately to a raft constructed from two dates— 1690 and 1912. The result is an unusually fragmented culture and a snarl of superficial or negative attitudes. A provincialism of the most disabling kind.

Although literary criticism is said to lead ultimately to an ideology or a theology (gnosticism in the case of Harold Bloom), it could be that the critic's position must always begin with a definite civil and cultural affiliation. The idea of balanced judgment which is, or used to be, such a strong feature of English literary criticism has obvious links with Anglicanism and English political history. My own critical position is eclectic and is founded on an idea of identity which has as yet no formal or institutional existence. It assumes the existence of a non-sectarian, republican state which comprises the whole island of Ireland. It also holds to the idea of sanctuary and to the concept of "the fifth province". This other, invisible province offers a platonic challenge to the nationalistic image of the four green fields.* Although I've occasionally caught glimpses of this cultural ideal—most recently in the report of

*For a definition of this idea see Seamus Heaney's preface and the editorial in *The Crane Bag Book of Irish Studies*. The New Ireland Forum Report (2 May 1984) offers a new political framework, or frameworks, for Ireland in which, 'All the cultural traditions in Ireland, North and South, would be guaranteed full expression and encouragement.'

the New Ireland Forum—it has for the most part the rubbed shine of the private hobby-horse, all reflections and obsessions, nothing else.

Belatedly, I've come to believe that class politics and proper democracy will only be possible in Ireland once the "national question" has been answered. It is a question, not of religious, but of secular values. England has a national church, but there can be no question of any church in an all-Ireland republic having a "special position". Once a full Irish identity has been established then some form of sceptical detachment —a repudiation of its possible narrowness—becomes necessary and obligatory. In my view it is impossible to achieve a wide and cultivated cosmopolitan outlook without beginning—like a diver kicking off a springboard—from the idea of a secular republic. Some northern Irish writers, whose work I admire, would disagree with this idea, and I will always respect them for doing so. But the question has yet to be debated properly. In a way, it is the equivalent of the English crisis.

The question, at least for me, involves a recognition that the Irish writer who publishes in Britain has a neo-colonial identity. And the central question which faces the neo-colonial and the post-colonial writer is—whom am I writing for? Here, the career of V.S. Naipaul is instructive.

Naipaul addresses a transatlantic audience to whom he explains that the Third World is, was, and always will be, a complete mess. In *India: A Wounded Civilisation* and in that shamefully bad novel *A Bend in the River*, Naipaul exposes India and Africa as awful, embarrassing, despicable. What comic people they contain! How feeble and ridiculous are their cultures! And Naipaul's audience is pleased to notice his disdain, because that disdain feeds its self-esteem, allays its guilt and confirms the Western sense of superiority. Indians and West Indians are hostile to Naipaul, but he does not write for them. Indeed, he writes for nothing and nowhere. He is simply against certain ghastly elsewheres.

The crucial problem for the writer who is an immigrant or *entryiste* is that such writers are rendered harmless by their lack of real affiliation. Otherness is a specialising feature, a distinguishing mark, but it can reduce the writer to an entertainer, a media clown. When this happens—as it happened to Wilde—irony can become an instrument of vengeance: 'Enter Jack followed by Algernon. They whistle some dreadful popular air

18

from a British opera.' Wilde's scene-direction is subversive; his great comedy and his tragic life have a terrible punitive integrity. Wilde is dissident, dandy, holy fool, the Victorian equivalent of life artist. His aesthetic rebellion was a version of Robert Emmet's, and it was also a principled rejection of the social role of the artist as lackey. That role—then, as now—involves being unconsciously stateless and nationless, an Estragon without Estragon's supreme knowledge and metaphysical despair. To be like this is to have an audience but no constituency. It is to have no place-names to cherish, no landscape or dialect where the gods are local and gentle and where it is possible to touch the earth and be at peace. Like Tom Moore, you sing for your supper and flicker through the gossip columns. Like Frank Delaney, you make a film for Joyce's centenary and wonder why Joyce chose a martello tower as the 'opening location' for *Ulysses*. You wonder, but you avoid mentioning the anti-colonial purposes to which Joyce put that tower.

Eliot must have considered this problem of disaffiliation when he came to England. His answer was to make an existential commitment by joining the national church. That 'moment in a draughty church at smokefall' is the instant of spiritual commitment which enabled Eliot to step inside the visionary heart of the culture. It enabled him to write these beautiful lines which would sound impossibly Georgian if we knew they had been written by a native English poet:

> We die with the dying:
> See, they depart, and we go with them.
> We are born with the dead:
> See, they return, and bring us with them.
> The moment of the rose and the moment of the yew-tree
> Are of equal duration. A people without history
> Is not redeemed from time, for history is a pattern
> Of timeless moments. So, while the light fails
> On a winter's afternoon, in a secluded chapel
> History is now and England.
>
> (*Little Gidding*, V)

This outsider's empathy with the heart of a culture always reminds me of the many books—especially collections of old photographs—which have been published in the North of Ireland during the last decade. Before the conflict started the province was lulled in a state of absence and aphasia, almost as

19

though its inhabitants were 'without history'. Eliot's lines suggest that the dead are resurrected as images in the cultural memory, that the past must be retrieved in acts of redemption and atonement.

Eliot wrote this invocation to the spirit of English culture less than a year after the Battle of Britain and it is essential to his vision that he should imagine culture as the resolution of conflicts within its society:

> These men, and those who opposed them
> And those whom they opposed
> Accept the constitution of silence
> And are folded in a single party.
> Whatever we inherit from the fortunate
> We have taken from the defeated
> What they had to leave us—a symbol:
> A symbol perfected in death.
>
> (*Little Gidding*, III)

Here, Eliot is contemplating the conflicts of the English Civil War, and the cultural unity he imagines—the 'single party'—is composed *inter alia* of Charles I and Cromwell, Lucius Carey and John Milton. It is an arch—gothic, rather than classical—which depends on the stress of opposites. In a sense it resembles Churchill's war cabinet of Socialist and Conservative politicians, and it therefore adumbrates an inclusive idea of national consciousness.

Eliot's career has certain affinities with Brendan Bracken's, but Bracken's cunning strategies are now outdated. Bracken pretended to be Churchill's illegitimate son and had a distinguished public career. No one entering Britain now would dream of making such a preposterous identification with the patriotic strain (Michael Schmidt's *Poetry Nation* began affirming its Anglican nationalism far back in the 1970s). English politicians now compete for the Irish vote in certain English cities by identifying with specifically Irish issues. In time, this may affect Irish politics, though it would appear that Livingstone and Benn are in advance of English public opinion. Nevertheless, it is clear that public opinion is now against British troops remaining in Northern Ireland. The relationship between Britain and its provincial satellite-state is changing, and an early indication of this realignment was the publication in 1980 of Paul Johnson's *Ireland: Land of Troubles*.

Johnson's history has the air of a summing-up, and at one

20

point he admits that Ireland has never attracted the services of Britain's 'best statesmen and thinkers'. He then offers a list of those who devoted their energies to solving the Irish question and concludes:

> Most of these men failed because Ireland was merely a passing episode in otherwise fruitful lives of public service and creative labour. But most of them accepted the fundamental misconception to which even the more enlightened British statesmen and pundits have clung: that if only Britain gave Ireland justice, prosperity and wise government, the British connection would be accepted by her people. Alas, it is of the essence of wise government to know when to absent itself. Britain has learned by bitter experience in Ireland that there is no substitute for independence.

Although that phrase 'bitter experience' is bound to perplex an Irish reader, Johnson's account must be seen as a concerned attempt to influence British policy. It is an admission of failure on the part of a notable Conservative polemicist which curiously anticipates the changed attitude to Ireland within the British Labour Party.

Another admission of failure is a revealing memoir which was published last year. In *Contact*, A.F.N. Clarke describes his experiences in Northern Ireland as an officer in the Parachute Regiment between 1971 and 1978. Clarke appears to have been conceived in a *Sun* editorial and his racist attitudes ('Mohammed, our pet Paki') must be familiar to anyone who has encountered English populism in action. With disgust and a strong sense of national superiority, Clarke describes an Irish slum like this:

> The dwellings, one could hardly call them houses, were typical of the ghettoes of Belfast, with two rooms upstairs, two down, an outside toilet and an alleyway backing onto the next row which faced another street. An assortment of sweating humanity lived in sordid conditions of filth, sinks full of greasy plates, cookers black with dirt and spilled decaying food. Bedrooms with a stench of unwashed bodies and bedclothes, full pots under the beds with the contents liberally sloshed onto the floor.

Several times Clarke refers to the 'grating sound of the ghetto Irish', at others he wishes for 'the powers the South African police have'. His swaggering frankness often makes him sound like a propagandist for the other side, especially in this description of a para camp:

As time drags on, the whole camp is praying for a contact. For an opportunity to shoot at anything on the street, pump lead into any living thing and watch the blood flow. Toms sitting in their overcrowded rooms putting more powder into baton rounds to give them more poke; some insert pins and broken razor blades into the rubber rounds. Buckshee rounds have the heads filed down for a dum-dum effect, naughty, naughty, but who's to know when there are so many spare rounds of ammunition floating about. Lead-filled truncheons, magnum revolvers, one bloke has even got a Bowie knife.

Although soldiers tend to boast and exaggerate, it's clear that this is a collage of separate incidents and authentic tricks of the trade.

This populist extremity is a version of the notorious Jak cartoon which appeared in the *New Standard** last year, but it enables Clarke to see a province entirely inhabited by Irish people (he hates Protestants as much as Catholics). At one point, he looks up at the Irish landscape and mutters 'it is so unfair that all this beauty should be wasted on these people'. Edmund Spenser had a similar thought several centuries ago and he recommended a policy of extermination. Clarke is less "thorough" in his outlook and seems to enjoy violence for its own sake:

We are getting high on violence now, the exhilaration of the chase, the feeling of uplift every time an Irishman goes down. We don't bother to take any prisoners, just zap them with the dick gun and trample over the prostrate forms. Let their own pick them up.

It is this central perception of the Irish as having accents and attitudes which are all 'their own' and in no sense British that causes Clarke to ask what his fellow soldiers are dying for. It is a question which must be asked, but it may be that only when Great Britain is a thing of the past will it ever be properly answered. These essays and reviews—written from within the belly of the system—are not intended as answers to that particular political question. Instead, I hope they will contribute something towards a tradition of critical independence. It must be possible to speak plainly for a new civility.

*The cartoon was of a poster advertising a film called *The Irish* and showed a series of monstrous simian figures with a strong resemblance to nineteenth-century cartoon-images of "The Paddy Irishman". The Press Council rejected a complaint that the cartoon was racist in intention.

The Making of a Loyalist

If there is a centre to Conor Cruise O'Brien's writing it must lie in the belief that politics and art are mutually absorbed in the production of historical fictions. Like Burke, he habitually views politics as theatre, and this habit has inspired him to write a number of plays which deal with political issues. His dramatic writings issue from a sub-Shavian rationalism and although this prevents them from being convincingly imaginative they do express his sense of the inseparability of politics and imagination. Recently, however, he has decided that they can be separated after all. In the last of the lectures in *Neighbours* he recommends that politics in the North of Ireland should be abolished. Those who talk of 'fresh political initiatives' are, he says, 'barking up the wrong tree'. They should instead offer prayers to a force called 'international attention'. That force will then establish an institution which as yet exists solely in O'Brien's imagination. This supreme fiction is called 'the Northern Ireland Fund' and in a revealing statement its author promises to pursue it 'as a private citizen with some international contacts and communications'.

This promise resembles that moment in Joyce's 'The Dead' when Gabriel Conroy tells his audience that the tradition of Irish hospitality is 'unique as far as my experience goes (and I have visited not a few places abroad)'. As he says this, Gabriel is thinking of the nationalist, Miss Ivors, who has earlier embarrassed him by calling him a West Briton because he writes a literary column for the *Daily Express* and refuses to visit the Aran Islands. His speech is an act of revenge against her and reveals him as falsely cosmopolitan, a timid, servile and self-conscious figure. Pitilessly, Joyce places him in relation to an influential strand of Irish culture and in doing so explores the dilemma of the Irish intellectual. Curiously, Joyce based the character of Gabriel's mocker, Miss Ivors, on a girl called Kathleen Sheehy who later married a Dublin journalist and gave birth to a well-known figure called Conor Cruise O'Brien.

Neighbours: The Ewart-Biggs Memorial Lectures, 1978-1979 by Conor Cruise O'Brien.

In O'Brien's writing, fact and fiction—or politics and imagination—often appear to merge in that ironical manner which is so characteristic of Dublin culture. And among the many ironies of this particular blurring is the spectacle of O'Brien respectfully addressing 'my friend Lord Goodman, and...the Fellows of University College, Oxford' in tones which relish their attention, as well as savouring the more international attentiveness which stretches beyond High Table. Part of that attention O'Brien promises to divert to the North of Ireland, and yet the student of his *Observer* column will search in vain for any evidence of his efforts.

In *Neighbours*, O'Brien supports an essentially loyalist position. In order to understand how he has reached it we must place this work in the context of his other writings. The act of placing raises complex questions of history, identity and intellectual freedom.

In the opening autobiographical section of *States of Ireland* (1972) O'Brien remarks that although historians normally write as if they are free of all conditioning factors, what they offer is mostly '*tribal* history'. Mixing anecdote with brisk name-dropping, he then recounts his own family history and pays an affectionate tribute to his father, Francis Cruise O'Brien, whom he describes as intellectual, agnostic, anti-clerical and gifted with 'the power to say wounding things in a memorable manner'. O'Brien senior emerges as the living image of his son and this is perhaps the most original quality of the memoir (most autobiographers try to establish that they differ from their fathers). However, Francis Cruise O'Brien died when his son was ten and this filial piety must be to a memory which O'Brien has at least in part invented. He has both submitted to the conditioning factors of the past and made an existential leap of the imagination which frees him from them. Put another way, he has combined Irish piety with European freedom.

Francis Cruise O'Brien ensured that his son received a Protestant education, and this tempered his inherited Catholic allegiances. In O'Brien's self-portrait we can see how the two traditions balance each other and allow that rare figure, the "objective" historian to emerge. This transcendental historian is able to voice and confirm Protestant fears of domination by a Catholic state. Reaching back into history, O'Brien seeks to corroborate those fears by emphasizing the sectarian divisions within the 1798 rebellion (and here he is echoed by the loyalist historian A.T.Q. Stewart in his study *The Narrow Ground*). Throughout *States of Ireland* O'Brien presents himself as the concerned but non-partisan commentator, and rebuts accusations that he is 'hyper-sensitive' about Protestants and indifferent to Catholics:

> It is to the Irish Catholic community that I belong. That is my 'little platoon', to love which, according to Edmund Burke (whose family were in the same platoon), 'is the first, the germ, as it were, of publick affections'.

It is a mark of O'Brien's continuing uncertainty about his identity that he must compare himself to, among others, Burke, Griboyedov, Milovan Djilas and 'Tolstoy's Prince Andrey on the field of Austerlitz'.

This last exalted comparison occurs in *To Katanga and Back* (1962), which opens with a question: ' "Who," Mr Macmillan was moved to ask one autumn day in 1961, "is Conor O'Brien?".' The answer might well have been 'An Irishman who is delighted to be noticed by the British Prime Minister.' The gratifying attention of Harold Macmillan helped to create O'Brien's image and this was an important stage in the promotion of a public personality which became a personal identity.

O'Brien would have the audience of *States of Ireland* believe that his identity is rooted in the Irish Catholic community, but the grouping is too wide to be helpful. In fact, he inadvertently reveals that there are really two Catholic communities when he admits that he writes 'specifically' from the point of view of the Southern Catholics. Nowhere does he point to the deep hostility which much of that community feels towards both communities in the North. Many Southerners—Catholic, Protestant and agnostic—are quite capable of believing in a United Ireland while at the same time regarding Northerners as members of what are sometimes scathingly referred to as "hill tribes". To the Southerner these tribes belong to an imaginative territory very similar to that symbolized by Galway and the West in 'The Dead'. They are beyond the pale and threaten the ironical civilities of Dublin.

Something of this is apparent in O'Brien's account in *States of Ireland* of a lecture which he gave to a Civil Rights meeting at Queen's University, Belfast, in October 1968. The main point of the lecture was 'that civil disobedience, in Northern Ireland, was likely to prove an effective lever for social change'. In the discussion which followed, the students criticised him 'quite heatedly' for mentioning 'the existence of two separate communities, Catholics and Protestants'. The student activists believed in working-class solidarity and they dismissed religion as 'irrelevant'. O'Brien's aim in his account of this meeting is to present himself as the objective historian, the *engagé* intellectual who is also disengaged by virtue of his superior wisdom. He presents the students as ignorant, idealistic and sloppy, and then reprints as part of his account an article which he published in the *Listener* that same October, where he compared the events in the North of Ireland to *Antigone*:

> Antigone's action was one of non-violent civil disobedience, the breaking of a law which she considered to be contrary to a higher law. The consequences of her non-violent action emerge in acts of violence: Antigone's own violent death; Haemon's turning of his sword first against his father Creon and then fatally against himself; the suicide of Eurydice, Creon's wife and Haemon's mother. A stiff price for that handful of dust on Polynices. Nor is it possible to put all the blame on Creon. Certainly his decision to forbid the burial of Polynices was rash, but it was also rash to disobey his decision...Ismene, who was Polynices' sister just as much as Antigone was, would not risk her life for the sake of her brother's dead body. It was Antigone's free decision, and that alone, which precipitated the tragedy. Creon's responsibility was the more remote one of having placed this tragic power in the hands of a headstrong child of Oedipus.

O'Brien published this interpretation of *Antigone* on 24 October 1968, and he lectured the students on the likely effectiveness of civil disobedience in 'late October'. He has never been slow to publish his lectures—why then did he not publish the lecture on civil disobedience? This is a most pertinent question because O'Brien informed the readers of the *Listener* that

> The disabilities of Catholics in Northern Ireland are real, but not overwhelmingly oppressive: is their removal really worth attaining at the risk of precipitating riots, explosions, pogroms, murder? Thus Ismene. But Antigone will not heed such calculations: she is an ethical and religious force, an uncompromising element in our being, as dangerous in her way as Creon, whom she perpetually challenges and provokes.

If O'Brien recommended civil disobedience in his lecture then he can hardly have told his audience that the injustices they were protesting against were 'not overwhelmingly oppressive'. Of course, this bland statement is attributed to Ismene but it is plain from his description of Creon's responsibility as 'more remote' and his description of Antigone as 'headstrong' that his sympathies—at least when not lecturing in Belfast—lay with the status quo.

There is yet another revealing omission from *States of Ireland*. It is the statement, 'Without Antigone, we could attain a quieter, more realistic world. The Creons might respect one another's spheres of influence if the instability of idealism were to cease to present, inside their own dominions, a threat to law and order.' These two sentences appeared in the article which O'Brien published in the *Listener*, but they were silently dropped when he reprinted it.

Possibly this was because a year after O'Brien suggested that Creon might have a change of heart, members of the RUC fired machine-guns indiscriminately at Divis Flats near the centre of Belfast, killing a nine-year-old boy and a young British soldier who was home on leave. The status quo was discredited and the British army arrived. From the perspective of 1971, the statement appeared both wrong and vulnerably naive, and so it disappeared from the text.

Reflecting on the *Listener* article in *States of Ireland*, O'Brien says that he is no longer in sympathy with its conclusion. That conclusion suggested that Antigone may express 'the essence of what man's dignity actually is', but now O'Brien rejects this:

> ...after four years of Antigone and her under-studies and all those funerals—more than a hundred dead at the time of writing—you begin to feel that Ismene's common-sense and feeling for the living may make the more needful, if less spectacular element in "human dignity".

Here Antigone (i.e. Bernadette Devlin and the Civil Rights movement) becomes responsible for 'all those funerals'. This means that the Unionist state is virtually absolved of all responsibility and Creon's hands appear to be clean.

O'Brien's political analysis is inspired and supported by his interpretation of Sophocles' great tragedy, so it is crucial to recognise how badly he misinterprets the play. According to Hegel, for whom *Antigone* was 'the perfect exemplar' of tragedy, the sacred laws which Antigone revered are 'the instinctive Powers of Feeling, Love and Kinship, not the daylight gods of free and self-conscious, social and political life'. As Hegel shows, in the play 'neither the right of family, nor that of the state is denied; what is denied is the absoluteness of the claim of each'. It is in the clash of these opposing 'rights' that the tragedy resides.

Antigone represents the absolute assertion of family against the state, and if O'Brien had truly felt that he and Bernadette Devlin belonged to the same 'little platoon' then he would have been unable to turn against a member of that extended family and assert the virtues of what Creon terms 'simple obedience'. But as Bernadette Devlin is a Northern Catholic he cannot feel any natural bond with her.

O'Brien's loyalties are to the 'daylight gods', and he sees the political conflict in the play as one of unequal values and unequal personal responsibilities. Creon, therefore, is both individual and institution, yet he appears to be more an institution, while Antigone, like St Joan, appears as an individual ahead of her supporters. She is 'headstrong' and therefore more responsible because she can supposedly exercise choice. So Creon is rendered almost innocent by his immobile precedence, his simply being there. This is a severe distortion of the tragic conflict and it provoked Hugh Lloyd-Jones to rebuke O'Brien in the next issue of the *Listener*: 'Tiresias makes it clear that Creon has offended against the laws of the gods.'

O'Brien ignored Lloyd-Jones's rebuke and also omitted to notice that Ismene eventually sides with Antigone. He has always attempted to occupy a middle position and his omission suggests that such a position is tenable here. But in recommending Ismene's common-sense he is really supporting Creon's rule of law. It is as though a future member of Creon's think-tank can be discerned hiding behind the unfortunate Ismene. Tragedy teaches no moral, but the analogy between the play and events in the North of Ireland shows us a terrible truth—neither Ismene, nor even Conor Cruise O'Brien, can prevent a civil war happening. O'Brien has often warned that such a war is imminent and he no doubt believes that so far he has helped to prevent it. But if it breaks out he will be able to say, 'I told you so.' That is the advantage of being pure.

Essentially, the thrust of O'Brien's argument is towards a position where he can be both politically influential and absolutely pure. Having once recommended a campaign of civil disobedience, and now believing that the campaign in the North of Ireland was responsible for political violence, he must prove that there is no blood on his hands. Throughout his published writings he returns obsessively to Yeats's famous question: 'Did that play of mine send out/ Certain men the English shot?' The question preys on O'Brien's mind, because as an international communicator and moulder of opinion he must believe in his power to influence history.

Yet as he observes in his first and best book, *Maria Cross* (1954), the relationship between 'the imagination and moral guilt' is by no means simple. This is an observation which issues from his sense of 'the oppressive domination of the rational faculties over the passions', and from his dislike of the 'levelling rational men' who set puritan reason against the imagination. In an earlier period, the puritan imagination created two great epics—*Paradise Lost* and *Clarissa*—but O'Brien rightly points to its subsequent lassitude. 'Modern Protestantism,' he remarks in *Maria Cross*, is 'dead from the waist down' and has nothing to offer the Catholic imaginations he is exploring. What is important, he argues, is that 'community of feeling' which enables Catholic writers to transform a private and incommunicable suffering 'into public utterance and communion with others'. Here, he writes in a manner that is passionately and warmly intelligent, and his prose is utterly unlike his later style. Where the mature style is rational, self-conscious and broguishly ironic, the early prose is lavish, ornate, agonized and often febrile. It sets the author's personality aside in order to explore a higher and more mysterious knowledge, and it swirls with cries of 'pain' and references to 'historical change', 'solidarity' and 'this revolutionary urge'. It is the intuitive pressure of the prose which guarantees O'Brien's assertion here that Sartre and Camus 'lack just that irrational instinctive force whose explosion made the greatness of Mauriac's prime'.

O'Brien has never written in this manner again. His work since *Maria Cross* has increasingly turned away from the instinctive and the intuitive towards the 'rational'. Possibly he was disturbed by his use of that metaphor of an explosion and wished to repudiate it by embracing an ideal of eighteenth-century reason. Another answer would be that the dazzling light of 'international attention' transformed him into a personality. Hammarskjöld read *Maria Cross* and admired it, and it was partly because of this that he selected O'Brien in 1961 as the United Nations Special Representative in Katanga. In an article in the *Observer* at the end of that year O'Brien dwelt on this 'somewhat eccentric element' in Hammarskjöld's choice. A journalist writing for an Arizona newspaper drew on this article in order to attack O'Brien and his criticisms provoked a vulnerable footnote in *To Katanga and Back* (1962):

> The emphasis, in the *Observer* article…was due, not so much to any real modesty on my part, as to the strategy of self-depreciation which one almost instinctively adopts when writing for a certain kind of English audience. I now realise that it is foolish for a foreigner to attempt this technique. Only a true-born Englishman knows the trick of being self-depreciatory without actually doing himself any damage—I only succeeded in making people as far away as Arizona think I was 'boasting'.

The Arizonans were right, but this is unimportant beside the hypersensitivity to other people's opinions which the statement reveals. O'Brien admits that his authorial personality owes much to his sense of his audience's expectations. It is little wonder that Macmillan asked who this shifting, 'almost instinctive' person was. He may have mistaken him for Brendan Bracken.

O'Brien offers the following self-portrait in the words of an attentive UN aide in *Murderous Angels* (1969), his play about the Congo affair: 'He's a trouble-maker ... Clever. Bumptious. Talks too much. The British say he's a Communist, but they just mean that he's Irish.' It's as though his identity is a figment of public opinion and since there are many opinions there must be many identities.

All the same, the anti-imperialism evident in the play also helped to inspire a lucid and brilliant study of Camus which was published in 1970. In it he demonstrates that Camus was far from being an exemplar of the truly independent intellectual and that his conception of 'Mediterranean culture' served to legitimise France's possession of Algeria. The court scene in *L'Étranger* similarly endorses this myth of French Algeria:

> What appears to the casual reader as a contemptuous attack on the court is not in fact an attack at all: on the contrary, by suggesting that the court is impartial between Arab and Frenchman, it implicitly denies the colonial reality and sustains the colonial fiction.

O'Brien's prose has a sweet rigour as he first explores Camus's sense of estrangement and unreality, and then places his work within a social context. This brief study displays O'Brien's cultivated intelligence at its most joyous pitch, and like *Maria Cross* it demonstrates his unique critical talent, but in the context of his other work it is remarkably inconsistent. Camus, he shows, criticised revolutionary violence but did not consider 'the question of violence used to defend the status quo'. Yet in his last book, *Herod: Reflections on Political Violence* (1978), O'Brien scorns the phrase 'institutionalised violence' and defends the status quo.

But two years before he published *Camus* he had suggested that the world would be quieter and 'more realistic' without Antigone. This idea is the reactionary equivalent of radical utopianism. It is a kind of negative idealism which argues that life would be better if only we could abolish part of human nature—in this case radical protest. Here, O'Brien emerges well to the right of Camus, who criticised revolutionary violence while O'Brien criticises non-violence by suggesting that it is responsible for political terrorism. And, as we have seen, that missing 1968 lecture on the effectiveness of civil disobedience adds a further inconsistency.

There is a yet deeper contradiction. It appears in the introduction to a collection of essays which O'Brien co-edited, entitled *Power and Consciousness* (1969). There he considers why 'sympathy with other people's revolutions is so deceptive' and shows how the sympathizer's retreat

> may become a rout, his disenchantment apostasy. Thus we may find that the man who has refused to make the decisive intellectual and moral sacrifices for the revolution will go on to make them for the status quo and in that cause proclaim: 'This sham is true, these injustices are just, these oppressed have all the opportunities of the free world.' These sacrifices, whether made for the revolution or for the counter-revolution, constitute, of course, the abdication of the intellectual.

The introductory essay in which this statement occurs was published in New York in 1969 and must have been written soon after his *Antigone* article. The reason for this contradiction must be that his warning against 'the abdication of the intellectual' was directed chiefly at an American audience. Here, he speaks in the persona of a New York intellectual, while in the *Listener* he adopts a Burkean mask and speaks of 'the instability of idealism'. The

Burkean mask is many-layered—as O'Brien points out in his introduction to *Reflections on the Revolution in France* (1968), Burke wrote 'in the persona of an Englishman', but was 'Irish to the marrow of his bones'. And in 1969 O'Brien discovered that Burke's education and origins were 'very similar to my own'. It seems that either O'Brien writes in the persona of a persona or that the Burkean mask looks almost exactly like his own face. This leaves no room for his other identities of New York intellectual, anti-imperialist, lecturer on civil disobedience and critic of Camus. Unless, that is, we adopt a Yeatsian theory of anti-types and regard his portrait of Camus as a self-portrait and its author as a shadowy opposite who is friendly with the New York intellectual.

Connected with the question of identity is that ideal of complete intellectual freedom which O'Brien appears to uphold in his writings. In arguing, for example, that Camus was not truly independent he implies that he himself is. And this is the theme of his introduction to *Power and Consciousness*, where at one point he mischievously suggests that it is 'perhaps' time to attempt a balanced consideration of Stalin's literary talent and then offers this striking comment: 'But of course it remains true that the exercise of power is incompatible with absolutely free intellectual activity, however powerful the intellect of the man in power may be.' What is remarkable about this deeply ingenuous statement is O'Brien's apparent belief that intellectual activity *can* be 'absolutely free'.

It was in 1969, as a New York intellectual, that O'Brien professed his belief in this absolute freedom. That same year he delivered the T.S. Eliot Memorial Lectures at Eliot College in the University of Kent. These were published as *The Suspecting Glance* (1972), and in his introduction O'Brien says they are the product of what he experienced in New York. The students he taught there were intelligent, serious and left-wing, but he was 'disconcerted...by the lack of suspicion in those bright, young eyes'. He therefore told them about Burke, rather than Marcuse or Shelley. Again, he approaches a Yeatsian struggle of opposites here—he writes as a radical in *Power and Consciousness* yet he redresses radical ideals in student seminars. Far from New York, in Eliot College, Canterbury, he catches the charred fragrance of Eliot's Anglican pessimism and begins to forge a new identity.

As always, the impression is one of balance. On the one

hand he addresses the important subject of how certain reactionary intuitions work against 'the optimism of the enlightenment'; on the other he criticises Burke for calling for a long counter-revolutionary war. His ambition is to provoke traditional left-wing thought into examining 'what man is actually like'. It is a salutary ambition, but as with that missing 1968 lecture on civil disobedience it appears to be tailored to the occasion.

The static and unfruitful contradictions in his thought are apparent in *Herod* (1978), an undistinguished gathering of reviews, lectures and short plays which looks queasy beside *Writers and Politics*, that melodious work of the mid-1960s. In one play, *Salome and the Wild Man*, Salome tells the sophist, Philo, that they are both 'lonely for the wild man'. O'Brien has discerned loneliness in Burke and we must assume that he is pointing to his own sense of isolation. The wild man believes in 'the politics of the impossible' and the drama in which he figures represents 'the high water-mark of the tendency to idealize the student revolution'. O'Brien admits to having once had this tendency, but he had it in New York, not in Britain or Ireland. The wild man is clearly related to Antigone, except that he has an American student base. However, as 'wild' is a word with a distinctive usage in Ireland he may be Irish-American. Where Yeats remembers the pre-revolutionary Constance Gore-Booth 'With all youth's lonely wildness stirred', O'Brien makes a division between loneliness and wildness and founds an idea of civilisation on that split. And Philo, the lonely sophist, represents civilisation, which is mistakenly identified with the status quo.

Philo is O'Brien in a toga and at the end of the play he confuses the wild man with Antigone's brother: 'We kill him, we bury him, we even *honour* him. And yet he always comes up again under a new name.' As the tragic action of *Antigone* springs from Creon's refusal to allow Polynices an honourable burial, this again demonstrates O'Brien's inability to understand the play. As with that phrase 'the politics of the impossible' which he puts into the wild man's mouth, O'Brien's cynical pragmatism rigs the entire analysis. The issues are always prejudged in Creon's favour, like votes in a one-party state.

Yet O'Brien admits to being lonely for the wild man, and this loneliness is apparent in a statement he includes in *Herod*:

'My liberal image, I am told by those who can tell such things, is in bits.' He then suggests that he is 'not too worried' about this, 'not being much of a one for images, having indeed some inclination to iconoclasm'. Here we can sense the loneliness of a performer: instead of honestly admitting that he has changed his convictions, he turns to contemplate his shattered liberal image. The image should be nothing, the conviction everything—unless you are a politician of the most opportunistic kind. As it happens, O'Brien was Minister for Posts and Telegraphs in the Irish government at this time, but it would be unfair to accuse him of political opportunism. He was not a successful politician and this was due partly to his iconoclastic habits and partly to his neglect of his constituency. Yet he regrets the disappearance of his liberal image because for him image is identity. However, he has now a new image-identity, and this personality can be understood as a kind of negative definition which has become a positive commitment. The free spirit, like the pure lovers in Donne's poem 'The Extasy', must eventually descend to 'affections and to faculties', and in O'Brien's latest work that commitment—or that descent—is made.

Neighbours consists of four lectures which O'Brien gave in memory of Christopher Ewart-Biggs. As these were public lectures and not private messages of condolence to the family of the dead ambassador, it is only with their public function that the reader can be concerned. The function of the lectures is partly a diplomatic one—to improve relations between Britain and Ireland, and in pursuit of that aim O'Brien insists on the links between the two countries. As an iconoclastic critic of Irish nationalism he also attacks the 'anglophobia' which some Irish people profess, and again this is part of a diplomatic stress on common interests.

It is here that we can see the free critical spirit making and revealing its commitment to an external structure. For all O'Brien's apparent diplomacy that structure is not finally the political system of the Irish Republic, nor is it some noble structure of ideas to which he has at last submitted his personality. It is a shaky edifice called 'the Union of Great Britain and Northern Ireland' and O'Brien has dedicated himself to its maintenance. He speaks in the persona of an Official Unionist, and like that fugitive and visionary politician, Enoch Powell, he has offered his services to a political party demoralised by its absence of talent and by the political skills of John Hume and Ian Paisley. Just as Camus believed that Algeria was actually part of France, so O'Brien believes that the North of Ireland is permanently wedded to Britain.

His Unionism has a nineteenth-century flavour and at times he writes as though the whole of Ireland is really incorporated within the British system: 'The sea which we think of as separating the two islands actually joins them.' This is the mental equivalent of walking on water and it issues from O'Brien's fatuous statement, ' "Break the connection," wrote Wolfe Tone. "Only connect," wrote E.M. Forster.' The fact that Forster was referring to a completely different issue—the relationship of the spiritual to the public life—is not mentioned by O'Brien. It is another significant omission.

O'Brien's intellectual method in these lectures is a kind of grisly comedy which revolves around an obsession with an opinion survey which was carried out in Dublin in 1972. Rather like Winnie addressing her toothbrush in Beckett's *Happy Days*, he directs his monologues at a brittle mass of statistics and quantified opinions. This is the terminal phase of political rationalism and it is bitter with a sense of intellectual dereliction. In the first lecture on Irish-British relations (delivered at Trinity College, Dublin), O'Brien considers how Dubliners responded to the statement 'I would be happy if Britain were brought to her knees.' A solid 79.3% disagreed while 17.1% of responders agreed. It is the smaller percentage which concerns O'Brien because it represents what he terms a 'pathological element in our life'. It is a figure which is 'startlingly and frighteningly high'. Yet it is a statistic which must be located in a specific period—1972. This was the year when the survey was conducted and it was also the year of Bloody Sunday, when British paratroopers shot dead thirteen civilians in Derry. From another point of view the 17.1% of anglophobic Dubliners could be described as curiously low.

When O'Brien does mention Bloody Sunday it is to further an essentially Unionist argument. Faced with the statement, 'British soldiers are generally cruel and brutal', 28% of Dubliners agreed and 57% disagreed. Here, O'Brien blithely remarks: 'considering that the interviewing was carried out within a year of Bloody Sunday, the majority disagreeing seems more significant than the 28% minority agreeing'. But of what is that 'majority' significant? It depends on the point of view of the interpreter, and it is likely that the 'majority' of the citizens of Derry would attach a different significance to these figures from the one which O'Brien implies.

There are many more statistics and percentages in his first lecture, and at one point he considers whether it is worth plodding on. Contemplating the 30% who agreed with the proposition that 'the world owes a lot to Britain', he remarks:

> Granted that Britain's contributions to the world have been enormous, so also the world's contributions to Britain have been enormous, and not always voluntary. Is it the world that is the net debtor, or Britain? How much does Shakespeare weigh against the slave-trade? How much does Britain's leading part in abolishing the slave-trade weigh against Britain's earlier part in carrying on the slave-trade? Who is to say, who owes who what—and what is the use of saying it anyway?

As with O'Brien's question in *Herod*, 'How many children is it worthwhile to kill to get rid of Derry Corporation?', or his linking of Wolfe Tone and E.M. Forster, the Shakespearian slave-trade is an impossible collocation. Bentham remarked 'quantity of pleasure being equal, push-pin is as good as poetry'. The scales in O'Brien's non-argument are those of the hedonic calculus and it is unfortunate that he avoids his Beckettian question, 'and what is the use of saying it anyway?'.

When he turns to consider the contribution of Irishmen to 'the building of the British Empire', he makes a very revealing mistake. He asserts that the 'most execrated figure in the eyes of Indian nationalists in the twentieth century was General O'Dwyer, who gave the order that brought about the massacre at Amritsar'. It is characteristic of his sloppy method of argument that he should mistake the English general called Dyer who gave the order, for the Irish colonial administrator O'Dwyer, who ratified it. O'Brien has an obsessively analogical imagination and the motive for this mistake becomes apparent when we remember that he referred to Bloody Sunday in order to further an anti-nationalist argument. For 'Amritsar' we should read 'Derry'. O'Brien wishes to exculpate the British Army of all responsibility for the shooting of the thirteen men there, and he does so by, as it were, blaming a nationalist called General O'Somebody who was actually Irish. This is a version of the argument that the army were replying to terrorist gunfire and so were justified in shooting non-violent demonstrators. Again, it shows how O'Brien's concept of personal responsibility enables him to blame such demonstrators for political violence.

It is only in the second of these lectures, 'The Northern Connection in Irish-British Relations', that O'Brien displays any real uneasiness. This is because, ten years after that lecture on civil disobedience, he is again addressing an audience in Queen's University, Belfast. He remarks that his audience are 'likely to agree' with his admission that he knows 'relatively little about Northern Ireland'. He then offers an Empsonian political analysis which involves 'six possible dual inter-relationships among the four entities'. He speaks of triangles, dualities, 'twelve sets of attitudes', invokes further opinion polls, and eventually emerges from this numbers game by declaring: 'Give direct rule a chance.' The essential frivolity of his historical aestheticism is revealed when he compares the political differences in the North of Ireland to a game of football between 'Micks' and 'Prods'.

His intention—and this is clear in the relaxed third lecture in New York—is to demolish the idea that Britain is preventing the formation of a United Ireland: 'This fantasy, proceeding from a brain oppressed by the Irish Republican version of history, is of course one that legitimises the IRA campaign in Northern Ireland.' Here, O'Brien's tactics work to lay responsibility for the IRA campaign at the door of everyone who believes that terrorist violence is the result of partition.

Does O'Brien's support of the Union mean that he condones the actions of terrorist groups which also support the link with Britain? Might those groups not receive succour and encouragement from a Ewart-Biggs lecture? Did O'Brien's lecture at Queen's University in 1978 send out certain men? Or his 1968 lecture? The relation between the imagination and moral guilt is not as simple as this.

Among the many percentages he cites there is one figure that particularly angers O'Brien—75% of the British people seem to be Irish republicans. At least, this is one way of reading the fact that only 25% of the population of Britain believe that the North of Ireland should remain part of the United Kingdom. O'Brien calls this percentage 'miserable' and he believes that it would be much increased if only people listened to the 'reasonable policies' he is advocating. Elsewhere he warns of the dangers of losing through compassion 'the power to think'. It is not compassion which has destroyed his much-vaunted intellectual ability, but an abiding affection for Creon and a mistaken identification of civilisation with the status quo. His defence of the free spirit now appears as a rearguard action fought in support of a permanent Unionist state, and these eccentric and self-regarding lectures are an attempt to persuade the British government to maintain that state. It is to be hoped that Creon's daylight gods ignore the advice he offers them.

A Professional Irishman

Tom Moore's Irishness made him very famous in his day. He was born over his father's grocery shop in Dublin, went to Trinity College where he dabbled in revolutionary politics, and then crossed to England with some translations of Anacreon in his baggage. A diminutive charmer, he soon gained access to the most exclusive London drawing-rooms and his sentimental songs reduced many a duchess to tears. He was a completely social being who, according to Leigh Hunt, was 'lively, bustling, full of amenities and acquiescences, into which he contrived to throw a sort of roughening of cordiality, like the crust of old port'.

His *Irish Melodies*, which were wildly popular throughout the nineteenth century, are mellifluous confections, all smiles, tears and fond retrospection:

Erin! the tear and the smile in thine eyes,
Blend like the rainbow that hangs in thy skies!
    Shining through sorrow's stream,
    Sadd'ning through pleasure's beam,
    Thy suns, with doubtful gleam,
        Weep while they rise!

The Irish weather, an exile's watery nostalgia, a vague but polite nationalism, all combine to create a sugary melancholy which delighted the fashionable and made Moore £500 a year for over a quarter of a century. As Hazlitt rightly complained, these winsome lyrics converted 'the wild harp of Erin into a musical snuff box'. And when Jeffrey criticised them in the *Edinburgh Review* for concealing corruption 'under the mask of refinement', Moore, who was always conscious of how he appeared to others, decided to behave like a pasteboard gentleman and challenge the moral Scot to a duel. They met at Chalk Farm, raised their pistols and were promptly arrested by the police. While waiting to be bailed out of Bow Street they began to talk about poetry and became friends for life.

It was always Moore's intention to gain an important public position through the influence of the aristocrats he so assidu-

---

Tom Moore: The Irish Poet by Terence de Vere White.

ously cultivated, and in 1803, five days after the execution of Robert Emmet (a friend of his at Trinity), he set sail for Bermuda where he mistakenly hoped to make his fortune as registrar of the naval prize court. He visited New England, met with the usual rapturous reception, and affected a cultivated disdain, noting that there was nothing to be seen in the streets 'but dogs and negroes', and the few ladies 'that pass for white are to be sure the most unlovely pieces of crockery I ever set my eyes upon'. Here, as Terence de Vere White points out in one of his few insights into Moore's utterly evanescent character, he 'writes as one of the establishment'—as someone whose merely token membership depends on an ability to season his witty conversation with predictable phrases like 'to be sure' which, by reminding his audience of his nationality, flatter its sense of amused superiority. As Hunt shrewdly noted, there was 'just enough of the Irishman in him to flavour his speech and manner'.

Singing sweetly at the centre of the English establishment, this 'innocent, good-hearted, idle fellow' existed for many years in a state of pleasing servility—he was 'always in a flutter about lords and ladies and lobsters'. Like any Irishman in English society he was expected to charm and amuse, to be just sufficiently the Celt without being offensive, and like Gulliver in Brobdingnag this small Dubliner believed he was taken seriously.

Moore's only place was on the fringes of the Whig aristocracy where, provided he could provoke their cultivated emotions, he would always be the recipient of a patronising tolerance. He transformed his country's political aspirations into lilting anapaests and managed to be popular in Ireland as a nationalist writer without ever offending any of the innumerable aristocrats that cram the pages of this biography. Crowds cheered him in the theatre, dinner invitations showered in, and the ladies doted on him—in Rome, Pauline Bonaparte showed him 'her beautiful little hands, which I had the honour of kissing twice, and let me feel her foot, which is matchless'. He dispensed superlatives wherever he went and received them back in the form of praise of his inimitable self. He seems to have been one of those deeply selfish people whose radiant self-love casts a brief, delighted spell on everyone they meet.

It's this, more than anything else, which makes Moore a disastrous subject for a biography—he lived so much in other people's opinions, and his personality was such a flimsy, frothy bundle of visiting cards and song sheets that it's virtually impossible to perceive any natural integrity in the man. He had an immense talent for friendliness—as distinct from friendship—and it was this dazzling superficiality which made him safe, emotionally undemanding and companionable. This Irish Skimpole was totally heartless, and yet by making the emotions wholly social he offered a persuasively pasteurised ideal of good-nature. Byron described him as 'the best-hearted, the only *hearted* being I ever encountered', and told Samuel Rogers that he had only one friend in the world and 'that was Tom Moore'.

A surface charmer who shied away from pain and suffering, who avoided the deathbeds of his children and took some girls out to Vauxhall Gardens after Byron's funeral, Moore became the recipient of some of Byron's most famous letters. Byron poured out his jokes, his hangovers, his loves—'I am just come from an hour's swim in the Adriatic; and I write to you with a black eyed Venetian girl before me, reading Boccaccio'—and received in return a short and belated note of the kind they exchanged when they used to live in London 'and talk laxly, and go to parties'.

What was it in this professional Irishman that made him Byron's ideal confidant? For Moore, Byron seems to have been just another lord in his collection—on his last day in Venice he and Byron sat up until two in the morning 'beside the Palace of the Doges, drinking hot brandy and laughing over old times', but when Byron tried to persuade him to stay longer Moore refused and set off for Rome, never to see Byron again. Perhaps it was Moore's complete immunity to suffering, his genial and entirely public personality, which made him the right recipient of some of the greatest letters in the language. The case is puzzling and fascinating, but unfortunately de Vere White's garrulous telegraphese doesn't begin to answer it. Instead, he complains that Moore's statue presides over the largest public toilet in Dublin. But, as Leopold Bloom mused, it seems appropriate enough: 'They did right putting him up over a urinal; meeting of the waters.'

The Cruelty That Is Natural

William Trevor is one of the acknowledged masters of the short story. He is an Anglo-Irish writer who now lives in Devon and so he is an exiled member of a disappearing social group whose complex contradictions he shrewdly places in this description of a small Protestant schoolroom in the Irish Republic:

> There were portraits of England's kings and queens around the walls, painted by some teacher in the past. There were other pictures, added at some later date, of Irish heroes: Niall of the Nine Hostages, Lord Edward Fitzgerald, Wolfe Tone and Grattan. Maps of Europe and of Ireland and of England, Wales and Scotland hung side by side.

This is Trevor's heritage and it is at once his strength and his weakness. It enables him to present with the most accurate sympathy that desperately principled Irish intransigence which in 'Another Christmas' makes an otherwise gentle Irish exile destroy a long-standing friendship. Dermot is unable to forgive his English friend for mildly disagreeing with him about Irish terrorism. His momentary fanaticism ruins the old man's Christmas and permanently scars Dermot's relationship with his wife. Trevor tells the story with that impartial economy which is one of the most remarkable features of his writing.

Often Trevor returns to that notoriously Irish condition of being trapped by racial memories and historical bitterness. Usually he treats this subject with a resigned detachment which is effective and appealing, but sometimes the contradictions that underlie his detachment make him the passive victim of a nostalgia for vanished decencies. In a trilogy of stories called 'Matilda's England' he describes an Englishwoman who hates the present and who believes that 'there's nothing wrong with living in the past'. Here, Trevor appears to be justly critical of that national nostalgia which keeps *The Country Diary of an Edwardian Lady* at the top of the bestseller lists—he seems, in other words, to be investigating an English

---

Lovers of Their Times by William Trevor.
Jake's Thing by Kingsley Amis.

fixation with the past. And yet the three stories are suffused with loving memories of lost summers and lush pastures, and there is a most curious moment when Matilda looks at old Mrs Ashburton whose husband was killed in the First World War:

> I understood her law of averages and her sitting alone in her dark kitchen, crying over the past. I cried myself, thinking of the grass growing on her tennis court, and the cruelty that was natural.

Trevor very rarely springs a fine and arresting phrase like 'the cruelty that was natural' on his readers, and it makes an excellent conclusion for the story. Unfortunately, the cadence of the phrase is unmistakably Irish and because the story is so deeply English it sounds badly out of context, as though Matilda has momentarily changed nationality. For Trevor, an obsession with the past is a kind of madness—Matilda's nostalgia eventually drives her mad—and yet there is a deep dislike of contemporary reality in his stories.

In 'Broken Homes', for example, the delinquent children who desecrate old Mrs Malby's flat assume a parabolic significance, and this is especially evident when Mrs Malby thinks of their school—Tite Comprehensive—and sees 'an ugly sprawl of glass and concrete buildings'. This is a succinct image of how the modern world appears to Trevor, and it would be wrong to dismiss it as reactionary. No opinion should interfere with an appreciation of the unforced artistry and superb economy of this brilliant story. The children's violation of the old woman's decent privacy is registered with such accuracy that one can only admire its narrative perfection.

In 'Torridge' Trevor establishes the personality of a naive and lonely schoolboy through a few conversational mannerisms: 'Dad's in the button business—Torridge's you know.' Torridge becomes a figure of fun who serves to seal the friendship of three contemporaries—Mace-Hamilton, Wiltshire, and Arrowsmith. None of the senior pupils ever selects Torridge as his 'bijou' or 'male tart' and so he remains isolated from that phase of male homosexuality which appears to be obligatory in all public schools. The years pass and Torridge's three contemporaries have periodic reunions at which their wives, and later their children, are forced to listen to their accounts of the old school and its assorted eccentrics— including Torridge who gradually becomes a myth within the three families. At last they invite him to one of their reunions.

The three schoolboys are middle-aged men by this time and life has been variously kind and unkind to them. When Torridge appears he is suave, confident and rather sinister: he is no longer the comic butt, the lasting joke that binds a triangular friendship, and he effortlessly destroys the shabby snobberies and forced hilarity of the reunion by revealing that he is homosexual, just as Arrowsmith and his cronies once were. And he also reveals that their schoolboy cruelty was responsible for the suicide of one of the senior pupils. Trevor's narrative has a ballad-like inevitability and momentum, and as in a folk-tale we watch the spectre of justice appearing at the feast. It's as though the Green Knight has appeared in the dining-room of the Woodlands Hotel, Richmond.

'Torridge', like 'Broken Homes', is a masterpiece, and yet there is a quality in Trevor's prose and characterisation which is curiously processed and ersatz: the characters speak in the clipped twittering accents of British films of the 1940s (a grocer asks, 'What can I entice you to, sir?'). Many of the characters—the Reverend Throataway, for example—are as flat as the butcher, the baker, the candlestick-maker in the card game of Happy Families, and the prose style somehow manages to possess both a spare simplicity and a superannuated drabness. Norman Britt and Marie in the title-story are more like meek Edwardians than lovers in the 1960s. All too often Trevor settles for a decent, tolerant, middlebrow obviousness, a kind of synthetic mustiness. It's rather like being presented with an exact reproduction of a bakelite wireless set, switching it on and hearing Alvar Liddell reading the 10 o'clock news. The oddly dated atmosphere of Trevor's stories is the main obstacle to a more complete—and more generous—appreciation of his talent.

Traditionally, John Bull is a bloody-minded, insular, beer-swilling, xenophobic philistine with a thick neck and a truculent manner. He hates wogs, he hates the young, and he wishes women would disappear as soon as it's over. Although this choleric figure has been lying low of late, he has dictated a novel to a battered amanuensis called Kingsley Amis. His novel has half a dozen good jokes, a brilliant title, but it is often tedious and sometimes insolently stupid. It tells the story of an Oxford don, Jake Richardson, who has been surprised by impotence in middle age and who is the vehicle for a series of complaints about scruffy girls, hotel meals, the

GPO, feminism, bloody foreigners, bad bus services and incompetent taxi-drivers.

As Amis—or John Bull—charts this banal hell of rancid grievances and utterly average sensuality he has the cheek to suggest that undergraduates today are a poor lot who are vandalising the English language. Some students undoubtedly write badly, but perhaps they will do better in time, and anyway it's nonsense to suggest that there was a golden age of good English before the advent of comprehensive schools. More of Amis's prose emphatically means worse. Take this sentence:

> Jake stood at the window in thought, though not of any very purposeful description, for a couple of minutes.

And this rasping description of girls passing in the street:

> Apart from their dirtiness, which was often no more extreme than a look of entire neglect as in a hermit or castaway, they tended to have in common smallness of frame that wasn't quite slimness, smallness of feature that went with roundness of head, dark-blonde colouring and nothing to shout about in the way of tits, so much so that the odd one here and there was probably a boy: anyhow, there were enough such to point to a large secret migration from (as it might have been) Schleswig-Holstein.

This desecration of a once noble language is evident throughout the novel. The sentences are often jammed with infinitives:

> Jake took him on to dessert and gave him port; to help to seem to be giving rather than plying with he took a small glass himself.

No undergraduate in my experience has ever written as badly as this. Reading Amis's prose is like getting kicked in the stomach—I found myself virtually retching at its sheer awfulness. And what does he mean by 'an O'Casey peasant'? Someone Irish, I suppose—the sort of chap who has a name like Synge and writes plays called *The Plough and the Stars*. Again, the kind of mistake that an undergraduate might be forgiven for making, but no one—except the small circle of Black Paper chums this novel glances at—will forgive Amis for writing so badly.

However, some of his targets are well chosen: academic laziness, waterlogged Brussels sprouts, the more lunatic extremes of the women's movement, and a certain Oxford don who writes plays. But throughout there is a huge imaginative slackness and a heavy obviousness. And behind the brusquely average cynicism there is a tone of plaintive self-pity and puzzled misogyny. It's as though all his life Amis has been obediently following the advice that every sergeant-major used to give his men before they left for a night on the town: a shit, a shave and a shampoo. Now, Amis has begun to wonder if this advice wasn't just a shade too basic, too functional, too stupid. But his total lack of imaginative distinction and fineness tells him that the sergeant-major was bloody well right and damn anyone who disagrees. Like the most vulgar materialist, the bullish national archetype has named all the parts, barked out a few orders, and that's the end of it. Women, Jake concludes, are a lot of foreigners anyway and they always were a waste of a man's time. And at the end of the novel, when Jake is offered a new treatment which will repair his libido, he responds by summoning every woman he has known onto his mental parade-ground.

> Jake did a quick run-through of women in his mind, not of the ones he had known or dealt with in the past few months or years so much as all of them: their concern with the surface of things, with objects and appearances, with their surroundings and how they looked and sounded in them, with seeming to be better and to be right while getting everything wrong, their automatic assumption of the role of injured party in any clash of wills, their certainty that a view is the more credible and useful for the fact that they hold it, their use of misunderstanding and misrepresentation as weapons of debate, their selective insensitivity to tones of voice, their unawareness of the difference in themselves between sincerity and insincerity, their interest in importance (together with noticeable inability to discriminate in that sphere), their fondness for general conversation and directionless discussion, their pre-emption of the major share of feeling, their exaggerated estimate of their own plausibility, their never listening and lots of other things like that, all according to him. So it was quite easy. 'No thanks,' he said.

It's a sad assertion of defeated machismo, and if anyone thinks that phrase 'all according to him' refers to Jake and not Amis, then they can't tell crude bad artistry from good.

National Myths

Myths are rare nowadays, possibly because we have become dull positivists who mistake imaginative explanations for lies. John le Carré, however, is a devout and brilliant myth-maker who has raised the jargon of office politics into the terms of a national epic:

> The Circus in those days was like a bombed-out building, [Smiley] remembered; its officers scattered, its agents blown or dead or laid off. Bill Haydon's unmasking was an open wound in everyone's mind: they called it the Fall and shared the same sense of primeval shame.

The hurt is to the English psyche and at the end of le Carré's masterpiece, *Tinker, Tailor, Soldier, Spy*, the wounded patriot, Jim Prideaux, avenges the betrayed consciousness of Albion. Not since Auden—whose early work le Carré most subtly draws on—has a writer succeeded in making the English landscape so intensely political. Le Carré's Cornish coastlines, vistas of dying elms, playing-fields around mouldering prep schools, juju men scanning the horizons, are haunted by ghosts from the public world of intrigue, vigilance and obscurely dirty tricks.

In many ways he resembles Spenser, whose mercifully unfinished epic offers a myth of the English consciousness struggling to achieve its Anglican identity. Karla is the Leninist equivalent of Spenser's Papal Archimago, while Ann Smiley is the false Duessa, a neurotic metamorphosis of Una who is Truth and the soul of the nation. Smiley is the Red Cross Knight who is given advice by an aged holy man called Contemplation:

> Then seeke this path, that I to thee presage,
> Which after all to heaven shall thee send;
> Then peacably thy painefull pilgrimage
> To yonder same Hierusalem do bend,
> Where is for thee ordaind a blessed end:

Smiley's People by John le Carré.
Northern Myths and Other Stories by John Morrow.
The Mangan Inheritance by Brian Moore.

For thou emongst those Saints, whom thou doest see,
Shalt be a Saint, and thine owne nations frend
And Patrone: thou Saint George shalt called bee,
Saint George of mery England, the signe of victoree.

Like the Dantean shade or 'compound familiar ghost' in Eliot's *Little Gidding*, Smiley is a shadowy absolute who incarnates the finest contemplative wisdom. And this is stressed when a devoutly religious police superintendent compares Smiley to an abbey which is 'made up of all sorts of conflicting ages and styles and convictions'.

If this suggests that Smiley is an establishment figure then we must very firmly distinguish him from what that term normally means—he will not be found sleeping off his lunch in the library of the Travellers' Club. The 'iron quietness' of his demeanour depends on a tough and unillusioned view of Western values ('I can see through Eastern values just as you can through our Western ones,' he tells Karla in *Tinker, Tailor*). He is a thirties intellectual—with, naturally, a European sensibility—who has made a severe commitment to the cause of social democracy, and yet he knows how mushy and contradictory that cause is in comparison with more definite ideologies: 'I am a thief of the spirit, he thought despondently. Faithless I am pursuing another man's convictions.'

The unique Englishness which Smiley represents is caught in this passage from the latest novel, *Smiley's People*, where he broods on a gnomic and urgent statement that has strange mythic echoes, '*Tell Max that it concerns the Sandman*':

> ...he still knew that it was just possible, against all the odds, that he had been given, in late age, a chance to return to the rained-off contests of his life and play them after all. If that was so, then no Ann, no false peace, no tainted witness to his actions, should disturb his lonely quest.

The significant word 'quest' links le Carré's story with that ancient imaginative world of wandering forests, fluid identities, and mysterious fortresses just off the beaten track. Le Carré's use of aliases—Gerstman becomes Karla who becomes the Sandman who is then 'too important to exist'—is curiously Ovidian, and if at times he emphasizes the protean too self-consciously it would be wrong to dismiss him as the Tolkien of espionage. He is a rigorously serious writer and his remark that Smiley 'knows that most of life is led below the surface, and that people are very secretive creatures—secret even from themselves'* connects the world of official secrets with the private world of emotional betrayals and evasions. An imagination capable of making such connections must be mythic in its ambitions, and it's this direction which gives his fictions their tantalizing permanence. He is not, therefore, the kind of writer whom Clive James has termed 'a prisoner of clarity'.

For le Carré, people are betrayed by whatever streak of personal tenderness they possess, rather like Adam in *Paradise Lost* whose commitment to Eve after she has eaten the apple is at once his downfall and the proof of his saving humanity. Thus Karla is both a committed absolutist and a flawed human being. Smiley, whose private wound is public knowledge, considers this paradox:

> And there is this other Karla, Karla of the human heart after all, of the one great love, the Karla flawed by humanity. I should not be deterred if, in order to defend his weakness, he resorts to the methods of his trade.

Smiley decides that Karla isn't 'fireproof' because he's a fanatic whose 'lack of moderation will be his downfall'. Essentially, le Carré is saying that deep down we are all squashy liberals, and the central inspiration of *Smiley's People* is an almost despairing wish to prove this and to assert the superiority of Western over Eastern values. Throughout le Carré's imagination has a quiet brooding heroic quality and a reined-in bitterness.

His mythic urgency is apparent in his presentation of Karla's daughter, who is mentally ill and spins tales which her nurse disbelieves:

> How her father was a secret prince more powerful than the Tsar. How he ruled at night, as the owls rule while the hawks are at rest. How his secret eyes followed her wherever she went, how his secret ears heard every word she spoke. And how, one night, hearing her mother praying in her sleep, he sent his men for her and they took her into the snow and she was never seen again: not even by God, He was looking for her still.

*From an interview with Miriam Gross. This compulsive secrecy is beautifully caught in a pun in *Tinker, Tailor* where Jerry Westerby lifts a finger to denote a Red Indian's feather before padding off 'into his own reserves'.

This schizophrenic myth brilliantly images the nature of power—how natural and cruel it is—and at the same time it explores Alexandra's equally natural hunger for a religious explanation of secular phenomena. In one extraordinary moment Alexandra tells Smiley that he represents 'the forgiveness of the authorities' and then asks him if he is God. No, he replies, 'I'm just an ordinary person.' But we remember the scene early in the novel where Smiley appears in the 'religious light between dawn and morning', and we remember, too, that he has been called 'an abbey'. He is therefore a saintly confessor, a divine, a human absolute whom we can trust. This is a complex and hard-won assertion of English superiority, and only a combination of le Carré's imaginative *gravitas* and Smiley's truly European cultivation prevents it from appearing absurdly and offensively patriotic (though anyone interested in the deep structures of the English mind would do well to consider le Carré).

In the closing pages of the novel we stare with Smiley across the Berlin Wall and see his strict mildness waver as an evil desire for revenge touches him. His companion, Guillam, reflects: 'It is a place of no compromise...a place of no third way. Whatever reservations he might occasionally have about the Western freedom, here, at this border, like most other things, they stopped dead.'

The Wall is like a great breach in nature, and Karla's defection to the West represents an unequivocal victory for good. Haydon's treachery—'the Fall'—is atoned for, and the divided and sceptical Western spirit is healed. Although le Carré writes magnificently here, I'm not convinced by what he says—Karla has to exist as an absolutist and cannot be broken in this humanly relativistic way. In any case, Karla is saving his own skin by defecting, and le Carré is trivialising Western values by identifying them with that wish.

The ending—and one doesn't have to be a committed Marxist to recognise this—*is* sentimental and I'm forced to recognise its weakness. Nevertheless, *Smiley's People* is a very fine novel—taut, subtle, exciting and deeply serious. After the flaccid and disappointing *The Honourable Schoolboy* le Carré has rediscovered his profound imaginative resources.

For John Morrow a myth is both an elaborate and strategic lie and a way of telling the truth. In his collection of contemporary folk tales he draws on a vigorous and seldom noticed oral tradition of northern Irish story-telling. Morrow is the author of a brilliant comic novel, *The Confessions of Proinsias O'Toole*, which treats the Ulster situation in a violently comic manner, and the folk memory which informs his art is that of the urban working class—a wild, often cruel imagination which eagerly absorbs the contemporary and transforms it into legend:

> Myth-making can be studied at its best in the morning riot courts, when first drafts are presented to wide-eyed magistrates. From these fantasy sessions one would deduce that Belfast has a sizeable population of unemployed stone-masons, company directors and horse-riders (see the *Belfast Telegraph*, July 1970) who frequently take off in the small hours, driven by a sudden whim to visit widowed/crippled/blind parents, to search for stray dogs, or to buy chips. This might be acceptable as yet another social problem of our unquiet times; but that every one of these night-strollers should then trip over semi-automatic pistols—which they lift to admire the workmanship—or milk bottles full of petrol—which they are about to put out of the childer's way when the Army arrives—is pure artistry.

Out of the surge of the folk memory come figures like Duncher McAnuff, Joe McConkey, Billy McCord and Savage Mary—figures who, in Yeats's phrase, 'engross the present and dominate memory'.

Central to Morrow's imagination is the sense that one of his narrators comes to share: 'At that time I had not yet outgrown some juvenile ideas about "Honour" and "Fair Play"— products, I might add, not of my Belfast slum environment but of the English public school myth propagated by *The Magnet* and *Boy's Own*.' And as in many folk-tales the ruthlessness that lies at the core of all experience is revealed. At times Morrow resembles the Kipling of 'Mrs Bathurst' and 'A Sahib's War', and this similarity is most powerfully apparent in 'Beginnings' where an adolescent's sexual fantasies are 'cribbed from an album of photographs his Da had looted from a dead Turk in the Dardanelles'. This historical reference is just one example of the mythically actual thread that runs through the stories— the Somme, the Titanic, the Dardanelles, Murmansk, all become intense images which locate the struggles, sufferings and energies of many generations.

In 'Savage Mary' an old woman's public flyting of her neighbours is tolerated by the community because she rep-

51

resents 'the vindictive Dark Powers', and in many ways these stories enact the bacchic release which story-telling provides in a tight community—as a force the narrative urge is both socially cohesive and wildly anarchic. It simultaneously binds the community together, draws on the communal past, and supplies a creative outlet for pent-up passions. Morrow's image for this narrative urgency (an urgency which most naturally depends on a live audience) is the experience of folk music, and this is most vividly apparent in the 'wild skirling climax' of the concert in 'Hunch'. Like Joyce, Morrow is in various senses tapping the primeval powers which manifest themselves in the last stanza of the ballad of 'Finnegan's Wake':

Jack Maloney ducked his head
When a bucket of whiskey flew at him;
He ducked, and falling on the bed,
The whiskey scattered over Tim.
Bedad, he revives, and see how he rises,
Finnegan rising in the bed saying
'Whirl yer whiskey around like blazes.
Thundering jazez! did yis think me dead?'

These lines fuse sex, death, resurrection, intoxication and wild brawling, and what is remarkable about the folk imagination is its way of overriding the great division between life and death. It locates the resurrection in the self-delighting wildness of sheer rhythm, or in the mesmeric fascination of narrative. Spontaneous comic hyperbole is one of the essential qualities of this fascination:

If disease can be seen as water, the child was a sponge; his "mentions" in *The Lancet* during the first eight years of his life equal the 'Hunch Shaughnessy' file in his press-cutting agency today; a score of doctors made reputations by merely diagnosing the maladies he played host to—one of which I've mentioned, the throat infection, last known as the curse of inbred Bulgarian royalty in the eighteenth century, which left behind a voice that can alibi the most abysmal lyric.

Another device of the mythic imagination is to relish the historical and barbaric "yawp" of certain words—thus the missing place-name in 'O'Fuzz' has a sound which is hilariously described as 'long and glottal, half-roads between a Gaelic battle-cry and a Planter's curse'. The third device—it is primarily associated with Savage Mary—is that of a lacerating rhetoric which possesses an operatic and inebriated violence and yet doesn't actually scathe anyone. Its literary tradition stretches back at least as far as medieval poetry.

Morrow possesses a prodigal imaginative intelligence which is brilliantly comic, sometimes rather too sprawling, but always fiercely certain of itself. He writes at a peak of inspiration, as though on a permanent binge, and his series of hyperborean myths deserves a wide readership.

Brian Moore's last novel, *The Doctor's Wife*, was in part a clever reworking of *Madame Bovary* which traced the defection of a middle-class Belfast housewife from her husband and society. Moore has always been gifted with an ability that Fay Weldon has recently denied male novelists can possess—the ability of imagining a woman's experience. In his new novel, *The Mangan Inheritance*, Moore displays a fine and reverberating irony as he takes the feminist subject of the discovery of identity by one partner in a marriage, and realigns it by making the dominant partner a successful actress (Beatrice Abbot) and the submissive partner a failed writer (James Mangan).

The opening section of the novel is a beautifully poised narrative which begins with the aftermath of the separation and then traces the experience of the marriage. Moore's prose is sharp and crisp as he recapitulates that experience—Mangan becoming more and more passive and self-effacing until he dwindles into the question, 'Aren't you Beatrice Abbot's husband?' Mangan's attempt to achieve his identity involves a traditional—even mythic—journey back to Ireland. There is a family tradition that the Mangans are descended from the famous Irish poet, James Clarence Mangan, and the rest of the novel is concerned with Mangan's search for proof of his ancestry. Unfortunately, Moore switches into a mode of Hibernian Gothic which reads like the exploration of a private obsession with guilt and 'the impure delight of the forbidden'. Dark Rosaleen, that enduring myth of Irish nationhood, makes a predictable appearance and behaves like a preposterous *houri*, and there is a great deal of merely ersatz Irishness.

At his best Moore is a quietly magnificent novelist, and two of his earlier novels, *The Feast of Lupercal* and *I Am Mary Dunne*, are masterpieces. The first hundred pages of *The Mangan Inheritance* are as good as anything he has written, but the rest of the novel is mostly kitsch. There are some fine and authentic moments among the rainswept fantasies, though Moore's sense of history is confused and superficial (he believes there was a Fenian movement at the time of the 1798 rebellion). It's perhaps this sentimental expatriate view of Ireland which accounts for the bogus nature of the story.

A Terminal Ironist

In 'Entropy' Derek Mahon included these images of the abject, almost snug moment before the final instant of cultural collapse:

> We have tried
> To worship the sun,
> To make gods of clay,
>
> Gods of Stone
> But gave up in derision.
> We have pared life to the bone
>
> And squat now
> In the firelight reading
> Gibbon and old comics.

These stanzas have been cut from the version of 'Entropy' which appears in *Poems 1962-1978* and so Mahon has 'pared...to the bone' a poem already dedicated to the terminal and minimal. This ruthless refinement is one of the essential qualities of all Mahon's verse and almost invariably he combines an exquisite absolutism with an arrogant nonchalance:

> I have been working for years
>   on a four line poem
>   about the life of a leaf.
> I think it may come out right this winter!*

Mahon aims at what Eliot terms 'A condition of complete simplicity/ (Costing not less than everything)', and his poems are remarkable for their purity of style, the subtle lucid singing intelligence they display.

At some point in his brilliant youth Mahon must have faced the choice between perfection of the life or of the work—he chose the latter and made a religion of art. Thus he is an intransigent aesthete who rejects life almost completely and considers only the flotsam and jetsam along its fringes. In his magnificent reworking of 'April on Toronto Island' he sees a 'litter of tin cans/ And oily fish-skeletons', and as groups of

*'The Mayo Tao'—a revised version of the prose poem 'A Hermit'.

people stand on the wintry shore:

> Their faces dream of other islands,
> Clear cliffs and salt water,
> Fields brighter than paradise
> In the first week of creation –
> Redemption in a wind or a tide,
> Our lives in infinite preparation.

These figures cannot conceive of any compromise with this life, because like Mahon they must dream always of a perfect elsewhere.

In all Mahon's work there is only one poem which might, for what the terms are worth, be called warm and tender. Rather like one of Yeats's early poems, 'Glengormley'* sets the virtues of quotidian ordinariness—'The terrier-taming, garden-watering days'—against the ideal reality of aesthetic heroism:

> The unreconciled, in their metaphysical pain,
> Dangle from lamp-posts in the dawn rain.

Mahon identifies with the unreconciled and the damned, and often there is a quality of still anguish in the bitter clarity and detachment of his work. Again and again he returns to motifs of silence, exile, utter clear-eyed despair, and versions of the artistic life. What he celebrates—and it's a celebration conducted in a temperature of absolute zero—is the perfection of art, an intense *quidditas* which exists outside history:

> Perfecting my cold dream
> Of a place out of time,
> A palace of porcelain. †

And he rejects any insistence that art should be socially relevant or politically committed:

> But the fireloving
> People, rightly perhaps,
> Will not countenance this,
> Demanding that I inhabit,
> Like them, a world of
> Sirens, bin-lids
> And bricked-up windows.

However, the poet and rioter share an occult identity in 'Rage for Order', and this is a version of Yeats's sense that every culture originally springs from the actions of 'violent bitter men'. Art, Mahon implies, has nothing to do with liberal ideas of decency, and his work has a quality that Yeats discerned in Joyce: 'A cruel playful mind like a great soft tiger cat.'

In order to arrive at his vision of art—'Our afterlives a coming true/ Of perfect worlds we never knew'—Mahon takes the negative way, and his rejection of sense experience is glanced at in 'The Voice' ‡:

> Do you hear the voice increase in volume
> and, as a March wind quickens the creaking trees,
> sing mildly to us without fear,
> content in the fact of death? Do you hear?
> What does it sing in the grey dawn? Nobody knows;
> but the voice is audible only to those
> whose hearts are emptied of property and desire.

This visionary voice is audible only to those who in Eliot's terms reject 'the practical desire' and follow this advice:

> To arrive where you are, to get from where you are not,
>   You must go by a way wherein there is no ecstasy.
> In order to arrive at what you do not know
>   You must go by a way which is the way of ignorance.
> In order to possess what you do not possess
>   You must go by the way of dispossession. §

And in some ways Mahon resembles George Herbert who characteristically creates a perfect poem which also abolishes itself in the last line ('Prayer' is the most obvious example of this self-annihilating technique). Herbert's poems set themselves aside in order to merge with the absolute reality of God, while Mahon's slip into the utter perfection of Art. Paradoxically, therefore, Mahon's work possesses an extraordinary humility—at the last moment his *non serviam* modulates into the finest idea of service. And perhaps his aestheticism has parallels with the dedicated fanaticism of a hunger-striker

---

*In *Night-Crossing* this is dedicated to Padraic Fiacc. Whatever the reasons for it, the dropping of the dedication consorts oddly with the merely dandyish danglers from lamp-posts. The significant absence is a complex historical and personal bitterness—Fiacc's, not Mahon's.

† 'The Last of the Fire Kings'.

‡ From 'Three Poems after Jaccottet'.

§ From Eliot's *East Coker*.

whose absolute personal pride must also involve a complete rejection of personal identity.

From his early poem, 'Unborn Child', to the great master-piece, 'A Disused Shed in Co. Wexford', Mahon is fascinated by a place of pure being which exists outside history. It's a Jamesian subject and is treated in a sophisticated and para-doxical manner—the unborn child wants 'to live' and yet knows its days are numbered, the mushrooms are woken by a 'flash-bulb firing squad' and still beg us 'To do something, to speak on their behalf'. In 'An Image from Beckett' history and the still split second are identical:

> They will have buried
> My great-grandchildren, and theirs,
> Beside me by now
>
> With a subliminal batsqueak
> Of reflex lamentation.
> Our hair and excrement
>
> Litter the rich earth,
> Changing, second by second,
> To civilisations.

This is one of Mahon's finest achievements and an example of his uniquely terminal imagination: death and art are virtually identical in his work and his mockery in 'Poets of the Nineties'* stems not from any moral criticism, but from an aesthetic position even more extreme than Dowson's and Lionel Johnson's. Mahon makes them seem like cosy rustic liberals, bland and incapable of a complete commitment to art.

Mahon's commitment is naturally evidenced in the type of book this is—somehow it feels like a selected and a collected edition, *and* a new volume. There is something terrifying about its wholeness. And yet if certain poems—'My Wicked Uncle', 'April on Toronto Island', 'Rage for Order', 'Entropy'—have been brought to perfection, others have been nagged and tinkered into something less than their original spirit. For example, in 'In Belfast' † the line, 'The spurious mystery in the knowing nod', becomes the too-obvious, 'The hidden menace in the knowing nod'. And in 'Bruce Ismay's Soliloquy' ‡ the

*Originally titled 'Dowson and Company'.   † Now titled 'The Spring Vacation'.   ‡ Originally titled 'As God is my Judge'.

cadence of the last line—'Include me in your lamentations'—is flat and drab compared with, 'Include me/ *Honoris causa* in your lamentations'.

With the exception of 'The Attic', 'The Return', and 'Three Poems after Jaccottet', Mahon's new poems are very disappointing—they tend to whine without much distinction. There is a very fine poem called 'Mythological Figure' which must have been dropped from *Night-Crossing* and which is included in this volume, and unfortunately Mahon's new poems don't match up to it. In it the mythological figure who 'ought' to have existed is condemned to sing whenever she opens her mouth. She begins to sing

> and her gestures
> Flowed like a mountain stream;
> But her songs were without words,
> Or the words without meaning –
> Like the cries of love or the cries of mourning.

Only a rare and extraordinary imagination could invent such a figure.

For the Ancient Britons: Edward Thomas

Edward Thomas often groaned under the tons of terrible light verse which postmen and literary editors conspired to dump on his doorstep. He once had to review a book called *Bungalow Ballads* and although he could be witty in the face of banality the pressures of literary journalism increased his melancholy. However, he had a wife and children to support and so he heroically churned out over a million words of reviewing, as well as nine full-length critical studies, various introductions, essays and anthologies.

It was only in the last two years of his life that he was able to write the poems for which he is now remembered. Since his death in the battle of Arras, those poems have always been in print and there have also been anthologies of his writings on the English countryside. This is the first prose selection to give pride of place to his criticism and it reveals what a uniquely gifted literary critic Edward Thomas was.

His reviews of Yeats, Synge, W.H. Davies, Pound, Lawrence and Frost all shine with that eagerly intelligent recognition which springs from the meeting of the right book with the right reviewer (his piece on Frost's *North of Boston* has the classic certainty of James on *Middlemarch*). Although Thomas referred to himself as 'a doomed hack' and 'a hurried man with little scholarship', he was in fact one of those rare critics whom Yeats called 'hearers and heartners of the work'. And as Edna Longley shows in her closely argued introduction, Yeats was Thomas's 'first hero of the modern revolution'. He followed Yeats in praising a passionate simplicity and a 'nonchalant grasp of life'. For Thomas, the best lyrics always appear to be 'the poet's natural speech' and good prose, too, must resemble speech in its method and effect.

Although Thomas never hits the pitch of great prose, his fascination with its 'music of ideas' lies at the foundations of his critical imagination. His polemic against Walter Pater is an exciting act of critical demolition and his praise of Shelley's prose is similarly fresh and provocative. Central to Thomas's

---

A Language Not To Be Betrayed: Selected Prose of Edward Thomas, edited by Edna Longley.

criticism is a delighted awareness of what he termed 'natural sweet cadence' and it was this expressive rhythm which he discovered in Yeats, Synge and Frost. Pater, he argued, pushed words around as if they were tin soldiers and the result was an 'exquisite unnaturalness', a form of trivial connoisseurship. Swinburne neglected vocal cadence in favour of musical jargon and kept 'a harem of words to which he was absolutely and constantly faithful'.

Thomas's prose and verse are both informed by a type of liberal anguish and uncertainty, a quality which in a review of Dowson's work he termed 'the comic terrible cry of the superfluous man'. At times he writes with a depressed decency which he knows belongs to 'a self-conscious civilisation, turning in disgust upon itself'. Thomas's dislike of Imperialism and his mystic introverted patriotism nourish his work and in his criticism he attempts to define a cultural identity which has nothing to do with bungalow verse. In a sense he tries to draw on that slightly chalky, insular spirit which informs the left-wing of the Labour Party.

Paradoxically, his best poems issue from the failure of that attempt and we can now begin to see how essential Thomas's critical prose is to a proper reading of his poems. Although he absurdly overpraised Doughty's epic of early Britain, his critical enthusiasm eventually helped him to shape the closing lines of 'The Combe':

> But far more ancient and dark
> The Combe looks since they killed the badger there,
> Dug him out and gave him to the hounds,
> That most ancient Briton of English beasts.

Thomas's symbol of the ancient rooted *British* badger replaces the more conventional imperial application of the term with a significance that is close to the historical vision of William Blake and the English Jacobins. He is attempting to imitate Yeats and draw on suppressed or vanished folk energies, on a kind of aboriginal Celtic essence which was buried beneath successive invasions of Romans, Saxons and Normans. Like John Clare, he is lamenting a vanished integrity and anyone who admires Thomas's work must be grateful for this fine and considered selection.

In Golden Mentmore: Henry James

There is an intense imaginative pitch which all of us perceive with varying degrees of rareness. Henry James appears to have known it every moment of his waking life, and it's this knowledge he describes in the great and noble letter of comfort which he wrote to Grace Norton:

> I don't know *why* we live—the gift of life comes to us from I don't know what source or for what purpose; but I believe we can go on living for the reason that (always of course up to a certain point) life is the most valuable thing we know anything about and it is therefore presumptively a great mistake to surrender it while there is any yet left in the cup. In other words consciousness is an illimitable power, and though at times it seems to be all consciousness of misery, yet in the way it propagates itself from wave to wave, so that we never cease to feel, though at the moment we appear to, try to, pray to, there is something that holds one in one's place...

In letter after letter he exercises that 'illimitable power' of consciousness and as a result everything he touches is brushed with the energy of absolute imaginative distinction. His taut rapid sweeping epistolary manner annexes whole territories of experience in a single sentence—there is a Napoleonic urgency and drive behind all that he says, and his unique sense of freedom seems to spring from what Hegel termed Absolute Spirit.

Like all great letter-writers, James speaks always with an intimate and varying responsiveness to the personality of the recipient—his voice is playful, respectful, teasing, lofty and almost always happy, for at its centre is a self-delighting eloquence. Thus in a letter from Paris to his father he says casually, 'You crave chiefly news, I suppose, about Ivan Sergeivitch,' and then gives a long witty account of a 'rigidly boresome' musical evening at Pauline Viardot's at which Turgenev acted charades and showed 'that spontaneity which Europeans have and we have not'. James naturally name-drops as he writes back to his family—he is friendly with Turgenev,

---

Henry James: Letters: 1875-1883, edited by Leon Edel.
Henry James: The Later Novels by Nicola Bradbury.

Zola, Daudet—and at the same time he speaks to them in a tender and nimble manner:

> I am delighted that Wilky's foot is better. Has he come to Cambridge? Tell Willy that I will answer his most interesting letter specifically; and say to my dearest sister that if she will tell me which—*black* or *white*—she prefers I will send her gratis a *fichu* of ecru lace, which I am told is the proper thing for her to have.

Here, he turns a kindly attention to his improvident and unfortunate younger brother, Wilky, then registers a grateful and dutiful, but perhaps slightly irksome obligation to William, before moving delightedly to his sister's future *fichu*. The letter concludes with an effect of rapidity which is held still by an especially intimate vocal shift: 'Ever, dearest daddy, your loving son, H. James Jr.' It's an eagerly affectionate conclusion and one which shows the extraordinary living presence of James's voice.

His relationship with William was close and difficult, and this is apparent in many letters (he often wrote to William from one of his London clubs and this must have been a way of impressing his elder brother). In a letter from the Athenaeum he writes:

> Yesterday I dined with Lord Houghton—with Gladstone, Tennyson, Dr Schliemann...and half a dozen other men of "high culture". I sat next but one to the Bard and heard most of his talk, which was all about port wine and tobacco: he seems to know much about them, and can drink a whole bottle of port at a sitting with no incommodity...Behold me after dinner conversing affably with Mr Gladstone—not by my own seeking, but by the almost importunate affection of Lord H. But I was glad of a chance to "feel" the "personality" of a great political leader—or as G. is now thought here even, I think, by his partisans, ex-leader. That of Gladstone is very fascinating—his urbanity extreme—his eye that of a man of genius and his apparent self-surrender to what he is talking of, without a flaw.

I quote this from Percy Lubbock's edition of James's letters because for some reason Leon Edel does not include it (though he quotes part of it in his biography of James). It's doubtful if this piece of splendid boasting made William envious and when he read *The Europeans* he fired off a critical letter which prompted this reply on Devonshire Club notepaper:

> I was much depressed on reading your letter by your painful reflections on *The Europeans*; but now, an hour having elapsed, I am

beginning to hold up my head a little; the more so as I think I myself estimate the book very justly and am aware of its extreme slightness. I think you take these things too rigidly and unimaginatively—too much as if an artistic experiment were a piece of conduct, to which one's life were somehow committed; but I think also that you're right in pronouncing the book 'thin', and empty.

William's unimaginative rigidity—his New England puritanism, Henry means—is reminiscent of the presentation of Caspar Goodwood in *The Portrait of a Lady*: 'His jaw was too square and stiff: these things suggested a want of easy consonance with the deeper rhythms of life.' And in many ways James's letters register his developing disaffection from American moral angularity and from the puritan attitude which personalises art as conduct.

And yet it's not as simple as this, because James's response to its Parisian opposite is initially enthusiastic, and then disillusioned. Writing to William Dean Howells, he speaks in a Strether-like manner: 'I am turning into an old, and very contented, Parisian: I feel as if I had struck roots into the Parisian soil.' Paris is a place of freedom where 'everything is accepted and understood', and yet when William rebuked him for his Gallic mannerisms he replied that he was now utterly bored by the French: 'I am done with 'em, forever, and am turning English all over.' In a letter which Edel omits, he told Charles Eliot Norton that the English are 'more complete than other folk, more largely nourished, deeper, denser, stronger'. And in a marvellous letter to his mother he describes a country house weekend at Mentmore where John Bright was also a guest:

> They are all at afternoon tea downstairs in a vast, gorgeous hall, where an upper gallery looks down like the colonnade in Paul Veronese's pictures, and the chairs are all golden thrones, belonging to ancient Doges of Venice. I have retired from the glittering scene to meditate by my bedroom fire on the fleeting character of earthly possessions, and to commune with my mammy, until a supreme being in the shape of a dumb footman arrives, to ventilate my shirt and turn my stockings inside out (the beautiful red ones imparted by Alice—which he must admire so much, though he doesn't venture to show it), preparatory to my dressing for dinner.

James says that the chief effect of '*ces gens-çi*' is to make him wish to distinguish himself by personal achievement—and so answer them—and then his imagination abruptly relishes his experience of the powerful basking in 'their atrocious good fortune':

> Lord Rosebery, however, with youth, cleverness, a delightful face, a happy character, a Rothschild wife of numberless millions to distinguish and demoralise him, wears them with such tact and bonhomie, that you almost forgive him. He is extremely nice with Bright, draws him out, defers to him etc., with a delicacy rare in an Englishman.

Here, James's fascinations are wealth, art, power, and the curious relativity of manners and customs—Rosebery shows a rare and delicate deference and James notes this very exactly.

He revels in national characteristics, pointing to the British dislike of being '*ironized* or satirised, from the American point of view', and noting how many people seem 'for the most part nothing but *surface*, and sometimes—oh ye gods!—such desperately poor surface!' He insists that London has 'all sorts of superior qualities', but it also shares with English life generally

> a certain number of great plump flourishing uglinesses and drearinesses which offer themselves irresistibly as *pin-cushions* to criticism and irony. The British mind is so totally un-ironical in relation to itself that this is a perpetual temptation.

James reveals a sensibility whose richness and sophistication depend on its deracinated alienation. His respect for English culture is tinged with an ironic and amused patronage—he knows that he is a social and artistic 'treasure' and his response is to gently pat the heads of those who pat him. It's a relationship of mutual acquisition, and James describes it in tones that vary from delighted gratitude to scornful exasperation.

His exasperation is apparent in various penetrating reflections on English politics:

> Dr Wilkinson came to see me a couple of days since, and wants them (the Irish) governed by the sword—by a reign of terror. This is all rubbish, as I think the rest of his opinions are. He thinks Disraeli wise and beneficent, Gladstone abominable, Bismarck a saviour of society etc. In short the politics of middle-class Toryism and the *Daily Telegraph*, mixed up with a queer, musty Swedenborgianism: an unsavoury compound.

This brisk and witty sketch issues from James's strategy of remaining slightly outside the cultural fabric he admires—it wasn't in order to become fully English that he joined various London clubs.

Although these letters can sometimes be exhausting in their beaming bachelor amiability, they are wonderful and fascinating—the lucid effusions of an illimitable consciousness. However, two vivid letters are missing from this volume—a volume which, Edel casually mentions, has been selected from 'great masses of correspondence'. And yet the dust-jacket makes the mendacious statement that Edel's edition is 'definitive'. How can a selected edition be definitive unless we're being led to believe it is in fact a proper collected edition? I know that I'm not alone in regretting the stranglehold which Edel has over James studies and this volume is merely another example of it. The most suffocating example of this is Edel's dim-witted and self-regarding biography of James.

Rather like Leon Edel, Nicola Bradbury appears to have become so besotted by James that she cannot bring herself to criticise him. Her study of the later novels belongs to that school of literary criticism which draws its inspiration from the agonized and self-delighting exquisiteness of James's late style. This type of criticism can best be described as the prose equivalent of an Ashbery poem—by saying nothing eloquently it aspires to exist as a display of supreme aesthetic sensibility. In many ways it represents a healthy and sophisticated reaction against the interpretative crudeness of those critics who demand that every work of art should have a moral significance—it breathes the traditional hedonistic atmosphere of Oxford and shrinks from the strenuous puritanism of Cambridge.

John Bayley is the ornate pontiff of this critical church and many of this pronouncements are elegantly and diffidently formal elaborations upon a beautifully organised void—he, too, believes he is a reincarnation of James. In his *Essay on Hardy*, especially, Bayley tastes the aroma of all possible judgements without every stooping to the vulgar act of discriminating between a good and bad piece of writing. He has attended so closely to James and the French symbolists that the result is a critical style which ripples with an intense awareness of itself.

Unfortunately Nicola Bradbury has been so influenced by Bayley's critical manner that her five essays (they pretend to be chapters) resemble that kind of nonsense-theology which wonders whether an infinity of angels dancing on a pinhead would perform a foxtrot, Viennese waltz, or maybe a brisk

Charleston. Her treatment of James represents a uniquely frustrating expense of sensibility in the dry desert of postgraduate research. Nevertheless, her original inspiration shows a proper respect for the reader's experience of a work of art:

> I do not want to overstress the difficulty of late James, but to show how this difficulty itself gives rise to some of the pleasure of reading, because in it is distilled the author's delight in writing: that sense of luxury which gives us access to "the quality of mind of the producer".

Pleasure in James's display of absolute imaginative pitch is one of the essential qualities in our appreciation of him and Bradbury is right to insist upon it. However, it's a virtually impossible task to evoke that display—a display that naturally bristles with its own pride—and not to give the impression of trying to wag a tail which is quite happy wagging itself. This kind of critical approach is rather like listening to someone singing in the bath—judgement is irrelevant to such a self-referring pleasure—and at one moment Bradbury actually has one of James's novels take a bath:

> In the golden luxury of a Kentish October at Fawns, the narrative itself sits up to its neck in a bath of opulence, and is helpless to move or see.

Everyone enjoys a warm bath, but it is pointless to compare those pleasures to a novel's delighted sense of its own existence.

Bradbury's tortured and paradoxical insistence on formal pleasure is really only an excuse for avoiding any kind of discriminating interpretation:

> The emotion generated during Mrs Stringham's imaginings and undercut by the narrative method, is here taken up again. The "logic" of this is poetic rather than analytic: it is an effect which works in reading but does not yield to critical analysis.

Like a small silver cannon loaded with a crimson smokeshell, that poor tired adjective "poetic" is wheeled into position in order to conceal the absence of any articulate critical vision. And Bradbury's sense of lectionary pleasure does not manifest itself in her own prose:

> Like Shakespeare's account of lust, 'mad in pursuit and in possession so,/ Had, having, and in quest to have, extreme' (Sonnet 129), or like Macbeth, the tragic hero, caught between

tenses and losing both present and eternity, Densher, knowing 'that he might on any other system go straight to destruction' (p.455), is reduced for a significant, though short, part of the novel, to the trap of a false position, and a riddling defence: 'he best kept everything in place by not hesitating or fearing, as it were, to let himself go in the direction, that is to say, of staying' (p.456).

The text is clotted with footnotes and references, and for all the aestheticism of the critical approach there are some oddly brusque moments:

> James's "international theme", his "money" theme, and the concern with power, which recur throughout his major works, besides the aesthetic question, a mode of considering the relationship of art to morality in a social context, are all presented in the first volume of *The Golden Bowl* with a dramatic immediacy, subtlety, and imaginative power which preclude easy dismissal.

Here the term "theme", which should never violate properly symbolist criticism, is dragged into the sentence and pushed about like a static counter. The sentence is slapdash and rhetorical, and although Bradbury displays taste and intelligence she has written a uniquely—and unconsciously—decadent work. Its passive quietism has a sort of mystic proneness, like an entranced fakir stretched upon a bed of nails.

The Writer Underground

Journalists sometimes present Solzhenitsyn as a combination of Tolstoy and Sir Keith Joseph. Like the Aims of Industry he stands for Freedom and all those other values which we in the West hold dear. Reading his work is rather like breaking the siege of the Iranian embassy—it makes people proud-to-be-British. And privately they remind themselves how nice it is not to be Russian.

This common distortion of Solzhenitsyn's work partly arises from an inability to perceive that his writings are addressed to his fellow Russians. He is proud of being Russian, William Whitelaw in proud of being British, and neither of them is the other. Thus for a journalist like Bernard Levin to transform Solzhenitsyn into Sir Keith Tolstoy is to practise a very familiar form of cultural imperialism. Anyone who finds the idea of Britishness grotesque must also be reminded of the extraordinary insularity and complacency of that culture. However, such smug appropriation may be inevitable unless the critic is deeply immersed in the Russian language and Russian culture. Here I must admit to being largely ignorant of the language and only sporadically read in its literature, so the account I have to offer is intended as a tentative approach to a figure who addresses his readers in a prickly volatile idiom which assumes they are part of the argument, not comfortable onlookers.

First of all, we must notice that Solzhenitsyn is closer to Dostoyevsky than to Tolstoy. He is a mystic Russian nationalist who scorns Western values:

> I put no hope in the West—indeed, no Russian ever should. If we ever become free it will only be by our own efforts. If the twentieth century has any lesson for mankind, it is we who will teach the West, not the West us. Excessive ease and prosperity have weakened their will and their reason.

There is an imperialistic ambition somewhere in this statement. But it is primarily informed by that ethic of suffering which

---

The Oak and the Calf: Sketches of Literary Life in the Soviet Union by Aleksandr Solzhenitsyn.

Russian writers emphasise so distinctively, and here it's essential to realise that, in the Russian imagination, suffering and the idea of the sacred are often identified. This and certain other distinctive qualities of that imagination are present in this poem by Osip Mandelstam, that great poet who died in a transit camp on the route to the Gulag archipelago:

> Cold spring, in starving Stary Krym,
> still with its guilt, as it was under Wrangel.
> Sheepdogs in the courtyard, patches on the rags,
> even the acrid smoke is the same.
>
> And the empty distance is as good as ever.
> The trees with buds starting to swell
> stand like shy strangers. The almond's pitiful,
> decked out in yesterday's silliness.
>
> Nature wouldn't know her own face.
> From the Ukraine, the Kuban, terrible ghosts.
> And the famished peasants, in felt shoes,
> stand guard at their gates, never touching the rings.

This poem is set in the terrible famine of 1932 and it combines remoteness, suffering and historical reference with admiration of nature and an insistent image of the starving peasants who are sacred and tragic figures. Mandelstam's vision has a kind of passionate eagerness, an exclamatory quality which is altogether different from the lyric melancholy it would probably possess if it were by an English writer and set in the Cotswolds. Of course, what I'm discussing here is a translation (the marvellous American translation of Clarence Brown and W.S. Merwin) and it may be that my reading of it is as much a distortion as Bernard Levin's version of Solzhenitsyn. However, this passage from the first section of these memoirs, 'The Writer Underground', has something of Mandelstam's visionary spontaneity:

> I strolled about now some ten metres from the bishop's arklike house, and those old linden trees, those immortal lindens under which I had paced back and forth, back and forth, back and forth, morning, noon and night, for three years on end, dreaming of freedom's bright distant dawn in other and brighter years, and in a brighter Russia.
> Now, on a clammy overcast day, in the sloppy November snow, I walked on the other side of the fence, along a path by which only

guards on their way to relieve comrades on the watchtower had trudged in the old days, and I thought: What have I done? I have put myself in their hands again.

Freedom's 'bright distant dawn' may not be a fresh image, but the reader must take it on trust and as with Mandelstam's poem notice how landscape, suffering and history combine to create what De Quincey terms an 'involute'—an inextricable compound of emotion, intellect and visual imagery. We must also recognise that Solzhenitsyn is not invoking a Western idea of freedom here.

Another reminder of how we should read his work comes from Mandelstam's widow, Nadezdha, who states in *Hope Abandoned*:

> The value of our main *samizdat* writer, Solzhenitsyn, is that he restores our memory of time past. This is the first step towards the recovery of one's sense of being human. Only after passing through this stage will people understand that the individual, the distinctive, stands for the whole or the general, and is a symbol of it. Literature can exist only where there is pain, and pain can be felt only by a human being, a personality. Where there is pain, people do not talk about "major" or "minor" works, about "style" or "subject matter", but only about pain—which itself knows how best to express itself.

Here, Nadezdha Mandelstam insists that aesthetic judgement is irrelevant to Solzhenitsyn's achievement, and what we must recognise, I think, is that he possesses a mnemonic imagination of epic dimensions. He has emerged from the underworld, like Aeneas, to speak for all the *zeks* who suffer there. And, like Dostoyevsky's persona in *Notes from Underground*, Solzhenitsyn addresses a fierce monologue to the reader (this kind of intimate and savage monologue is a characteristically Russian form). His voice is that of the *muzhik*—a folk voice, though that adjective sounds hopelessly twee in this context and is again a reminder of how difficult it is for the Western reader to approach the Russian experience. He speaks in tones that are spiky, passionate, lacerating and ironic, as in this passage from his open letter to 'the Secretariat of the R.S.F.S.R. Writers' Union':

> Dust off the clock face. You are behind the times. Throw open the sumptuous heavy curtains—you do not even suspect that day is already dawning outside. We are no longer in that muted, that

sombre, that hopeless age when, just as compliantly, you expelled Akhmatova. We are not even in that timid, shivery period when you expelled Pasternak, howling abuse at him. Is this not disgrace enough for you? Do you want to make it blacker yet? But the time is near when each of you will seek to scratch his signature from today's resolution.

Here, as so often in Russian writing, we seem to be eavesdropping on an intense family quarrel. Culturally, that enormous country appears to be passionately provincial—everyone knows each other and there is much malicious gossip, sudden tenderness and equally sudden rage.

Solzhenitsyn's peasant voice is often bitter and righteous, and it hurls itself against corrupt institutions, codes of conduct and manners. He identifies it with two personalities whom he greatly admired:

> I cannot say that I had precisely planned it, but I did accurately foresee that the *muzhik* Ivan Denisovich was bound to arouse the sympathy of the superior *muzhik* Tvardovsky and the supreme *muzhik* Nikita Khrushchev. And that was just what happened: it was not poetry and not politics that decided the fate of my story, but that unchanging peasant nature, so much ridiculed, trampled underfoot and vilified in our country since the Great Break, and indeed earlier.

Tvardovsky (the courageous editor of *Novy Mir*) emerges in this memoir as a most noble and tragic figure, and Solzhenitsyn's friendship with him was close and difficult. Tvardovsky's natural instinct tore against his ideological loyalties; he loved the magazine he edited and for the sake of its 'humane voice' he took 'all the brickbats, the kicks, the spittle' (a phrase that must echo what Mandelstam terms 'the wicked and gay sibilance of Russian verse'). Tvardovsky accepted humiliation, losing power, honours and his health. He smoked constantly, tried to relieve his tension in long drinking bouts, felt lonely, embittered and betrayed. Even after an operation for cancer he chain-smoked.

Solzhenitsyn loved him and saw him as inseparably linked with Khrushchev:

> Khrushchev had told Tvardovsky that three volumes of documents on Stalin's crimes had now been collected, but that they were not being published for the present. 'History will pronounce judgement on what we have tried to do.' Khrushchev always became

solemn and subdued when he spoke of our common mortality, and of man's limited span. This note could be heard in his public speeches too. It was a Christian trait in him, of which he was unconscious.

The Christian trait is strong in Solzhenitsyn and his ebullient rhetoric must be partly modelled on Khrushchev's political style. He greatly respected him and was profoundly shaken by his overthrow. His mission is an imaginative continuation of Khrushchev's liberating attack on Stalin. And again we must notice how Solzhenitsyn refuses to conform to our prejudices—despite a certain grudging admiration Khrushchev figures fairly prominently in Western demonology.

Solzhenitsyn confesses to making various mistakes in handling the power which his fame gave him and he admits that he did not use his power to the best effect. This was because of 'a mistaken sense of obligation to *Novy Mir* and Tvardovsky', and Solzhenitsyn's analysis of that mistake implicitly refutes a Western notion of personality and individual heroism:

> My point of departure should always have been that I did not belong to myself alone, that my literary destiny was not just my own, but that of the millions who had not lived to scrawl or gasp or croak the truth about their lot as jailbirds and their later discoveries in the camps. Troy, after all, does not owe its existence to Schliemann, and our many-layered camp culture makes solemn demands of its own, so that I, who had returned from the world that never gives up its dead, had no right to swear loyalty either to *Novy Mir* or to Tvardovsky.

That reference to Troy reminds us that Solzhenitsyn has been vouchsafed an epic imagination by the experience of those millions. He is setting his own personality aside, and insisting that we do likewise. Here, we need only remember the ending of the film *Holocaust* in order to recognise the way in which an optimistic Western notion of personal freedom can trivialise and sentimentalise.

Another quality of Russian culture which I've only glanced at is the importance which Russians attach to memory. A.R. Luria's *The Mind of a Mnemonist* is a classic account of one example of this phenomenon (it is a study of a man known as 'S' who possessed a memory so naturally powerful and also keenly trained that he felt damned by his gift of absolute recall). Solzhenitsyn describes how in prison he committed thousands of lines of his own verse to memory and devised 'decimal counting beads' as a mnemonic aid. As he approached the end of his sentence, he grew more confident of his powers of memory and began writing down and memorising prose: 'But more and more of my time—in the end as much as one week per month—went into regular repetition of all that I had memorised.' He mentions that Akhmatova kept her 'Requiem' in her head for 24 years, and in her memoirs Nadezdha Mandelstam tells how she memorised all her husband's poems.

Where there is ruthless oppression and where the written word is so respected and feared by those in authority that they must seek to control it, then a trained memory is essential to a living culture—a necessarily *samizdat* culture. Therefore the underground writer and the mnemonist are twins. In the West we tend to devalue memory and this means that various ancient mnemonic skills have been almost completely lost. I doubt if a Russian would be very impressed by Coleridge's famous distinction between the unmethodical memory (Mistress Quickly in her dolphin chamber) and Hamlet's 'methodising intellect' which selects and arranges. In Russia the mnemonist is essential to 'the recovery of one's sense of being human'.

If Solzhenitsyn sometimes appears to be remembering too much in these memoirs, we must consider the enormous pressures on him and his consuming obligation to those millions who perished during 'the great dark epoch'. Both he and Nadezdha Mandelstam ramble and digress in their memoirs because they must follow the inspiration of their recollections. For them it is a sin to break with the past and forget. This means that the Western reader must learn to respect their mnemonic compulsion—in order to recognise suffering on a scale so vast it must be remembered very accurately, for it cannot be imagined.

The Man from No Part: Louis MacNeice

On a cold morning some years ago I was sitting on a bench outside an Oxford college. An Irish tramp came and sat beside me, asked for the price of a drink and then began to talk. He asked me where I was from and I told him. And then, stupidly, I asked him what part of Ireland he came from. His answer was sad, evasive and very honest. 'I'm that long out of Ireland,' he sighed, 'you could say I come from no part.'

In all kinds of ways—except that of social dereliction—Louis MacNeice's life was like that. His ancestors came from the West of Ireland, he was born in Belfast and educated in England where he lived for the rest of his life. As he says in 'Carrick Revisited', he was

> Torn before birth from where my fathers dwelt,
> Schooled from the age of ten to a foreign voice,

and in his childhood 'interlude' he lived in Carrickfergus, on the shores of Belfast Lough. He is buried in Carrowdore churchyard, Co. Down.

MacNeice visited many countries, taught for some months in America at the outbreak of war and spent a year in Athens in the early fifties, and there is a sense in which he was a visitor everywhere, the man from no part. For the English reader he appears to be Irish, while for certain Irish readers he doesn't really belong to Ireland (he is given a cold and grudging welcome in John Montague's *Faber Book of Irish Verse*—four pages of MacNeice, as against six of Montague). And in a clever and perverse essay Derek Mahon has argued that the English public school system processed MacNeice into an Englishman. He was 'a fully paid-up member of the British academic, artistic and administrative establishment' who 'had no place in the intellectual history of modern Ireland'. The Irish sense of place is very exacting and intransigent, and many people can never forgive the man who goes, in that tantalizing phrase, 'across the water'.

MacNeice is always crossing the water, and the feeling of unease and displacement, of moving between different cultures

---

Louis MacNeice: Collected Poems, edited by E.R. Dodds.

and nationalisms, which he paradoxically returns to in his poetry, means that his imagination is essentially fluid, maritime and elusively free. He cannot identify himself exclusively with one or other part of the island: the North of Ireland is 'devout and profane and hard', while the South is 'a gallery of false tapestries'. And in *Autumn Journal* he asks

> Why should I want to go back
> To you, Ireland, my Ireland?
> The blots on the page are so black
> That they cannot be covered with shamrock.
> I hate your grandiose airs,
> Your sob-stuff, your laugh and your swagger,
> Your assumption that everyone cares
> Who is the king of your castle.

Ireland, he concludes, is 'both a bore and a bitch'. Her children 'slouch around the world with a gesture and a brogue/ And a faggot of useless memories'. His dismissive celebration is wild and melancholy, gay and sober—a series of passionate Irish contradictions.

Of course the lines are deliberately journalistic, and Mac-Neice's technique of setting clichés dancing to a hurdy-gurdy rhythm can be tedious. This throwaway lyricism—'the beer-brown spring/ Guzzling between the heather, the green gush of Irish spring'—often resembles a commercial jingle and the images are frequently stale or received, like the contemporary surfaces he was so fascinated by and on which they are partly modelled. In 'When we were Children' he compares laburnum blossom to scrambled eggs, and his witty copywriter's eye often pins down such slick gimmicky images. The urban rootless world of rootless urban clichés, consumer durables and advertising hoardings is an essential part of his imagination, and while he sometimes recycles images of the Irish landscape like a tourist board official eager to woo 'the sentimental English', few Irish writers have totally resisted the temptation to export their Irishness. And in any case Irishness is a sometimes clownish commodity which depends on being transported elsewhere.

It's wrong to condemn MacNeice for his deracinated, even at times ersatz quality because it's something which is implicit in the Irish landscape—the West of Ireland, for example, is strewn with derelict cottages abandoned by emigrant families and it's also covered with breezeblock suburban bungalows built with money brought back from abroad. Landscape and journeys fray against each other, and it is a shore and a seascape crossed by a journey which is at the centre of MacNeice's imaginative vision. From his first mature poem, 'Belfast', to his last poem, the stoic 'Thalassa', his imagination is caught by ships and 'the salt carrion water':

> Down there at the end of the melancholy lough
> Against the lurid sky over the stained water
> Where hammers clang murderously on the girders
> Like crucifixes the gantries stand.

Here the eye crosses Belfast Lough to the gantries in Harland and Wolff's shipyard which stand over the quays where the passenger ferries and cargo boats dock. The image catches the provincial introversion, the puritan work ethic, the cruelty and injustice of the stagnant society MacNeice only peripherally belonged to. The unfinished ships, he implies, stand in their scaffolds, and this fuses birth and death in a manner that is distinctively Irish (like Joyce's puns in his title, *Finnegans Wake*, or like Beckett's gravedigger's forceps). Although the view here is down the lough towards the city, because ships are launched there and other boats leave from the quays the image also looks out towards the open sea and England.

MacNeice responds to an idea of doomed freedom, the emigrant's ship leaving 'the husk of home' as he says in 'The Left-Behind', one of a sequence of poems which investigate the dilemma of the displaced exile who is condemned to be a tourist in the land of his birth. With a characteristic mixture of freedom and fatalism he says in this poem that his youth is a 'tall ship that chose to run on a rock', and in 'Death of an Old Lady' he makes a most complex image from this:

> At five in the morning there were grey voices
> Calling three times through the dank fields;
> The ground fell away beyond the voices
> Forty long years to the wrinkled lough
> That had given a child one shining glimpse
> Of a boat so big it was named Titanic.

The Titanic was built in Belfast and in this marvellous elegy for his stepmother MacNeice returns to the shores of Belfast Lough, the estuary of birth and death where 'shipyard voices' travel over the wet fields:

They called and ceased. Later the night nurse
Handed over, the day went down
To the sea in a ship, it was grey April,
The daffodils in her garden waited
To make her a wreath, the iceberg waited;
At eight in the evening the ship went down.

This poem has a terse stoic clarity and a beautifully managed cadence (there is a perfectly controlled anapaestic lilt which sweetens the abrupt iambics), and it is somehow both placed and displaced. This is also true of 'The Strand', an elegy for Bishop MacNeice, his enlightened and liberal father. Here the Irish strand is a 'mirror of wet sand' which once caught 'his shape' as it now catches that of his son. 'But then as now,' MacNeice says, the foam blotted 'the bright reflections—and no sign/ Remains of face or feet when visitors have gone home'. A strand is never quite a place, a really rooted locus, and that word 'visitors' is filled with a sense of dispossession—it is the word used in the West of Ireland to describe tourists.

On the page opposite 'Death of an Old Lady' in the *Collected Poems* there is a short and little-known poem called 'House on a Cliff' which is one of MacNeice's finest achievements:

Indoors the tang of a tiny oil lamp. Outdoors
The winking signal on the waste of sea.
Indoors the sound of the wind. Outdoors the wind.
Indoors the locked heart and the lost key.

Outdoors the chill, the void, the siren. Indoors
The strong man pained to find his red blood cools,
While the blind clock grows louder, faster. Outdoors
The silent moon, the garrulous tides she rules.

Indoors ancestral curse-cum-blessing. Outdoors
The empty bowl of heaven, the empty deep.
Indoors a purposeful man who talks at cross
Purposes, to himself, in a broken sleep.

The hard boxed circling rhythms build a terrible stoic isolation. The voice is variously and tautly cadenced in a cross between stress and quantitative metre—that word 'cross' stretches bitterly in so many directions—and there is a mysterious openness within or beyond the poem's mirror-like reflections of a dead closed universe. If this is one man facing his lonely mortality on the far extremity of an unnamed place, the 'ancestral curse-cum-blessing', the cross purposes and the broken sleep, suggest that the house is Ireland. Again, the silent moon and the garrulous tides obliquely suggest a Yeatsian reference to cold fanatic ideals and mob action. As in 'Death of an Old Lady', MacNeice recapitulates some of his favourite symbols—sirens, sea, wind, clock—in a manner that is almost playful. Although the demand for "meaning" will discover and insist that 'the blind clock' is the pulse of an indifferent and mechanical universe—the earth's compulsion—the poem is best appreciated in terms of voice, atmosphere and a pure symbolism. It is a bitter and tragic poem with a freedom in its intensity that transcends its unflinching sense of cosmic indifference, malignity or mischief—the 'winking signal' of the lighthouse and MacNeice's favouritely ambiguous 'the siren' simultaneously warn and lure. If this poem fits that baffled and contradictory term "Irish", it also has an asocial, even a derelict, quality which makes it difficult to place. It subverts any comfortable notion of belonging and this is true of all MacNeice's poetry. The anguished sense of displacement that is so fundamental to his imagination means that many readers glance at him and then hurry on. Instead he needs to be read and cherished. There are many places that should be proud to lay claim to him.

In the Salt Mines

In the early days of radio drama two of the most successful plays were Tyrone Guthrie's *The Flowers Are Not For You To Pick* and Richard Hughes's *Danger*. Guthrie's play employed the device of a drowning man's recall of his past life—voices from his past alternated with the sound of the waves—while Hughes wrote about three people trapped in a mine. Interestingly, Louis MacNeice's last radio play, *Persons from Porlock*, has several scenes set in 'Skrimshank's Cave', and its central character, an artist called Hank, is a keen potholer who suffers from claustrophobia. Before the play was recorded MacNeice went on an expedition to the Yorkshire Moors to record potholing effects for the production. It was there that he caught 'that cold' as Auden calls it in 'The Cave of Making', his wise and beautiful tribute to his dead friend. The play was broadcast as MacNeice lay ill in hospital, his sister listened with great foreboding, and four days later MacNeice died.

For anyone interested in the life of this remarkable poet, these facts must combine in a tantalizing and ultimately mythic manner. This is because radio drama and MacNeice's life have a common image—the cave. At its best, radio drama is essentially an intimate, even claustrophobic, form, and so it is no accident that two pioneering radio playwrights should have chosen the sensation of being trapped as their subject. They must have known intuitively that for the radio listener slow asphyxiation is more convincing than the din of sword blades or the gadzooks of trumpets. Although a radio play can be set anywhere in the great outdoors it always sounds bogus when it is—the ear suspects that the clatter of horse's hooves is only a couple of coconuts plocking together, and the inner eye is puzzled by this deception. And so radio drama works best when the voices of its characters are contained within an echoing hollow—a cave, a tunnel, a pothole, or a living-room.

In MacNeice's imaginative topography it was the cave which dominated: his childhood was spent in Carrickfergus, a small town on the coast of Co. Antrim, an area noted for its

---

Louis MacNeice in the BBC by Barbara Coulton.

basalt formations and caves. In 'Carrickfergus' MacNeice describes the place like this:

> I was born in Belfast between the mountain and the gantries
>   To the hooting of lost sirens and the clang of trams:
> Thence to Smoky Carrick in County Antrim
>   Where the bottle-neck harbour collects the mud which jams
>
> The little boats beneath the Norman castle,
>   The pier shining with lumps of crystal salt;
> The Scotch Quarter was a line of residential houses
>   But the Irish Quarter was a slum for the blind and halt.

The salt on the pier came from the local salt mines, and the metaphoric significance of those mines begins to show in Barbara Coulton's introductory account of MacNeice's early years:

> A dream that he recalled much later followed a holiday visit to a salt mine which was like a subterranean cathedral, the men 'like gnomes in the clerestories'. In the dream he was imprisoned by the gnomes, and could escape only by finding a certain jewel.

As in 'Carrickfergus' this is partly an image of Unionist Ulster (there is a beautiful variation on that particular provincial servitude in Seamus Heaney's 'The Singer's House'). The jewel is probably referred to in one of the potholing sequences in *Persons from Porlock*: 'I noticed a funny bit of crystal in there in the wall of the tunnel—No, my God, it's submerged!' And the submergence of that crystal must denote Hank's inability to find the jewel and so break out of the cave-system (he loses his life-line, which is a version of Ariadne's thread). Trapped in this labryrinth Hank tries to swim against the underground stream—MacNeice is clearly reworking the 'caves of ice' and 'sacred river' in 'Kubla Khan'. In a sense, therefore, his 'persons from Porlock' are whatever private hobbies or distractions prevent the artist's exercise of the imagination, his discovery of the jewel.

MacNeice treats this subject in 'Hidden Ice' where routine existence is overrun by the private hobby which should be free and separate from it:

> One was found like Judas kissing flowers
> And one who sat between the clock and sun
> Lies like a Saint Sebastian full of arrows
> Fathered from his own hobby, his pet hours.

This fascination with the absorbing madness of the unchecked private hobby is an important theme in MacNeice's work, and *Persons from Porlock* is his final oblique version of it. In it, MacNeice refers to his dream of the salt cathedral and he means that the mine of busy gnomes is really the institution in which he'd spent more than twenty years of his life—the BBC. Barbara Coulton astutely links the play with another of MacNeice's radio dramas, *Prisoner's Progress*, which involves a 'tunnelling to freedom, through a neolithic passage grave'. And this subject becomes dramatically clear once we place it in relation to *Rasselas*—MacNeice is exploring the dilemma of someone who knows he is trapped in the Happy Valley and wants to break out of it.

From this it should be apparent that I am by no means convinced that MacNeice's long and distinguished career in the BBC necessarily benefited his poetry. Certainly he made an immense and brilliant contribution to radio. Under Laurence Gilliam, the Features Department was a remarkable gathering of talent, and during the first six years of the Italia Prize 'of fifteen entries chosen as the outstanding works of those years, fourteen came from Features Department'. The programmes MacNeice scripted and produced were of the highest quality, and the position he occupied in relation to society was the egalitarian equivalent of a court poet. His plays and features are like masques created for a mass democracy, and his commitment to radio issued from his belief that the poet 'is only the extension of the common man'. In his working life he was applying the socialist and documentary aesthetic of the 1930s.

However, we must realise that all masques are designed simply to glitter in the moment. Like a piece of journalism, they are created for a particular occasion and though they may be repeated their original freshness will always be missing. They are part of what MacNeice termed 'the yeast of culture', but they are ephemeral. If MacNeice was applying many of the ideals of the 1930s—commitment to a group, closing the gap between art and journalism—we still have to choose between his two identities of poet and distinguished servant of the BBC. And the problem is that those identities first overlapped and then fed off each other during his middle-age: his radio features sound like poems, while many of his poems sound like features.

Take his introduction to a programme called 'Portrait of Athens' which begins with the tinny note of a bell and the Visitor's comment:

> So this is Athens. A nagging bell and a glaring sky. A box on the ear. A smack in the eye. Crude as a poster. Hard as nails. Yes, this is Athens—not what I expected.

There is a rich personal accent in these beautifully managed, knockabout speech cadences. And the ear gladly recognises a punchy couplet in:

> A nágging béll and a gláring ský.
> A bóx on the éar. A smáck in the éye.

That pyrrhic foot—'and a'—introduces the ghost of quantitative metre into the play of iambs and anapaests, and this mixed metre is characteristic of MacNeice's best poetry ('House on a Cliff', for example). Again, that last phrase, 'not what I expected', is both a dying fall and a superb moment of arresting colloquial thoughtfulness. It is magnificent radio journalism precisely because it comes so close to MacNeice's poetry.

However, if we transpose the relationship between journalism and art and examine these lines from the sequence of poems, 'Our Sister Water', we can see that their ersatz quality is the result of the application of documentary techniques to a subject that, at this point in the poem, should have passed beyond the journalistic:

> Best in the West
> Squelching round ankles, dousing the nape of the neck,
> Ringing the jackpot of colour out of the mountains;
> Best in the large or best when a girl in a shawl
> Barefoot and windblown staggers her way through the bog
> With a bucket of windblown gold.

The image of the shawled girl is a piece of kitsch Irishness, while the 'jackpot of colour' is passable as a throwaway metaphor in a broadcast commentary—in cold print a sunset of fruit machines looks queasy and banal. When MacNeice admitted 'This middle stretch/ Of life is bad for poets', he also meant that it was quite fun for boozy journalists—those tempting figures who wait beyond that famous line about the drunkenness of things being various. Journalism aims to live and die with the moment, but an art which addresses itself to the quotidian has to be intensely detached, intensely sure of itself—as MacNeice's vision usually was until broadcasting work began to invade his imagination.

He was a gregariously lonely man, and he appears to have needed team work and its inevitable concomitant, pub life, with increasing desperation. Two years before he joined the BBC he described his dream of community in the last canto of *Autumn Journal*:

> Where the individual, no longer squandered
>   In self-assertion, works with the rest, endowed
> With the split vision of a juggler and the quick lock of a taxi,
>   Where the people are more than a crowd.

And he came close to realising that dream in his work for Features which he described like this:

> In this age of irreconcilable idioms I have often heard writers hankering for some sort of group life...we cannot but envy playwrights, actors or musical executants. And here again I for one have found this missing group experience, in a valid form, in radio. Radio writers and producers *can* talk shop together because their shop is not, as with poets, a complex of spiritual intimacies but a matter of craftsmanship...we are fully entitled to discuss whether the dialogue rings true, whether the dramatic climax is dramatic, how well the whole thing works. This is refreshing for a writer.

MacNeice's need to belong must in part have been due to his sense of deracination—he had left a society of salt mines and this meant that there was no existing community with which he could identify (it's crucial to recognise that he was born before partition and never came to terms with a divided Ireland). He dramatized his 'hankering' for group life in the figure of Hank in *Persons from Porlock*, and that life became a warm burrow which was also the great cathedral of the BBC.

Barbara Coulton's study is a valuable account of MacNeice's life as a creative member of an institution, and although her appreciation of his poetry is limited by that unhelpful term "moving", she offers a diligent and comprehensive survey of his broadcasting career. Her chapter on MacNeice's Indian journey is excellent, and throughout she shows a warm and cherishing regard for her subject. There is in MacNeice's creative personality something that calls forth a strong and tender admiration, and the man himself was deeply loved by his many friends. This study should do much to rekindle interest in his life and work.

Disaffection and Defection: W.H. Auden

Perhaps there can be no extended consideration of Auden's life and work without a preliminary analysis of English upper middle-class culture, the public school system and the nature of the English establishment. In 1934, discussing his own public school, Auden wrote:

> Everyone knows that the only emotion that is fully developed in a boy of fourteen is the emotion of loyalty and honour. For that very reason it is so dangerous ... The best reason I have for opposing Fascism is that at school I lived in a Fascist state.

Although this is a characteristic Auden overstatement (his dogmatic and provocative pronouncements issued from what he termed the 'mad clergyman' in his personality), it is a significant rejection of the ethic of loyalty. Here Auden is speaking as a typical member of his generation because, like Orwell, like Philby, Blunt, Burgess and innumerable others, he is rejecting his background and education and the socio-cultural values that inform them. How far such a rejection is a conscious dedication to a systematic ethic of disloyalty, and how far it is part of the culture it appears to reject, is open to question, as a glance at the reaction to the Blunt affair will demonstrate.

When the English establishment had finally to admit that, yes, the Keeper of Her Majesty's Paintings had been a KGB agent for a very long time, what surfaced—at least on the backbenches of the Parliamentary Labour Party—was a resentment against an establishment that appeared to be run for and by a group of what were termed 'upper-class bisexuals'. From this point of view, the English establishment is an enormous gay charade in which the old boys of various ancient public schools all dress up in splendid costumes and mouth patriotic words while smirking secretly at each other. To the public at large it appears that a dignified group of personalities and institutions are engaged in an elaborate and ceremonial dance, while to the participants it is all a piece of sheer pointless fun

---

Early Auden by Edward Mendelson.
W.H. Auden by Humphrey Carpenter.

where the Archbishop of Canterbury is dressed like Mother and will shortly go to bed with the Head of the Civil Service. The qualities that distinguish the participants in this great cultural game are an insouciant and provocative irony, a ruthless aestheticism and an eager nihilism which sometimes—as in the case of Sir John Betjeman—subsides into a cosy but queasy sentimental kitschiness.

Auden knew Betjeman at Oxford, and they both shared an enthusiasm for High Anglicanism, Victorian Gothic and obscure Victorian poets. 'I can never make up my mind,' Auden said, 'whether Mr Betjeman was born after the flesh or whether he was magically conceived by myself in a punt on the Cherwell one summer evening in 1926. I have no memory of company on the outward journey on that occasion: I only know that *two* of us returned. Since that day, Mr Betjeman has indubitably existed,—but I *wonder*.' This is a beautifully calculated put-down and it is perfectly in tune with the finely polished bad manners of their class. Auden was able to see that class with forensic detachment, while possessing an insider's knowledge of how it operated, and as a disaffected upper middle-class intellectual he suffered, like many of his generation, from that self-disgust which inevitably accompanies disloyalty. Like Guy Burgess, he appears to have punished himself by being perpetually stimulating and stimulated, like an eternally precocious undergraduate. Just before he fled the country, Burgess twice tried to phone Auden at the Spenders' and one can only wonder if Burgess regarded him imaginatively as being in some sense his "control" (the police later detained Geoffrey Grigson and Spender's brother Humphrey on suspicion of being Burgess and Maclean).

All this is highly reminiscent of John le Carré and his fiction is among the best criticism of the poetry that there is (the work of Samuel Hynes and John Fuller is also essential to an appreciation of Auden). Anyone who admires Auden's work must recognise the marvellous and daring subtlety with which le Carré draws on his vision of decaying public schools, the English landscape, a haunting idea of Europe, and a chill and pervasive atmosphere of secrecy and surveillance. School is at the centre of this vision of culture and early Auden was both a schoolmaster and a severe critic of education. He argued that education, whatever it pretends, can do nothing for the individual because it is 'always social', and that the failure of modern education lies in the fact that 'nobody genuinely believes in our society, for which the children are being trained'. It was impossible, he insisted, to train children to be good citizens 'of a state which you despise', and two years later he was arguing that the state has to train its children not only to be good citizens but to change it, 'i.e. to destroy its present existence'. Educationalists, he concluded, 'must always be revolutionaries'.

Accompanying this revolutionary rejection of the existing educational and social system was a rejection of the romantic and liberal ideas of personality. Auden was fascinated by a remark of Lenin's about how the self must learn to be indifferent, 'to go hungry, work illegally and be anonymous', and he was attracted by communism's demand for 'self-surrender'. Linking Lenin with T.E. Lawrence, he stated that they 'seem to me the two whose lives exemplify most completely what is best and significant in our time, the most potent agents of freedom and to us, egotistical underlings, the most relevant accusation and hope'. For Auden, romanticism and liberalism were egotistic and in that pervasive metaphor of his generation he argued that 'unconsciously the liberal becomes the secret service of the ruling class, its most powerful weapon against social revolution'.

No doubt, somewhere in Moscow there is a KGB file on Auden which contains various strictures on the bourgeois illogicalities of his Marxist-Leninism, and perhaps that file concludes that he is/was a promiscuous and alcoholic liberal. This is beside the point because Auden's fascination with politics and psychology was a voracious quest for an intellectual structure that would satisfy him long enough to write a poem. Once the poem was written he either jettisoned the structure or tacked a new idea onto it. His attitude to ideas, like his attitude to sex, was extremely brisk and matter of fact ('Off to Oxford tomorrow for a quiet fuck,' he wrote to a friend, adding in a postscript, 'Monday. Returned having had it'). As with any attitude that is buoyed in the now, a strong element of fashion is involved and here Auden's attitude to politics is of much greater interest than his study of psychology. Although Edward Mendelson offers a great deal of information about Auden's debt to Freud, Homer Lane and John Layard, he ties his research so closely to the poems that the effect is rather like a reading of Yeats in terms of *A Vision*. It's certainly true that Auden constructed a ramshackle, flexible system out of borrowings from various psychologists, D.H. Lawrence, Gerald Heard and others, but the system isn't of much interest in itself—it's a private bore-hole designed to tap hidden imaginative resources, not a mythological system with a wide general applicability. But perhaps I'm saying this because no one nowadays is interested in psychology, while politics is a more or less inescapable condition.

Although Mendelson does mention the Wall Street Crash and a number of other historical events, he overemphasises Auden's interest in psychological theories with the result that the poems seem to dissolve into a volatile and lymphatic medium. A more satisfying approach would have been to see Auden as adopting the kind of strategy which Burgess or Philby adopted and to explore the idea that he, too, was a defector from both his class and, in 1939, from his country. In a tantalizing parallel between Auden and Wilde, Mendelson says that each 'was the son of a doctor father and formidable mother, and his aesthetic was partly intended *pour épater les parents*'. Mendelson fails to pursue this, yet, as his adapted phrase acknowledges, the personal struggle of child against parents is also a social struggle because to reject one's parents is to reject their social and cultural values.

Auden tried to replace the values of the Edwardian family with a form of group loyalty and again this was characteristic of his generation (the Group Theatre with which Auden was associated is another example). Nowadays the equivalent of the term "group" is "collective", though they differ in that the earlier term has associations with the public school ethic it is apparently intended to subvert. In an intriguing stanza which Auden dropped from his 1932 poem, 'Now from my window-sill I watch the night', he prayed:

Permit our town to continue small,
What city's vast emotional cartel
Could our few acres satisfy
Or rival in intensity
The field of five or six, the English cell?

Mendelson discusses Auden's interest in group-life and quotes from his 1934 essay on the Oxford Group where Auden explores the attractions and the limitations of a group-ethic. That curious phrase, 'the English cell', is a paradoxical combination of Marxist language with a patriotic cosiness and it sounds rather like Betjeman as a Comintern agent, which is probably why Auden dropped it. A cell is a political unit, a biological term, and it also suggests a monastery, which connects with Auden's interest in anonymity and self-surrender, his austere rejection of personality. It is also an attempt to conserve Englishness without the class system and it is close to that vein of patriotism and anti-Americanism which appears to have motivated Philby and Maclean.

Mendelson considers Auden's 'half-serious fantasy of himself as a secret agent behind enemy lines', but he fails to examine why he indulged it or to relate it to the other more famous agents who belonged to Auden's generation and whom Auden knew. More than this, his use of the term 'half-serious' assumes a division between the "light" and the "serious" which Auden never made. For all his moral imperatives and schoolmaster's manner, Auden had much the same attitude as Wilde to an Arnoldian seriousness—he would have considered it *petit bourgeois*. It is part of the paradox of Auden's personality, however, that he is capable of combining a Hooperish fascination with machinery with the gay aestheticism and strenuous frivolity of a Sebastian Flyte. Indeed, Auden and Waugh are very similar figures, though few critics have noticed how much they have in common. Although Mendelson does show Auden's debt to Yeats and his connections with Brecht, there is throughout his work a sealed-off, practical-critical, explicative approach which sets Auden outside the swim of history and literary tradition. Mendelson often paraphrases and the result is an extended reader's guide to the poems. These sentences are representative:

> A month after 'I have a handsome profile', he wrote the monitory ballad 'O what is that sound which so thrills the ear'. This is a quietly terrifying dialogue between two lovers, a ritual exchange of anxious questions in long lines of verse and calm cold answers in shorter ones. At the end, the betraying lover escapes the pursuit of the scarlet soldiers, leaving the betrayed to the mercies of the state.

This is null paraphrase, not literary criticism, and it ignores where the poem is set (Scotland), why Auden cast it as a ballad, and its relation to European politics. It relates, too, to that theme of disloyalty which runs through Auden's generation.

Although Mendelson offers many highly intelligent insights

they are always, in Leavis's phrase, 'local', and so fail to form part of a unified vision. His introduction, however, is clever and stimulating, and he rightly, if unsurprisingly, argues that Auden is a 'civil' rather than a 'vatic' poet. He offers a cogent interpretation of *The Ascent of F6*, but he fails to enjoy or explore *Letter to Lord Byron* which is one of Auden's finest achievements. The result is a scholarly but disappointing work.

Humphrey Carpenter's enormous tome belongs to the little-England tradition of literary biography and it passes the first test of bad biography on page 131 when Mr Carpenter informs us that Auden once ate six eggs for supper (Charles Osborne's earlier account of the life also passes when the broken eggshells in Auden's bedroom are noted). In a foreword, Carpenter modestly insists that his is not 'a book of literary criticism', though he immediately passes the second test of bad biography when he adds that he has tried to show that Auden's writings often 'arose from the circumstances of his life'. This denial of imaginative free will results in an account, not of a great English writer, but of a great English eccentric, a cross between Tom Driberg and Betjeman. However, it should be said that two friends of Auden's have told me how brilliantly the book captures Auden's personality. To them, it brings back the carpet-slippered, nicotine-stained man they knew, but this is little help to those readers who didn't know Auden and who are primarily interested in the poet. The great vice of the English tradition of biography is that it exalts precisely those qualities of personal egotism and eccentricity which Auden sought to escape in his early period. It makes its subjects less than human by humanising them, listing their foibles and personal habits, and sweeping up the detritus of their lives.

Like Mendelson, Carpenter minimises Auden's interest in politics and allows Late Auden to reshape the experience of Early Auden. Carpenter's account of Auden's participation in the General Strike is patiently exculpatory: 'Even now that he had taken sides in the strike,' Carpenter remarks, 'he did not really appreciate what he was doing.' Quite what that word 'really' means I'm not sure, but it is one example of Carpenter's bland and sloppy style. Again, commenting on the poem which begins 'Get there if you can', Carpenter suggests that there is 'a lot of exaggeration' in its vision of derelict industry:

...or at least there would be if it were meant to be a picture of Britain in the grip of the Depression. In fact the poem owes a lot to Auden's private landscape of abandoned lead mines, and soon reveals itself as not really concerned with the present state of the country but with the defective emotional condition of the middle-class intellectual, for which the ruined industrial landscape is a symbol.

This is to completely privatise Auden's work and effectively to immobilise his imagination. His is not a neurotic vision and it does not devour external social reality in the way that, say, Sylvia Plath's imagination does. Carpenter's insular post-war outlook distorts Auden into a strangely consistent and decent figure:

> Auden's time at the Downs School had been the happiest period of his life so far. He had lived and worked there in a state of contentment, and his poetry had entered a period of extraordinary fertility. On the other hand he had been in an ideological muddle. His earlier enthusiasm for the Layard-Lane-Lawrence-Groddeck doctrines had faded (though it had not vanished entirely), and he was as yet unable to replace it with any other dogma which he could use as a firm base for his poetry. Neither Gerald Heard's explanation of the ills of society nor the Communism of friends like Edward Upward proved to be more than passing attractions to him. He played with them in his poems, but quickly realised he should not pose as a propagandist.

Here the biographer runs Auden's life through a hedonic calculus and then seeks out a consistent identity behind 'ideological muddle' and passing enthusiasms. What poet since Dante has had a 'firm base', an unmuddled ideology, to sustain his imagination? Certainly not Auden.

Carpenter has gathered a great many facts together and there are some delightful anecdotes among them, as well as crisp quotations from the letters: 'The school gathers mildew. Numbers down, the headmaster partially blind, his wife growing gradually mad in a canvas shelter in the garden. I spend most of my time adjusting the flow of water to the lavatories.' The details have a bizarre clarity and Auden the amateur plumber is a witty version of his view of the poet as a responsible maker, a kind of social engineer. This is the side of Auden which exulted with Kipling in the builders of dams and bridges; it is the aesthete's tribute to Hooper's world of sludge and lead-pipes. Perhaps some day a critic who is also a social historian will rise up to describe and invent that Auden.

The British Presence in *Ulysses*

'In the beginning was something called Formal Authority and something called history, then came Practical Critic and history became an extrinsic irrelevance (somewhere was Marxist who said poems were functions). Then there was Structuralist and the literary work became a cultural artefact, like a plastic ashtray. In the end there was neither art, scholarship, nor criticism and a great crisis happened . . .'

Perhaps some future oral historian will tell a similar story around a fire of contiboard shavings; for the moment I want to offer a primitive reader's-guide, a brief act of mnemonic rescue.

The first book of *Ulysses*, Telemachus, is saturated with a sense of oppression and lack of freedom. Stephen is staying in a government watchtower – one of many that ring the coast of Ireland and which were built in 1804 to guard against a French invasion. When Buck Mulligan explains to his English friend, Haines, that William Pitt had the towers built 'when the French were on the sea', he ironically implies his attitude to them by echoing the famous song from the 1798 rebellion which celebrates the French landing at Killala:

'Oh the French are on the sea,' says the Sean Bean Boct,
'Yes the French are on the sea,' says the Sean Bean Boct.
'The French are in the bay, they'll be here without delay,
'And the English will decay,' says the Sean Bean Boct.
'Yes the English will decay,' says the Sean Bean Boct.*

The rent of the martello tower is paid to the Secretary of State for War and this underlines the way in which Stephen's existence in Dublin is trammelled by the British connection. He sees himself as someone who is humiliated by a double service: 'I am the servant of two masters...The imperial British state...and the holy Roman catholic and apostolic church.' Both ignoble services fuse as Stephen lifts Mulligan's shaving-bowl and is reminded of the boat of incense he carried at mass at school: 'I am another now and yet the same. A servant too. A server of a servant.'

*In *Ireland Sings* Dominic Behan explains: 'Sean Bean Boct, Poor Old Woman – a code name for Ireland, Shan Van Vocht.'

The bowl also becomes like a loyal address presented to the king – Mulligan has just been mockingly singing a song about the coronation of Edward VII, and in the previous year Dublin corporation had decided by a narrow majority against presenting a loyal address to the king when he visited Ireland. Yeats affirms a similar anti-colonial attitude in the title-poem of *In the Seven Woods* which was published in 1904, the year in which *Ulysses* is set. He cunningly pretends to have grown quiet and apolitical:

> I have forgot awhile
> Tara uprooted, and new commonness
> Upon the throne and crying about the streets
> And hanging its paper flowers from post to post,
> Because it is alone of all things happy.

Although Buck Mulligan appears to share this scornful attitude, Stephen regards him as a servile figure and as Stephen is momentarily Mulligan's servant he, too, is 'a server of a servant'. Also, the Roman Catholic Church is here presented as a servant of Britain – so Stephen is doubly the server of a servant. Almost comically, he considers the action of refusing to take Mulligan's shaving-bowl down as a revolutionary act – a *non serviam*. The shaving-mirror, too, assumes a colonial significance as Stephen regards it as a 'symbol of Irish art. The cracked looking-glass of a servant.'

This insistence on the national indignity of service is provoked by the presence of Haines in the tower – he is a symbolic usurper and is the butt of petty revenges. The atmosphere is nervous, edgy and highly self-conscious. Haines attempts to be sympathetic when he says, 'We feel in England that we have treated you rather unfairly. It seems history is to blame.' Here, Haines sounds lofty and patronising, and Stephen later transforms him into a symbol of naval supremacy: 'The seas' ruler. His seacold eyes looked on the empty bay.' As he visualises Haines in this Nelson-like manner, Stephen is listening to Mr Deasy – an authority figure who has a portrait of Prince Albert in his room. Deasy is a Unionist and his loyalist remarks spark a series of images for Stephen: the phrase, 'Glorious, pious and immortal memory' evokes the loyalist culture of Orange banners and gable-ends (it refers to William of Orange), while the phrase 'Croppies lie down' is the refrain from a sadistic loyalist song of 1798:

In Dublin, the traitors were ready to rise
And murder was seen in their lowering eyes.
With poison, the cowards, they aimed to succeed,
And thousands were doomed by Assassins to bleed
But the Yeomen advanced, of Rebels the dread
And each Croppy soon hid his dastardly head.
  Down, down, Croppies lie down.

Stephen is shown in reaction against the Unionist atmosphere of the school and his history lesson inevitably assumes a political significance. Asked to define a pier, one of the pupils replies, 'A kind of bridge. Kingstown pier, sir.' Stephen answers wryly, 'Yes, a disappointed bridge.' Because Kingstown (now Dun Laoghaire) is a port near Dublin the idea of a connecting link with Britain is suggested. Yet a pier is not a bridge, and the boy's mistake seems natural for one who cannot think outside the connection between the two countries.

Like many present-day Unionists, Deasy is anti-English – he tells Stephen that he has 'rebel blood in me too' – and Joyce emphasizes the essentially racist nature of this attitude by giving him anti-semitic views (Haines is similarly anti-semitic). Deasy also anticipates the nationalistic racism and anti-semitism of the Citizen who will abuse Bloom in the Cyclops section. Deasy's conversation is another history lesson and Stephen reacts against its tedium by saying, 'History...is a nightmare from which I am trying to awake'. This effort to 'wake' is essential to Joyce's inspiration because the epic imagination – which the heroic Stephen possesses – draws on history in order to free itself from the past, to make the leap into imaginative freedom.

In the Proteus section, Joyce implies a parallel between the epic modernist artist and the revolutionary activist in Stephen's memories of his stay in Paris. The fashion for cropped hair began in Paris during the French Revolution and was imitated by Irish revolutionaries (hence the pejorative term "Croppies"), and for many generations Paris was regarded as both the symbol and centre of imaginative freedom – Wolfe Tone went there to organise the invasion of Ireland and Parnell often met his colleagues there. Stephen associates Kevin Egan, the old Fenian whom he visits, with the explosion at Clerkenwell Prison in 1859 and with these lines from 'The Wearing of the Green':

I met with Napper Tandy and he took me by the hand,
Said he, 'How is old Ireland and how does she stand?'
'She's the most distressful country that ever could be seen,
For they're hanging men and women for the wearing of the green.'

Napper Tandy was one of the leaders of the 1798 rebellion and like Wolfe Tone he sailed to Ireland in a French warship. Egan, Stephen reflects, has been forgotten by the Irish, 'not he them. Remembering thee, O Sion.' Here Joyce introduces one of the first biblical parallels between the Irish and the Jews – the Promised Land is Irish freedom, Egypt is the bondage of British imperialism. Stephen's visit to Egan is an act of piety, and Egan's taking of him 'by the hand' is like a paternal blessing in an epic – old Anchises encouraging his pious son, Aeneas. Thus Stephen, the artist-hero, is the inheritor of a long tradition of political rebellion, and Joyce saw Parnell's stern, cold, 'formidable' nature as a paradigm of the true artist's integrity. Indeed, the epic inspiration of Joyce's art resembles that which informs Parnell's famous statement: 'No man has a right to fix the boundary of the march of a nation; no man has a right to say to his country – thus far shalt thou go and no further.'

If Stephen is the future epic artist – the uncrowned king – it is Bloom who carries the historical consciousness in *Ulysses*. As he moves through the streets of Dublin, personal and historical memories are triggered by buildings, statues and casual passers-by. Bloom associates the sun with the sun of Home Rule (his son, Rudy, is dead) and with Arthur Griffith, the editor of the radical paper, *The United Irishman,* and a friend of Joyce's. Griffith was the inventor of the famous 'Hungarian Policy' – i.e. 'the policy successfully pursued by the Hungarian patriot, Franz Déak, who organised a massive abstention of Hungarian representatives from the Imperial Diet at Vienna in order to secure the establishment of a separate Hungarian parliament at Budapest'. Significantly, Joyce makes Bloom's father Hungarian and credits Bloom with giving Griffith the idea for Sinn Fein. Here, the personal and the political are identified, as they are again in Bloom's fantasies of orange groves in Jaffa where an ideal sexual fulfilment and the promised land of Irish freedom are fused. Both frustrations are present when the mourners wander round Glasnevin Cemetery after the funeral of Paddy Dignam and agree that Parnell will 'never come again'. And Bloom's sexual impotence reflects the political impotence of sentimental Parnellites like Joe Hynes.

Both Daniel O'Connell, the 'breedy man', and Parnell are presented as potent liberators, and Joyce associated Parnell with Christ whom he imagined, in Blakean terms, as a revolutionary saviour. The parallel is implied in the cave of Aeolus section when a minor character called Brayden passes through. Brayden has a 'solemn beardframed face' and one character asks, 'Don't you think his face is like Our Saviour?' Here, the bearded face of Parnell is superimposed on Christ's. Joyce hints parallels between Moses and Bloom, and between Stephen, Christ and Parnell. Biblical scholars see Moses as the precursor of Christ, and imaginatively Stephen is Bloom's son, the substitute for Rudy who has sunk out of sight like the sun of Home Rule. The parallels cross and melt because Parnell is also associated with Moses.

In the newspaper offices Bloom reads some type backwards and his mingled personal and political obsessions are again triggered: 'papa with his hagadah book, reading backwards. Next year in Jerusalem...All that long business about that brought us out of the land of Egypt and into the house of bondage.' And the advertisement Bloom designs has itself a mild and virtually invisible political implication – the two crossed keys symbolise both the grocer called Keyes and 'the Manx parliament. Innuendo of home rule.' Passing a squad of constables, Bloom immediately recalls the day he took part in a demonstration against Joseph Chamberlain (Parnell called him 'the man who killed Home Rule'). Bloom's Parnellism is then ironically subverted when he almost immediately passes someone who is in a sense Parnell's ghost – his brother, Joseph Howard Parnell. The brother was a kindly, harmless, rather stupid man and Bloom remembers Simon Dedalus saying earlier that when they put him in parliament Parnell would come back and lead him out of the House of Commons. The effect of this is to stress the mock-heroic, anti-epic world which is Ireland after Parnell's death.

At the end of the Lestrygonians section Bloom passes a placard which contains the phrase, 'His excellency the lord lieutenant', and this is immediately followed by the startled, 'Straw hat in sunlight. Tan shoes. Turnedup trousers. It is. It is.' Bloom has glimpsed Blazes Boylan and grown fearful – in the lovely phrase Joyce uses, his heart 'quopped softly'. This establishes the first association between the Lord Lieutenant—the chief representative of British rule in Ireland – and Blazes Boylan, the usurper of Bloom's marriage bed. The association is developed two pages later in Scylla and Charybdis where Stephen's thoughts chime with Bloom's: 'Cranly's eleven true Wicklowmen to free their sireland. Gap-toothed Kathleen, her four beautiful green fields, the stranger in her house.' Boylan is the stranger in Bloom's house.

The Kildare Street Library, where Stephen reflects on these nationalist images, is the centre of Dublin literary culture and it's presented as a mixture of the cosmopolitan and the provincial. It is gossipy, sometimes silly, and yet there is a firm sense of an emergent literary culture. 'Our national epic', we hear, 'is still to be written', and with a curious kind of simultaneous hindsight we see its author-hero inside this epic as Stephen adds to the rambling, self-conscious, precious conversation. At one point, he politicizes Shakespeare: 'His pageants, the histories, sail fullbellied on a tide of Mafeking enthusiasm.' Like Bloom, who shouted 'Up the Boers!' at Joseph Chamberlain, Stephen momentarily identifies with the Afrikaaner cause and transforms Shakespeare's mystic English patriotism into British jingoism.

The two masters in whose service Stephen writhes jostle through the Wandering Rocks section in the shape of Father Conmee and the vice-regal cavalcade – both are greeted by 'obsequious policemen'. Father Conmee – the rector of Stephen's old school, Clongowes – has a hollow and polite conversation with Mrs David Sheehy and this is, implicitly, a moment when the forces of reaction preen and consolidate themselves. David Sheehy was an Irish MP who adopted what his grandson, Conor Cruise O'Brien, describes as 'the Catholic and clericalist position' and voted against Parnell. Joyce was a frequent visitor to the Sheehy household and in the Wandering Rocks the Sheehys represent that pious respectable tyranny which he, as a politicized aesthete, hated.

The vice-regal cavalcade is a moment of arid and tyrannical dullness. It is 4 p.m. and there is a slack, neap feeling of demoralisation or defeat. Tom Kernan muses:

Down there Emmet was hanged, drawn and quartered. Greasy black rope. Dogs licking the blood off the street when the lord lieutenant's wife drove by in her noddy.

The sense of squalor and defeat is increased as the prose describing the vice-regal cavalcade takes on the 'toady' style of the *Irish Times*, and as Blazes Boylan moves in counterpoint towards his assignation with Molly: 'jogjaunty jingled Blazes Boylan'. Meanwhile Ben Dollard is singing a rebel song of 1798, 'The Croppy Boy', to a bar-room audience that is lost in sentimental pity. Ironically, Ben Dollard is metamorphosed into 'Big Benaben Dollard, Big Benben' – far from being a rebel he becomes the symbol of imperial authority.

By leaving the hotel at this point Bloom refuses to serve that symbol and his reaction to the portrait of Robert Emmet which he sees in a shop window is a rejection, less of Emmet's example, than of sentimental nationalism and martyrology. Joyce had an intense dislike of Pearse and Bloom's flatulent 'I have done' echoes Pearse's echo of Emmet's last words.* Like the *pok-pok* of the corks in 'Ivy Day in the Committee Room', Bloom's fart belongs to a beery mock-heroic world.

In his famous speech from the dock, Emmet said:

> I have but one request to make at my departure from this world. It is the charity of silence. Let no man write my epitaph. When my country shall have taken her place among the nations of the earth, then, and not till then, let my epitaph be written.

In a very important sense, *Ulysses* is that epitaph because its epic scope and classic perfection gave Ireland a national and international identity. To insist on this is not to make a narrowly nationalistic point, partly because the identity Joyce forges is in advance of Irish political reality (it absolutely has to be in advance of *that*) and partly because of his manner of presenting the Citizen. The Citizen sees a wholly green Ireland through his bigoted Cyclopean vision, and the effect of this is to make Bloom an alien in his own country. Bloom symbolises the Irish as the Jews enduring Egyptian bondage, so it is ironic that there is no place for the Irish in the Citizen's patriotic Ireland.

During a long servile curse against the English, the Citizen asks, 'Where are the Greek merchants that came through the pillars of Hercules, the Gibraltar now grabbed by the foe of mankind?' Gibraltar, we remember, is Molly Bloom's birthplace and so we recognise that Joyce chose it not just for the Homeric reference but because it symbolises imperial occup-

*See Dominic Manganiello's invaluable study, *Joyce's Politics.*

ation. In her great sleepy monologue Molly scorns all Bloom's 'blather' about Home Rule and bathes in a collusive admiration for the Union Jack, redcoat soldiers and gallant English officers. She finds Britishness erotic.

In the Oxen of the Sun episode there is a drunken definition of British imperialism: 'Beer, beef, business, bibles, bulldogs, battleships, buggery and bishops', and past uprisings are re-enacted in Circe when a navvy shouts 'Come on, you British army!' and sings a snatch of patriotic song. In this wonderfully neo-colonial phantasmagoria Bloom becomes a castle Catholic and a voice calls him a 'turncoat' and reminds him that he once shouted 'Up the Boers!' Bloom replies stuffily, 'My old dad too was a J.P. I'm as staunch a Britisher as you are, sir.' And he claims to have fought for King and Country in the Boer War. Frightened by the street violence, Bloom abases and humiliates himself before the fantasy-jury of his conscience. He has, however, an alternative fantasy of himself as a Parnellite liberator, though he is only able to express this in a borrowed literary style which comically subverts it. Joyce offers a hilarious parody of Shakespeare's histories where John Howard Parnell appears, raises a royal standard and declaims, 'Illustrious Bloom! Successor to my famous brother!' Bloom's habitually Fabian and utilitarian attitudes are set aside and he begins to speak in a melodiously patriotic English accent: 'We thank you from our heart, John, for this right royal welcome to green Erin, the promised land of our common ancestors.' Bloom becomes God and announces that the 'new Bloomusalem' is at hand. In a recapitulation of Parnell's downfall, the mob threatens to lynch Bloom and a parallel is suggested with *The Playboy of the Western World*. Synge's play is a symbolic version of Parnell's career and its first audiences reacted in a predictably vengeful manner that reflected the villagers' treachery towards Christy Mahon, the liberating 'Christ Man'.

In Circe, history becomes farce as innumerable atavistic images circle round a brawl on a Dublin street. Stephen taps his brow and says, 'But in here it is I must kill the priest and the king', and this provokes a riot which is the parodic equivalent of Emmet's failed uprising, or 'scuffle on a Dublin street' as it is often referred to.

As in the Oxen of the Sun episode, Joyce is fascinated by the trapped and servile consciousness which is doomed to a hell of brilliant parody (in Hegel's commentary on Diderot this protean imitative brilliance is embodied in Rameau's nephew). And as the language of *Ulysses* tires, he pays an extended, ironic, loving and exasperated tribute to Defoe by reducing "reality" to a gigantic inventory. Joyce deeply admired Defoe's work (he owned his complete works), but he also saw Robinson Crusoe as the 'true symbol of the British conquest...the prototype of the British colonist'. In this inventorial sentence we see Bloom's idealistic vision of Home Rule trapped in a plain factual colonial reality:

> a butt of red partly liquefied sealing wax, obtained from the stores department of Messrs Hely's Ltd., 89, 90 and 91 Dame street: a box containing the remainder of a gross of gilt 'J' pennibs, obtained from the same department of the same firm: a sealed prophecy (never unsealed) written by Leopold Bloom in 1886 concerning the consequences of the passing into law of William Ewart Gladstone's Home Rule bill of 1886 (never passed into law): a bazaar ticket No.2004, of S. Kevin's Charity Fair, price 6d. ...

For Matthew Arnold – he appears in *Ulysses* as a gardener mowing a college lawn – the Irish imagination is always in revolt against 'the despotism of fact', and that positivist tyranny is given an enormously detailed elaboration here. Molly Bloom's monologue breaks that factual boredom and Poldy's prophecy is finally unsealed in her great closing affirmation

> and then he asked me would I yes to say yes my mountain flower and first I put my arms around him yes and drew him down to me so he could feel my breasts all perfume yes and his heart was going like mad and yes I said yes I will Yes.

The French Are on the Sea

At the end of Yeats's *Cathleen Ni Houlihan* the news of the French landing at Killala Bay in 1798 charges the play with a strict and dedicated passion, that 'curious astringent joy' which both terrifies and inspires.

Thomas Flanagan's remarkable historical novel tells of the French landing to assist the United Irishmen in their rebellion against the Crown. The story is mediated through several narrators—each of whom has a different viewpoint and style—and in this way Flanagan overcomes most of the standard objections to the historical novel. Through the narrative of an English clergyman we see a civil and decorous eighteenth-century mind attempting to understand the native Irish who combine 'a grave and gentle courtesy with a murderous violence that erupts without warning'. The Revd. Arthur Broome is horrified by the excesses on both sides, and he emerges as a decent, sympathetic, if ineffectual, character who speaks for the powerless centre of Irish politics—he is unobtrusively modelled on Conrad's elderly language teacher in *Under Western Eyes*.

Flanagan has an unerring sense of the parallels between the political situation in 1798 and the events in Ulster over the last ten years. Thus the Mayo yeomanry are the shadowy and bigoted forerunners of the B Specials, the secret society called the Whiteboys of Killala is the Provisional IRA, while the brief 'Republic of Connaught' parallels Free Derry nearly two centuries later. Flanagan has considerable sympathy for the aims and ideals of the United Irishmen, but he is also aware of what happens when ideology is translated into action:

> How could we have supposed a connection to exist between our ideas, city bred, and the passions of the peasants? Theorems advanced in a Rathfarnham villa, beneath the cool, benign skies of a Dublin evening, are transformed by the airs of Connaught, country people hanged by indifferent dragoons, pikes piercing the horizon, an Irish-speaking priest bawling out his bloody sermons.

The net of contemporary parallels tightens as the local

The Year of the French by Thomas Flanagan.

gentry prefigure the Ulster Unionists, and when the English general, Cornwallis, decides that he must get rid of the Dublin parliament and its 'venal legislators' there is a clear analogy with the prorogation of Stormont. The Act of Union is the elder twin of direct rule, and Cornwallis's 'My God, what a country!' echoes Reginald Maudling's notorious 'What a bloody awful country!' Particularly interesting is Flanagan's presentation of Owen MacCarthy, the Gaelic poet who is caught up in the revolution. Through MacCarthy (he is partly based on Seamus Heaney) Flanagan explores the difficult relationship of poetry to politics in Ireland, and he expresses the historical reality which informs Heaney's powerful conclusion to 'Triptych':

> How we crept before we walked! I remembered
> The helicopter shadowing our march at Newry,
> The scared, irrevocable steps.

Through the eyes of the sceptical historian, George Moore, we see how Ireland has always been 'a maidservant to others':

> When James and William, the two kings, faced each other at the Boyne, the game was Europe, and Ireland but the board upon which the wagers were placed. The history of Ireland, as written by any of our local savants, reminds me of a learned and respectable ant, climbing laboriously across a graven tablet and discovering there deep valleys, towering mountains, broad avenues, which to a grown man contemplating the scene are but the incised names of England, Spain, France.

Thus the French general, Humbert, becomes a prototype of those American congressmen who periodically interfere in Irish politics. Flanagan is also subtly aware of the "equivocal" nature of Loyalism, and by admitting every shade of political opinion he builds a rich, intelligent and exciting fiction. Although there are purple passages and moments of costume-drama in this novel, it is a heartening achievement which must prove influential and enduring.

Life Sculpture: Patrick Kavanagh

Patrick Kavanagh was a difficult, devout, very innocent man who was known in witty Dublin as 'the ploughman-about-town'. He grew up on a small farm in Co. Monaghan where he worked 'among poetry, potatoes and old boots'. In his brother's memoir Kavanagh emerges as a sincere man who pretended to be 'a country gobshite' in order to protect the holy simplicity of his personality. His devious ebullience concealed a shy and delicate imagination.

In one of his finest poems, 'Kerr's Ass', Kavanagh offers a vision of the great good place, the home townland which his imagination names from the exile of 'Ealing Broadway, London Town':

> Morning, the silent bog,
> And the God of imagination waking
> In a Mucker fog.

In these lines, a unique place-name (it derives from the Irish for 'pig') mediates between the individual imagination and what Coleridge called 'the infinite I AM', and so helps body out a visionary statement which is close to the first line of *The Great Hunger*: 'Clay is the word and clay is the flesh'. Like Coleridge, Kavanagh spent much of his life avoiding giving any direct vision of the infinite I AM and as a result he is a figure of great promise, rather than firm achievement. There's something peculiarly *intact* about Kavanagh's imagination, and this is reflected in the subject of *The Great Hunger*—the frustrations and inertia of Irish rural life. Its sad hero, Patrick Maguire, is praised by his mother for making 'a field his bride', and remains a frustrated rural bachelor:

> He stands in the doorway of his house
> A ragged sculpture of the wind,
> October creaks the rotted mattress,
> The bedposts fall. No hope. No lust.

For all the poem's insistence on boredom and sexual frustration, it has a quality of hectic acceptance—Maguire has remained

---

Sacred Keeper: A Biography of Patrick Kavanagh by Peter Kavanagh.

true to 'the enclosed nun of his thought'.

Kavanagh often denounced Irish society as 'mediocre' and yet he also complained that there was 'no protection in Ireland anywhere for anybody with a poetic talent'. It's a most perverse complaint—Ireland is packed with philistines who nevertheless ought to protect the poet—and it surfaces again in this daft remark to his brother: 'I applied in an insulting way for one of the Script Writers jobs on Radio Eireann, 750 per annum and was not even asked for an interview.' Here, the source of his contradictory annoyance can be traced in his adaptation of a common Monaghan phrase, 'an iron fool'. According to Peter Kavanagh the phrase is used to describe someone who pretends to be a fool 'only to protect himself', and Kavanagh originally chose it as the title for his marvellous autobiographical yarn, *The Green Fool*. His brother states that he altered the title because he felt the word 'iron' would be incomprehensible to most people, but the real reason must have been that he wanted to conceal and protect his imaginative strategy. Instead of admitting irony, he chose to present himself as a naive innocent, a holy fool, or as someone green in judgement. His wearing of the green was also a deliberate dressing up in motley and this memoir is rich in Kavanagh's denunciations of 'sentimental patriotism' and 'bitter barren minds'. However, he was in some ways the victim of the partition of Ireland—like Cavan and Donegal, his native Monaghan was severed from the rest of Ulster and cast into a kind of historical limbo. For all its closeness to rural life, Kavanagh's imagination has an oddly stateless quality—he knew what he was against, but like some of his northern contemporaries he saw no possible culture he could be for.

Patrick's canny evasiveness is apparent in his advice to his brother not to 'let everyone know your business', and something of his contrary nature informs Peter's heartfelt memorandum of the first cancer operation:

> The first object he saw as he came out of the anaesthetic was the head of a friend peeping over the curtain! His privacy invaded! It was a violent insult to his ease of mind, but he refused to be bitter about it.

He must have been an exasperating friend and a typically dominating elder brother. In all kinds of ways Patrick speaks through Peter's account and their relationship is very similar to the mutual dependency of James and Stanislaus Joyce.

There is a particularly vivid sequence of letters which shows Patrick mounting his assault on literary London from a café in Gerrards Cross:

> I have had my coat cleaned and that will be money. I wonder if you would be able to raise ten bob for me by return—to arrive by second post on Tuesday morning. In my other letter which I wrote yesterday and may not arrive so soon I told that H. Macmillan wrote a friendly letter. I'll hear from him and you'll hear then.

Peter was his trusted confidant, and although this memoir by 'the brother' resembles a collage of photographs, old bus tickets and unpaid bills, the result is a portrait which has an extraordinary quality of absolute verisimilitude—like a Duane Hanson figure.

Lawrence after Fifty Years

During the First World War, Lawrence remarked, 'We are, have been for five centuries, the growing tip. Now we're going to fall. But you don't catch me going back on my whiteness and Englishness and myself. English in the teeth of the world, even in England.' Although he may well have changed his mind the next day and proclaimed that he was, and always had been, an Assyrian or a Pict, this assertion of Englishness must be taken at its face value and its distinctive oddity noted— Lawrence a distinctively *English* writer? English like Orwell, or Edward Thomas, or Jane Austen? The Lawrence who wrote 'England, My England' belongs to the England which begins at the river Trent, that great hyperborean tundra of mills, mines and factories which dreams itself as the territory of fierce, passionate, authentic feeling. For some reason, that northern part of England never seems quite English, and I don't think it did to Lawrence—he sought parallels for it in other countries, other cultures, different ways of feeling. In doing so, he obviously had to adapt a received concept of Englishness, and he did this by offending, deliberately and often, against one of the central tenets of Englishness—the idea that there is ultimately a law to which we are responsible, a law which is invoked in that mystic phrase "you're going too far". This admonition not to go too far is linked with the notion of decency and with the idea that there is a version of experience which is indecent and which lies "beyond the pale".

That phrase "beyond the pale" is a metaphor which derives from the English settlement of Ireland and it denotes 'that part of Ireland over which English jurisdiction was established'. And obviously the phrase has ancient colonial significances— to go beyond the pale is to stray beyond the bounds of Englishness and to join the ranks of what Kipling, the Lawrence of imperial engineering, terms 'lesser breeds without the Law'.

How, then, did Lawrence go beyond the pale? One example—it's a famous one—is the letter he wrote to Katherine Mansfield when she lay dying: 'You revolt me, stewing in your consumption.' Another example, is a letter of 1912 which he wrote to Edward Garnett from near Munich:

I had rather a nice letter from somebody—'Hugh Walpole'. Is he anybody? Could I wring three ha'porth of help out of his bloody neck? Curse the blasted, jelly-boned swines, the slimy, the belly-wriggling invertebrates, the miserable sodding rotters, the flaming sods, the snivelling, dribbling, dithering palsied pulse-less lot that make up England today. They've got white of egg in their veins, and their spunk is that watery it's a marvel they can breed. They *can* nothing but frog-spawn—the gibberers! God, how I hate them! God curse them, funkers. God blast them, wish-wash. Exterminate them, slime......Why, why, why was I born an Englishman!—my cursed, rotten-boned, pappy hearted countrymen, *why* was I sent to *them*. Christ on the cross must have hated his countrymen. 'Crucify me, you swine,' he must have said through his teeth. It's not so hard to love thieves also on the cross. But the high priests down there—'crucify me, you swine'.—'Put in your nails and spear, you bloody nasal sour-blooded swine, I laugh last.' God, how I hate them—I nauseate—they stink in sourness.

They deserve it that every great man should drown himself. But not I (I am a bit great).

This Calvinistic curse is directed simultaneously against the English social and literary establishment and against Ernest Weekley; and the terrible phrase 'Exterminate them, slime' is so close to Kurtz's scrawl, 'Exterminate all the brutes', in Conrad's *Heart of Darkness*, that Lawrence appears to be consciously modelling himself on that demonic emanation. He appears to be living the disintegration of liberalism, and ironically we have to consider whether Lawrence's murderous directive is an essentially primitive attitude or whether it's not a naturally colonial attitude which happens to be turned against its own culture?

For Lawrence, such a curse was an invocation to the savage god, and we can see this in another letter which he wrote to Garnett five days later:

I don't want to come back to England. For the winter I shall get something to do in Germany, I think. F. (that is, Frieda) wants to clear out of Europe, and get to somewhere uncivilised. It is astonishing how barbaric one gets with love: one finds oneself in the Hinterland der Seele, and—it's a rum place. I never knew it was like this. What Blasted Fools the English are, fencing off the big wild scope of their natures. Since I am in Germany, all my little pathetic sadness and softness goes, and I am often frightened at the thing [originally 'savage'] I find myself.

Obviously this passage is a celebration of the delights of

barbarism—of living beyond civility—though what's curious about it is the way Lawrence *socialises* love while at the same time denying social or civil values. It's as if the act of love becomes a revolutionary act against the English class system—indeed, against the whole of European civilisation. And of course love across the barriers of class, culture, race, is often seen as a form of subversion.

What is fascinating about this letter is the way in which two voices play against each other in Lawrence's rapid sentences—the voice we hear in that phrase 'it's a rum place' is distinctively English in its attitude of decent, slightly ironic stoicism. The second voice is Frieda's—'Since I am in Germany, all my little pathetic sadness and softness goes'. The syntax here isn't English ('*Seit Ich in Deutschland bin*', it would begin in German), and so this sentence, both in its grammatical structure and its content, expresses a very different attitude. It's almost as though the entire von Richthofen family is speaking in a bad translation here. The spirit of Nietzsche and of Prussian militarism has momentarily possessed Lawrence.

Another significant influence which modified Lawrence's Englishness was that of Synge, whose work he read during the Croydon years. *Riders to the Sea*, Lawrence said, 'is about the genuinest bit of dramatic tragedy, English, since Shakespeare, I should say'. And in a letter to Garnett he states:

> I believe that, just as an audience was found in Russia for Tchekov, so an audience might be found in England for some of my stuff, if there were a man to whip 'em in. It's the producer that is lacking, not the audience. I'm sure we are sick of the rather bony, bloodless drama we get nowadays—it is time for a reaction against Shaw and Galsworthy and Barker and Irishy˙ (except Synge) people—the rule and measure mathematical folk. But you are of them and your sympathies are with your own generation, not with mine. I think it is inevitable. You are about the only man who is willing to let a new generation come in. It will seem a bit rough to me, when I am 45, and must see myself and my tradition supplanted. I shall bear it very badly. Damn my impudence, but don't dislike me. But I don't want to write like Galsworthy nor Ibsen, nor Strindberg nor any of them, *not* even if I could. We have to hate our immediate predecessors, to get free from their authority.

That last recommendation—'We have to hate our immediate predecessors, to get free from their authority'—is in several ways connected with the admiration of Synge which Lawrence expresses early in the letter. This is because Lawrence and Synge both deal with essentially Oedipal conflicts between a passionate instinct for freedom and a Law which they see as imposed, as not belonging to the essential conditions of life. Thus Synge praises the natural *sprezzatura* of the Aran islanders like this:

> The absence of the heavy boot of Europe has preserved to these people the agile walk of the wild animal, while the general simplicity of their lives has given them many other points of physical perfection. Their way of life has never been acted on by anything much more artificial than the nests and burrows of the creatures that live round them, and they seem in a certain sense to approach more nearly to the finer types of our aristocracies—who are bred artificially to a natural ideal—than to the labourer or citizen, as the wild horse resembles the thoroughbred rather than the hack or cart-horse. Tribes of the same natural development are, perhaps, frequent in half-civilised countries, but here a touch of the refinement of old societies is blended, with singular effect, among the qualities of the wild animal.

This is Yeats's 'dream of the noble and the beggarman' and it is accompanied by a celebration of passionate rage, a rage which is nevertheless a communal activity: 'This grief of the keen is no personal complaint for the death of one woman over eighty years, but seems to contain the whole passionate rage that lurks somewhere in every native of the island.' And describing an eviction, Synge writes: 'these mechanical police, with the commonplace agents and sheriffs, and the rabble they had hired, represented aptly enough the civilisation for which the homes of the island were to be desecrated'. Were Synge not an influence upon Lawrence, we might describe this remark— especially the words 'mechanical', 'rabble', 'civilisation'—as clearly Lawrentian in tone. The quality both writers share is also apparent in the folk tale which Synge describes and which provided the immediate inspiration for *The Playboy of the Western World*:

> Another old man, the oldest on the island, is fond of telling me anecdotes—not folk-tales—of things that have happened here in his lifetime.
>
> He often tells me about a Connaught man who killed his father with the blow of a spade when he was in passion, and then fled to the island and threw himself on the mercy of some of the natives

with whom he was said to be related. They hid him in a hole—which the old man has shown me—and kept him safe for weeks, though the police came and searched for him, and he could hear their boots grinding on the stones over his head. In spite of a reward which was offered, the island was incorruptible, and after much trouble the man was safely shipped to America.

This impulse to protect the criminal is universal in the west. It seems partly due to the association between justice and the hated English jurisdiction, but more directly to the primitive feeling of these people, who are never criminals yet always capable of crime, that a man will not do wrong unless he is under the influence of a passion which is as irresponsible as a storm on the sea. If a man has killed his father, and is already sick and broken with remorse, they can see no reason why he should be dragged away and killed by the law.

Such a man, they say, will be quiet all the rest of his life, and if you suggest that punishment is needed as an example, they ask, 'Would any one kill his father if he was able to help it?'

Some time ago, before the introduction of police, all the people of the islands were as innocent as the people here remain to this day. I have heard that at that time the ruling proprietor and magistrate of the north island used to give any man who had done wrong a letter to a jailor in Galway, and send him off by himself to serve a term of imprisonment.

The conflict, clearly, is between artificial civil law and natural passion, between Pentheus and Dionysus, and Lawrence gives this an extreme expression in 'The Prussian Officer' where the young orderly's 'blind, instinctive sureness of movement' is contrasted with the officer's harsh rigidity. It is his celebration of this wild and lawless principle which makes Lawrence an essentially unEnglish writer, and some idea of this other essence can be perceived in a wry and gentle short story by V.S. Pritchett called 'The Fig Tree'.

The story is told by a nurseryman who remarks, 'It is well known, if you run a nursery, that very nice old ladies sometimes nip off a stem for a cutting or slip small plants in their bags. Stealing is a form of flirtation with them.' And then he reflects on this delicately erotic situation:

There was a myth at our Nursery that when a box of plants was missing or some rare expensive shrub had been dug up and was gone, this was the work of a not altogether imaginary person called Thompson who lived in a big house where the garden abutted on our wall. Three camellias went one day, and because of the price he was somehow promoted by the girls and became known as 'Colonel' Thompson. He had been seen standing on a stepladder and looking over our wall.

In mythic terms this thief, the not-altogether-imaginary person called Thompson, is Autolycus, and what's fascinating about this passage is the way it demonstrates how a naturally lawless principle can be easily accommodated within the English class system. When Thompson daringly steals something enormous—three camellias—he is immediately promoted to Colonel, and so Autolycus becomes an English gentleman who somehow exists both within and beyond the law. Lawrence's opposition between the officer and his Dionysian servant is wittily circumvented. It's a curiously Burkean perception.

As a nonconformist, Lawrence cannot rest content with this type of evasive Anglican compromise. He believes in a romantic puritan ethic of 'sincerity and a quickening spontaneous emotion' and rejects the idea of reserve. Partly this issues from that dissenting chapel-culture which Matthew Arnold so disdained, but it must also be an expression of that new climate of feeling and behaviour which George Dangerfield examines in *The Strange Death of Liberal England*. One of the starkest examples of this is the end of 'The Fox' where the young soldier allows a tree to fall on March's possessive companion, Banford. Human relationships, for Lawrence, are a form of bloodsport in which the weakest are destroyed, and his savage puritan romanticism might be summed up in the remark with which Heathcliff justifies his treatment of Isabella Linton: 'I have no pity! I have no pity! The more the worms writhe, the more I learn to crush out their entrails! It is a moral teething.'

Although Lawrence's enormous hatreds appear to belong to a Nuremberg rally, it might be more accurate to regard them as distinctively neo-colonial. Synge's Christy Mahon, for example, is a Parnell-figure who tries to strike the father dead and is then turned on and betrayed by his supporters, while Lawrence's Oedipal hatred of the establishment is that of someone who feels that he belongs to another country, or at least to a disadvantaged culture. It expresses something more than class antagonism and is perhaps an extreme form of puritan individualism. And in arguing that the 'big wild scope' of human nature is something which the English 'fence off',

Lawrence has moved outside the pale into Synge's western world or into a German cult of the *völkisch*.

Lawrence embodies a Cromwellian opposition to formality and this is one reason why his work appeals to Leavisite puritans rather than to Oxford scholar-critics. For example, Lawrence would reject vehemently this characteristically Oxford remark of Anthony Cockshut's: 'reticence is so undeniably necessary to civilised life, since without it the whole idea of what is fitting is lost'. Commenting on this statement, Russell Davies has remarked that it represents 'the extremely English concept, widespread throughout our society, though most Europeans would call it aristocratically conservative, of appropriateness as an ideal in itself—the notion that situations impose their own moral order, and that to respect this, and to pattern one's behaviour accordingly, is to make one's optimum contribution to the health of civilisation. By this creed, there is a decorum beyond decorum, beyond convention; its demands are unspoken, and its essence is tact.' Lawrence is fundamentally opposed to decorum and convention—reticence is merely priggishness for him—and he everywhere insists on the untactful expression of personal emotion. Preaching out of an evangelical culture of moral fervour and plain speaking, he often resembles a demonic version of John Bunyan. In a sense he has succeeded in internationalising that world of nonconformist provincialism which offended Arnold so deeply.

One of the most damaging results of Lawrence's insistence on intense experience is that his work is regarded as a body of doctrine which compels a moral assent. His writings are seldom discussed in a formal aesthetic manner, and Lawrence is seen throughout as a preacher who exhorts us to live. The work, therefore, can only be discussed by making "life" into a critical term—which is what Leavis does—and this means that critical writing about Lawrence is often comically and stupendously naive.

To take one example, in a recent essay on the short stories D. Kenneth M. Mackenzie points shrewdly to the parallels between Lawrence's 'You Touched Me' and *Washington Square*. However, he concludes by expressing a preference for Lawrence's story on the grounds that James's novel 'resigns itself to a spinsterish fortitude'. Once you accept the Lawrentian imperative of experience then you have to believe that married people are somehow morally better than spinsters or bachelors (puritanism is traditionally hostile to the unmarried and the celibate). It also means that when you reach one of the decisive tests of literary sensibility—the end of *Washington Square*—you are bound to fail precisely because you judge Catherine Sloper to be a failure. That last sentence—'Catherine, meanwhile, in the parlour, picking up her morsel of fancy-work, had seated herself with it again—for life, as it were'—is a life sentence, but it is not what Lawrence or Leavis mean by life. It has nothing to do with some managerial notion of positive thinking or with the insistence that it is everyone's moral duty to have sexual experience, or any form of experience.

Looking through the shelf upon shelf of Lawrence criticism, I've begun to realise that his critics believe that he wasn't an artist at all—instead, he was an inspired natural genius whose experiences simply fell out onto the page. In his study of *The Prussian Officer*, for example, Keith Cushman draws these moral lessons from the stories. 'Odour of Chrysanthemums' is a 'moving statement about the human condition' and the two lovers in 'Daughters of the Vicar' embody 'the human salvation available through the dark mystery of the body'. In a rare aesthetic judgement, Cushman remarks that the 'highly visible symbolic framework' of the chrysanthemums is 'perhaps a little overdone'. However, he fails to notice that when the flowers make their last appearance—one of the men carrying the miner's body into the room knocks the vase over—Lawrence is deliberately killing off his leitmotif with a neat self-conscious flourish (that vase of chrysanthemums is resurrected in Virginia Woolf's 'The Shooting Party' which is obviously inspired by Lawrence and Synge).

Again, although Cushman makes the important point that *Riders to the Sea* helped Lawrence shape his story, he must retreat from the idea of tradition, culture and conscious craft which this implies by adding, 'nevertheless the main creative impulse came from Lawrence's own experience'. Here, Cushman is attempting to be true to what he believes is Lawrence's ethic and actual artistic practice, for to the romantic critic experience is all, and art is mere dishonest artifice. By identifying experience with the imagination, Cushman suggests that as an artist Lawrence was complete and entire unto himself—he didn't need to learn from anyone else. Yet, as Cushman has discovered, 'Odour of Chrysanthemums' went through *five* major revisions—Lawrence didn't rest content with the first published version but continued to alter, change and perfect it. And perhaps at last he felt able to pare his fingernails like Joyce's aesthetic god.

Lawrence's story is remarkable for its formal perfection, for the manner in which he develops the irony of Elizabeth Bates's remarks:

> 'But he needn't come rolling in here in his pit-dirt, for *I* won't wash him.'
>
> 'They'll bring him when he does come—like a log. And he may sleep on the floor till he wakes himself. I know he'll not go to work tomorrow after this.'
>
> 'No!—I expect he's stuck in there.'

These ironies are drawn together when the body is at last brought home and one of the children shouts down, 'Is he drunk?' With great sureness, Lawrence builds a sense both of narrative inevitability and ordinary event—a stagnant afternoon, routine actions, waiting and foreboding. And then, as Elizabeth goes to enquire of her neighbours, there is this tense and evasive narrative uncertainty—do the neighbours know or suspect that there's been an accident? Why are they so furtive, helpful, rather embarrassed? Are they really trying to avoid her? And the manager's remark when the body is brought home—'He'd no business to ha' been left'—throws us back to Rigley's self-justifying speech:

> 'Ah left 'im finishin' a stint,' he began. 'Loose-all 'ad bin gone about ten minutes when we com'n away, an' I shouted "Are ter comin', Walt?" an' 'e said, "Go on, Ah shanna be but a'ef a minnit," se we com'n ter th' bottom, me an' Bowers, thinkin' as 'e wor just behint, an' 'ud come up i' th' next bantle—' He stood perplexed, as if answering a charge of deserting his mate. Elizabeth Bates, now again certain of disaster, hastened to reassure him.

Though they are in no way derivative, Lawrence's delight in Rigley's dialect and the fatalism that is felt here and throughout the story, owe much to *Riders to the Sea*. What is unusual is the way in which Lawrence appears to have set his puritan belief in personal destiny and individual salvation aside and to be inspired by a pagan fatalism.

However, to talk of Lawrence's debt to other writers, to notice his irony and his delight in conscious art is—at least in the lost world of Lawrence studies—to entirely miss the point. For the Lawrentian critic all that matters is the "doctrine" and this turns out to be merely a few catchphrases about the 'dark mystery of the body' and 'wonderful naked intimacy'. Lawrence the man is Lawrence the artist, his prose style is the biological energy of the life-force, the expression of pure, natural, original inspiration. Here, then, is one of the greatest English short story writers and yet there is hardly a critical book on the stories (Lawrentian critics find the novels a much softer option and this softness has spread far and wide over the academic study of literature with terrible destructive consequences).

In my view, one of Lawrence's most formally satisfying short stories is 'Samson and Delilah', a story that was surely inspired as much by *The Playboy of the Western World* as by the fluid gods of experience. Synge's play and the story share similar settings—a dark Celtic night, a man arriving at a lonely pub near the sea, the woman who keeps the bar, his relationship with her, her urging the men in the bar to tie him up. Lawrence uses the adjective "celtic" several times in the story and he does so for reasons which any Cornish nationalist would approve. This imaginative territory is outside the pale, another country like Northtrentland. And its different ethic emerges when the sergeant reflects on Nankervis's return: 'A dirty action,' said the sergeant, his face flushing dark. 'A dirty action, to come after deserting a woman for that number of years, and want to force yourself on her! A dirty action—as isn't allowed by the law.' This speech is made, significantly, at closing time, the time when the law tries to control Bacchus. Nankervis replies, 'Never you mind about law nor nothing,' and here he speaks like one of Synge's peasants. In *The Aran Islands* Synge describes the islanders' hostility to the law, and in *Playboy of the Western World* the widow Quin says to Christy's father, 'Let you give him a good vengeance when you come up with him, but don't put yourself in the power of the law, for it'd be a poor thing to see a judge in his black cap reading out his sentence on a civil warrior the like of you.' Like Nankervis, Synge's characters scorn or refuse to recognise the law.

Subtly, Lawrence shows Mrs Nankervis using legality as a weapon against her husband. Concealing her personal anger against him, she calls out in a bright business-like voice, 'Time, please. Time, my dears. And good-night all!' He then sets this vocal tone against a more personal tone as Nankervis refuses to obey what he terms 'orders' and leave:

> 'I'm stopping here tonight,' he said, in his laconic Cornish-Yankee accent.
>
> The landlady seemed to tower. Her eyes lifted strangely, frightening.
>
> 'Oh! indeed!' she cried. 'Oh, indeed! And whose orders are those, may I ask?'
>
> He looked at her again.
>
> 'My orders,' he said.
>
> Involuntarily she shut the door, and advanced like a great, dangerous bird. Her voice rose, there was a touch of hoarseness in it.
>
> 'And what might *your* orders be, if you please?' she cried. 'Who might *you* be, to give orders, in the house?'
>
> He sat still, watching her.
>
> 'You know who I am,' he said. 'At least, I know who you are.'
>
> 'Oh, you do? Oh, do you? And who am *I* then, if you'll be so good as to tell me?'
>
> He stared at her with his bright, dark eyes.
>
> 'You're my Missis, you are,' he said. 'And you know it, as well as I do.'
>
> She started as if something had exploded in her.
>
> Her eyes lifted and flared madly.
>
> '*Do* I know it, indeed!' she cried. 'I know no such thing! I know no such thing! Do you think a man's going to walk into this bar and tell me off-hand I'm his Missis, and I'm going to believe him?'

Really, this is an operatic passage—the anger on her part is furious and intense, and yet what is taking place between them is a form of courtship. Like lovers in an opera, they are conscious of their audience—'"Yes," *sang* the landlady, slowly shaking her head in supreme sarcasm.' The young soldiers look on 'in delight', the sergeant smokes 'imperturbed'. When Nankervis is seized by his wife and she and the soldiers tie him up there is a curious description of the couple swaying together like a 'frightful Laocoon' (so the woman is a sea serpent, the man is Laocoon who offended Apollo by marrying and having children). The rope is the Law, is Justice, because Nankervis is being punished—at least this symbolism holds true until he frees himself and we learn that the rope is made of 'a kind of plaited grass' which soon frays and breaks. It has associations with natural magic, with the plaits tied round corn stooks or haystacks (in Irish such a rope is a *sugan*). Until this point the rope is punitive, the instrument of Nankervis's humiliation and apparent rejection by his wife. Yet paradoxically she is also laying claim to him—the door which she shut 'involuntarily' earlier is surprisingly unbolted.

Also, if their first argument is a form of courtship, the tying-up is a form of marriage service with the sergeant deputising for the priest. Afterwards, when they're reunited in the kitchen and Nankervis uses the variously ambiguous phrase 'I take you' we can almost hear the by now extremely ironic words 'as my lawful wedded wife'.

Thus we witness a ceremony, a form of decorum, and see that their experience has a natural pattern. In the end, it's a comic story with a wonderfully banal love-speech from Nankervis which insists on being read ironically—Nankervis's coarse cloying 'mindless' stupidity, his macho weakness and almost clucking admiration are beautifully created. However, at least one Lawrentian critic I've read sees Nankervis as the perfect epitome of natural aristocracy, a moral lesson to follow. For such critics—they are numerous and influential—Lawrence's work is remarkable for an inchoate intensity, and not for a formal beauty, a ceremonial irony. It's a rum do, Lawrence criticism.

The Earnest Puppet: Edward Carson

Early in 1981 Ian Paisley mounted a midnight demonstration on an Antrim hillside where 500 men gathered to threaten the British government with firearm certificates. When a puzzled journalist asked him exactly what he was playing at, Paisley told his interviewer to go away and acquaint himself with the life and times of Sir Edward Carson. Here, then, is the book which political journalists and their uninformed public may have been waiting for—a life of that grim and righteous figure whose ghost stalks through the North of Ireland now.

Carson was born in Dublin in 1854 and was descended from 'Honest John' Lambert, one of Cromwell's major-generals. A tall, ungainly, dyspeptic figure whose schoolfellows called him 'Rawbones', his personality suggests many of the darker aspects of puritanism—he was a joyless barrister, a canny hypochondriac, a brooding philistine, a savagely destructive politician. He knew Oscar Wilde at Trinity and appeared a dull and conscientious plodder beside his brilliant contemporary (many years later he vengefully destroyed Wilde in a famous cross-examination). He was a histrionic advocate who loved to simulate a stony integrity, and his favourite ploy—both in the court-room and in the Commons—was to lose his temper and walk out. Without irony, without subtlety, he possessed a peculiarly harsh and negative will which was stoked by huge bunkers of moral self-righteousness.

In 1910 he gave up the chance of leading the Tory Party and became the parliamentary leader of the anti-Home Rule Irish Unionists. Soon this distinguished KC and former Solicitor-General was supporting Loyalist gun-runners and doing his fanatic best to undermine the legal and political institutions he claimed to revere. According to George Danger-field—a compelling authority who is oddly absent from this study—Carson possessed a nature which 'ought never to be allowed within the walls of a Parliament'. He was one of the rough beasts who assisted at the death of liberal England, a case-hardened lawyer who was so passionately and uncompromisingly lawless in his utterances that his seditious rhetoric

Edward Carson by A.T.Q. Stewart.

won the admiration of Patrick Pearse and Sir Roger Casement. It was the Loyalist rebellion of 1912 which Carson led that helped to inspire the 1916 Easter Rising, and this paradox finds contemporary expression in the admiration which David O'Connell, one of the Provisional IRA leaders, feels for the most extreme Loyalist leaders.

Carson's public life was a long and relentless success-story and yet he felt he had been a failure. His maiden speech in the House of Lords is a spectacular example of the contradictory, self-pitying, childish and festering sense of grievance which is at the centre of the Loyalist mentality. Addressing the Lords in 1921, he first attacked the government for negotiating the Treaty with Michael Collins and then turned to lambast his colleagues in the Tory Party. He complained bitterly that the Tories had merely used the Unionists during the previous thirty years: 'I was in earnest. What a fool I was! I was only a puppet, and so was Ulster, and so was Ireland, in the political game that was to get the Conservative Party into power.' It's a naive and anguished political testament which never arrives at the perception that Unionist MPs at Westminster must always have the status of political whores. Lord Randolph Churchill, Austen Chamberlain and Lord Birkenhead all used the Unionists ruthlessly, and when Edward Heath betrayed them many years later they glumly sold their votes to the Labour Party—a party which will never repeal their constitutional veto, despite its vague and contradictory gestures towards Irish unity.

Although Stewart's biography is a useful addition to Gill and Macmillan's welcome series, it is a sometimes sentimental piece of loyalist hagiography whose style is well below his characteristic standard. Stewart assumes the integrity of the Ulster Unionists' quarrel and although he quotes A.J.P. Taylor's verdict that Carson was dangerous in opposition but ineffective in office, he fails to explore the glaring and obvious limitations of Carson's Loyalist credo. He does, however, comment on the incompatible nature of Carson's cultural allegiances, and on the manner in which he became the prisoner of the Ulster Unionists. Carson's costive self-importance was founded on the belief that the Tory Party was 'earnest' about the Union with Britain. He came to believe his own theatrical gestures and so failed to notice the element of fantasy and games-playing in public life which was so clear to the ironic intelligence of his old enemy, Wilde.

Nineteen Twelve

George Birmingham was once a well-known writer, but all his books—with the exception of *The Red Hand of Ulster*—are now out of print. His name was the pseudonym of James Owen Hannay who was born in Belfast in 1865, studied at Trinity College, Dublin, and became a minister of the Church of Ireland which he described as 'that rigid, somewhat arid branch of the Anglican communion'. During his long life he published many novels, as well as essays, travel books, journalism and an autobiography. He was a remarkably wise and witty writer, and in *The Red Hand of Ulster* he offered an ironic and sympathetically intelligent account of Ulster politics which is still relevant today.

His novel is about the Home Rule Crisis of 1912 and he began writing it on 2 April that year. He finished it two months later and it was published the following month. The speed of composition and publication shows how urgently Birmingham responded to current political events. Like Orwell and Auden in the 1930s, he was forced to become a type of journalist and to reflect actual events imaginatively, as well as interpreting them politically. His novel is a kind of documentary as well as being an amusing fantasy—and here again it anticipates the documentary realism and satirical fantasy of much 1930s writing.

Just a week after he began writing his novel, a huge demonstration against Home Rule was held in Belfast. While the novelist wrote in his study, a Loyalist crowd gathered under an enormous Union Jack—it measured over a thousand square feet. They listened to a speech by Bonar Law, who assured them that they would save the British Empire by their example. Clearly he was wrong—the Empire has gone, but Ulster remains—and Birmingham understood Bonar Law's mistake very shrewdly. In *An Irishman Looks at His World* (a wryly intelligent work which ought to be reissued), he remarks that Belfast's captains of industry 'care for their trade' more than they love the Union Jack, 'or perhaps they love the flag chiefly because trade follows it'. Indeed, Frederick Crawford, one of the Loyalist military chiefs, echoed this when he remarked that if Ulster were put out of the Union with Britain he would 'infinitely prefer to change his allegiance right over to the

Emperor of Germany'. And so that enormous Union Jack which was hoisted over Belfast in 1912 symbolised a loyalty that was less than absolute—a loyalty that was being protested rather too much.

Ulster Loyalism, Birmingham shows, issues from a deeply rebellious culture, and he explores this paradox by making the narrator of his novel an amateur historian called Lord Kilmore of Errigal. Lord Kilmore is engaged in writing an account of every Irish rebellion and he sets this historical work aside in order to describe the rebellion of 1912. Although Birmingham is a much lighter novelist, his fictional atmosphere has a Turgenevian fragrance—characters wander through the grounds of Kilmore's country house, gossiping, talking politics, and picking strawberries.

Birmingham stoutly resists a political analysis which suggests that the Irish conflict is essentially a tribal one, and instead offers an economic analysis of the rebellion. Thus, Lady Moyne, one of the Unionist leaders, says how 'splendid' it is to have a cause which will 'bind our working classes to us and make them loyal to those who are after all their best friends and natural leaders'. And her argument is echoed by another character—a Belfast businessman called Cahoon—who prophesies 'doleful things' about the paralysing of business under a Home Rule Parliament.

The attention which Birmingham draws to business values throughout the novel demonstrates how closely he understood the Loyalist cause. He shows that business values and political idealism are mutually exclusive—businessmen are pragmatists who ask only that the government leave them alone, so that they can get on with making money. This emerges starkly in a rhetorical overstatement which James Craig, the Loyalist leader and a wealthy businessman, made in April 1912, the month Birmingham began his novel. Craig said that there was a growing feeling in Ulster that Germany and the German Emperor would be preferred to an Irish Nationalist government. His loyalty to Britain was therefore conditional and contradictory. And Birmingham explores the paradox of Unionist loyalty—rebelling against Britain in order to remain British—by inventing a newspaper called *The Loyalist*. This newspaper recommends its readers to imitate the Boers and 'shoot down regiments of British soldiers' rather than be false to the Empire. Of course this isn't possible, but neither, Birmingham implies, is it possible to rebel violently against Britain in order to stay British.

The documentary strength of Birmingham's fiction lies partly in his deft placing of the Loyalist rebellion within a historical tradition which the rebels are not consciously aware of. This placing is made by Lord Kilmore when he remarks that his great-grandfather was a captain of the volunteers in 1780—the Irish volunteers secured a form of parliamentary independence for Ireland which ended with the Act of Union of 1801. Significantly, the year after *The Red Hand of Ulster* was published the Loyalist army of citizen volunteers became known as the 'Ulster Volunteer Force' and this title was taken more recently by a Protestant terrorist group. The volunteers of 1912 belonged, Birmingham shows, in a tradition of rebellion against Britain. And as he knew and wrote about in his novel, *The Northern Iron*, Belfast in the eighteenth century was a revolutionary city. The Society of United Irishmen was formed there in 1791 with the aim of overthrowing British rule in Ireland, and it was the United Irishmen who organised the rebellion of 1798. The rebellion of 1912, Birmingham implies, was a distorted expression of that stubborn and enduring northern radicalism. And it is this tradition which nourishes his imagination in *The Red Hand of Ulster*.

At the time, many observers argued that the Loyalists would not fight against British troops in order to remain British—it was therefore up to Asquith and his Liberal government to stand firm. Here, Birmingham moves into the mode of documentary fantasy as he imagines what might have happened if the two rival armies had confronted each other.. Reading his words now is like exhuming a historical record of dreams, hopes, anxieties and speculations—the flimsy litter and remnants that are some of the more corruptible parts of history.

He describes the centre of Belfast where, at first, all is quiet. The two armies patrol the streets, but keep their distance. Then a Loyalist meeting is broken up by the cavalry and shooting breaks out. Are the Loyalists fighting against the forces of the Crown? Not quite—the dragoons charge, the Loyalists open fire, but they do so 'without a shout' and watch their enemies fly 'without a cheer'. An English war correspondent called Bland is puzzled by this behaviour. The shooting, he says, is '"damned bad...damned bad on both sides"', and he wonders if they mean to shoot straight. The answer is—they don't. The troops have been ordered to fire over the people's heads, while the Loyalists are firing short. And the Loyalist bullets dig 'a curious kind of shallow trench' halfway down the street.

That little trench on a street in the centre of Belfast is a potent symbol of rebellious bluff. Yeats's well-worn lines from 'The Second Coming'—'Things fall apart; the centre cannot hold;/ Mere anarchy is loosed upon the world'—have frequently been applied to Irish politics during the last fifteen years. Journalists tend to quote them in order to prove that the Ulster situation is intractable. Yet in Birmingham's novel we see the centre holding in that 'little trench' in the centre of Belfast.

There are casualties, however—stray bullets fired by British soldiers kill an innocent woman and child, and in retaliation three British soldiers are killed and a number wounded. But the British troops don't fire back at the Loyalists, so perhaps the centre is holding after all.

Because Birmingham is essentially offering a solution to the Ulster crisis, it is necessary for the opposing forces to pass beyond this tricky equilibrium into a different relationship. Instead of recommending the monetarist policies which are currently making some Unionists wonder if the British connection is worth it, Birmingham imagines that standard imperialist ploy—sending in the gunboats. And as a British battleship steams down Belfast Lough a Loyalist crowd gathers in the shipyards. In silence the crowd watches the 'black ironclad parading sluggishly' before their eyes. Suddenly the ironclad swings round and fires a single shell over the heads of the crowd. A few people scream, there is silence, and then a moaning sound which grows and gathers. Soon the crowd is singing the hymn which was the Loyalist party-song in 1912— 'O God, our help in ages past'. The ironclad steams back up the Lough harried by Loyalist gunfire from the hills above the northern shore. That geographical location is important because it activates memories of the Antrim rebels of 1798, and again it is also reminiscent of a more recent episode—the waving of 500 firearm certificates on an Antrim hilltop.

Birmingham's imaginative documentary now considers a political solution—a solution which is based on his intuitive understanding of the psychology of Loyalism. He describes how the single shell fired by the battleship hits an ironically appropriate target—the statue of Queen Victoria which stands to this day outside the City Hall in Belfast. Here, the contradiction between loyalty and rebellion becomes dramatically apparent, and Birmingham's presentation of the Loyalist reaction is acute and daring. He knows that these Protestant volunteers belong to a tradition of rebellion which dates back to the eighteenth century when Presbyterian revolutionaries walked the streets of Belfast. And he chooses as the inheritor of that tradition an angry and confused Loyalist called McConkey.

McConkey is the foreman of a scutching-mill and he is intensely proud of his machine-gun—and very disappointed that he has missed the chance of firing it at the battleship. He remarks that the shell from the battleship 'made flitters of the statue of the ould Queen that was sitting fornint the City Hall'. And McConkey rages at the British government which he says is 'thick with rebels and papishes'.

This is the authentic voice of the dominant tradition of Ulster Protestantism, but McConkey's constitutional distinction between British Government (bad) and British Queen (good) is ultimately untenable. Birmingham is saying that you must either accept both or reject both. If you try—as the Loyalists try—to be loyal to the monarchy and disloyal to the government then you can only go so far before you have to accept both or neither.

Here, the middle-ground is beginning to melt away, for there is no place where people can somehow choose and not choose. This the Loyalists—hard-headed though bigoted radicals that they are—ultimately come to realise. And Lord Kilmore comments that by blowing up Queen Victoria's statue the British government has succeeded in destroying Ulster's loyalty. The graven image has gone and there is nothing left.

The Loyalist leaders then repeat the slogan 'We will not have Home Rule', but they tie their rejection of Home Rule to a demand for a complete British withdrawal from Ireland. A Liberal politician called Clithering—his name is derived from "dithering"—offers to pay for the repair of Queen Victoria's statue. Lord Kilmore agrees to convey this offer to the people of Belfast. But he issues a significant warning: 'They may not want that exact statue again. We're not quite as keen on Kings and Queens as we were.'

Birmingham's prophecy of a Loyalist rejection of British rule remains to be fulfilled. As so often with prophecies and "political solutions" the historical facts speak differently. What actually happened was that in 1914 the British govern-

124

ment planned to move troops into Ulster to ensure the acceptance of Home Rule. In what became known as 'the Curragh Mutiny' General Gough and 57 officers stated that they would resign their commissions if they were ordered to march North. The government backed down, but General Gough said later that if he had been simply ordered to march North he would have done his duty and gone. Because the government had given him the choice he had followed his personal preferences.

Thus the confrontation between British troops and Loyalist volunteers, which Birmingham imagined, never took place. But the Loyalists had shown that the threat of violence could work, and in his recent study of Irish history Paul Johnson argues that the lasting consequence of their bellicosity was to undermine the position of the constitutional Nationalists at Westminster. This increased the importance of those Irish Nationalists who sought a decision by force—and, indeed, Birmingham predicts this when he subversively makes the editor of his Loyalist newspaper an extreme Irish Nationalist. There is therefore an influential line which stretches between Easter 1912 in Belfast and Easter 1916 in Dublin.

Five years later, in 1921, a Home Rule Bill was passed which divided Ireland in two. In *The Red Hand of Ulster* Birmingham offers a vision of complete independence, and the partition of Ireland was never intended to be permanent. Neither of the Loyalist leaders—Edward Carson and James Craig—believed that Ireland would always be divided. Carson thought the link with Britain might last for fifty years, and Craig, who became the first Prime Minister of Northern Ireland, believed it would last for only thirty years.

Over sixty years later we know that they were both wrong. And so was George Birmingham when he imagined the British connection being broken in 1912. Yet this gentle Church of Ireland clergyman, who was also an engagé writer, had a profound understanding of northern Protestant culture. It is his intuitive sympathy, allied to a mischievous and engaging irony, which makes *The Red Hand of Ulster* such a fascinating analysis of a dramatic event—an event which remains so obstinately alive that it cannot simply be termed "historical". It is a fiction which offers both political commentators and historians an almost mythic insight into the complex contradictions within the Loyalist position.

Those Foul Ulster Tories

When Stormont fell in 1972, the Northern Ireland Civil Service continued to function with an efficient anonymity. However, some of its more senior members were prone to feelings of guilt—they had loyally served a set of mediocre politicians and had used their talents to run an unjust state. Somehow, they must justify themselves without appearing to support a now-defunct political system. In 1978, a retired permanent secretary, John Oliver, published *Working at Stormont*, an account of his 40 years with the service, but the code of absolute confidentiality prevented him from being indiscreet and the result is a largely self-regarding memoir which draws a veil over both the Unionist and the direct-rule administrations. Now another retired permanent secretary has published his autobiography and although it isn't scandalously indiscreet, the story it tells is fascinating.

Patrick Shea's earliest memory is of sitting in class writing the date, 1912, and his account covers the period from the Unionist rebellion against the third Home Rule Bill to the present troubles. He remembers Easter 1916, has listened to speeches by Maud Gonne and Countess Markiewicz, and he gives a vivid and subtle account of civil disorder, atrocities and political change. He joined the Northern Ireland Civil Service as a clerk in 1926 and in 1969 reached the top rank of permanent secretary—the first Catholic to do so since A.N. Wyse in the 1920s. During his long career he was several times passed over for promotion and a senior civil servant once told him that their bigoted political masters would probably deny him further advancement. He resolved to work as hard as possible because it would be 'foolish to make life easier for any who might wish to undervalue me or to make injustice look respectable'. The irony is that his subsequent career did in a sense 'make injustice look respectable' and he was accused of being a token Catholic in a Protestant administration.

Shea mentions the 'malevolent' influence of the Orange Order on the Unionist Party and argues that it is the duty of some Protestant civil servants to reveal what went on in 'those

Voices and the Sound of Drums: An Irish Autobiography by Patrick Shea.

locked rooms'—being a Catholic he was denied access to the secret places of power. Unfortunately, the Northern Ireland Civil Service has yet to disgorge a mole and it looks as though it never will—Oliver's account doesn't contain a single mention of the Orange Order.

Patrick Shea has a hospitably ironic intelligence and he writes deftly about a personal experience that has been crossed again and again by great political events. One of the most startling personalities in his account is a legendary Belfast radical called Harry Midgeley who was a passionate socialist orator and an apparent opponent of Unionism. Midgeley eventually persuaded himself into the Unionist Party and became a member of Brookeborough's cabinet. Shea sketches him with a loving exasperation and his portrait develops a consciously ironic parallel with another impassioned socialist who has always supported Unionism—Michael Foot. Indeed, the British Labour Party has had a perverse love affair with that band of politicians whom Lord Randolph Churchill long ago termed 'those foul Ulster Tories'. Brookeborough used to take Herbert Morrison fishing and it was Attlee who gave the Loyalists a cast-iron guarantee. More recently, Don Concannon has slavishly supported the Unionist cause.

Shea is particularly interesting in his account of the strike which destroyed the power-sharing Executive and he remarks on the craven manner in which the middle class cooperated with the strike and so confirmed his belief that the Northern Ireland Unionists are a 'possessive, unbending remnant of a powerful ruling class'. Although he is characteristically more generous than this—and sometimes rather politically short-sighted—*Voices and the Sound of Drums* tells a tantalizing story and should become a local classic. In many ways Patrick Shea resembles Owen in Brian Friel's play *Translations* and in his sophisticated ambivalence and tough reasonableness he might almost be the model for Friel's linguistic diplomat. As a historical witness he is profoundly wise, often amusing, and lucidly intelligent. Many Labour politicians who are currently trapped in the policy of 'me-tooism' would benefit from reading this autobiography.

The Disloyalist

There have been signs recently that the Northern Ireland Civil
Service contains a number of moles, or republican sleepers,
and it now appears that many years ago the Ulster Unionist
Party was also penetrated by a proto-republican. His name is
Desmond Carson and he's the central figure in Roy Bradford's
curious and fascinating account of Ulster politics. Bradford is a
native of Belfast who studied languages at Trinity College,
Dublin, served with British Army Intelligence during the war,
and later worked as a television producer and writer. In the
1960s he suddenly emerged as a Unionist politician and he
later became a minister in the Stormont Government. On the
evidence of this work he is an intelligent ex-intelligence
officer who has an acute understanding of the mentality of the
secret agent or "disloyalist".

In *The Last Ditch* he offers a semi-fictional account of the
affair between a Unionist cabinet minister (Desmond Carson)
and a female civil servant called Josephine Scanlon: 'her name
alone revealed her tradition'. By cleverly conflating various
actual events—the abolition of the B Specials, the suspension
of Stormont, the fall of the power-sharing Executive—Bradford
creates a subversive atmosphere of political intrigue and sheer
Unionist desperation. It's a witty combination of journalistic
fact and wild fantasy which at times resembles the vision in the
verse dramas of Guy Burgess's old friend, W.H. Auden. And
although Carson appears as a typical member of the Old Gang,
he is essentially an undercover radical who sees the necessity of
doing 'a deal with the South'. He is a composite figure based
on two well-known Unionist politicians and Bradford presents
him as a kind of gut intellectual who is fed up with being a
member of a 'puppet regime'.

Carson suffers from the 'self-disgust' which many thirties
intellectuals appear to have felt and this means that he is an
invisibly corrosive element within a divided and demoralised
ruling class. He is friendly with a southern Irish politician
called Ryan who is rather too obviously based on Garret
FitzGerald and he is attracted by Ryan's teasing offer of '*real*

The Last Ditch by Roy Bradford.

sovereignty'. Carson's alter ego—a politician called 'the Rooster'—gives this definition of Unionism in its terminal phase: 'We Unionists are doomed, Desmond. Doomed! We're a race of Flying Dutchmen, condemned to roam the seas forever, seeking a spiritual and political home'. And although Carson agrees, he is trapped by his ostensible loyalism and fear of being exposed as a kind of closet Parnellite. He also lacks the 'theological cast of mind' which one of his SDLP opponents fortunately possesses and this makes him into a restless maverick figure who oscillates between establishment and anti-establishment opinions.

Bradford, unfortunately, is no Brian Moore, and large sections of *The Last Ditch* are written in a form of Rotary Club prose—a great deal of pheasant salmi, Black Bush and fine port are consumed, and the lavish sexual descriptions are often hilarious. Although the fantasy element is vulnerable and tedious, there's an almost spring-like promise beyond its jaded prurience—Carson knows that the link with Britain has frayed to snapping-point and he is concerned with the future political structure. In a recent interview Bradford argued that Unionists are 'clinging now to a one-sided relationship with Britain. There's not the same feeling of kinship and we've got to face it.' Although this has been obvious for a long time, Bradford at least shows himself to be more flexible and prescient than Michael Foot, who may yet find himself elevated into the pantheon of Orange heroes.

Bradford deftly exposes 'the hypocrisy of Unionist attitudes' and he probes the uncomfortable sense of inferiority which the more reflective exponents of those attitudes share. He is anxious—anxious in an almost Jamesian manner—to display his taste and sensibility to his readers. His epicurean descriptions of drunken receptions, quotations from Baudelaire, and references to the visual arts, must all be construed as crude attempts at cultural definition. He is insisting that some Unionists are embarrassed by their reputation for narrow and philistine attitudes and implies that a few of them are Belfast Acmeists nostalgic for world culture and envious of their sophisticated southern neighbours. Bradford's aesthetic sense is rather less than fine, but he has at least helped to further discredit the Unionist cause.

Formal Pleasure: The Short Story

Although there are no great short stories which aspire to be novels, there are great novels which dream of becoming short stories. In last last paragraph of *Middlemarch*, for example, the epic narrative disappears into an invisible short story. Dorothea Brooke's

> ...finely-touched spirit had still its fine issues, though they were not widely visible. Her full nature, like that river of which Cyrus broke the strength, spent itself in channels which had no great name on the earth. But the effect of her being on those around her was incalculably diffusive: for the growing good of the world is partly dependent on unhistoric acts; and that things are not so ill with you and me as they might have been, is half owing to the number who lived faithfully a hidden life, and rest in unvisited tombs.

Here, we have a fine and poignant definition of the different ambitions of the two forms. Where the story story, in Frank O'Connor's argument, deals with a 'submerged population group', has never had a hero, and often has an atmosphere of 'intense loneliness', the novel depends on figures like Dorothea who appear 'widely visible' both to the reader and to society. The novelist believes that there is a shaping, mutually sustaining relationship between the individual and history, while the short story writer is an unillusioned quietist who describes the hidden lives of powerless people. In his eyes, the novel is a trendy, optimistic, slapdash form held together by the affairs of history men and history women, while the short story, like the rest of us, is powerless before what happens to happen.

When Dorothea is presented as a failed public figure she quits the society of the novel and joins that submerged population from which the short story draws its characters. Yet George Eliot cannot quite let go of that Whig interpretation of history which sustains the nineteenth-century novel. Although Dorothea disappears into the private life she has still somehow the power to influence history—her actions may be "unhistoric" but they are nonetheless contributions to progress. In her ordinary social and domestic life she assists 'the

The Short Story in English by Walter Allen.

growing good of the world'. It's as though we are asked to believe that the National Health Service was created not by political action but by small subscriptions of individual decency over a long period of time. On one level, the tantalizing ghostly conclusion of *Middlemarch* advances a nineteenth-century liberal argument for private philanthropy, and a 1980s version of the story would stress the monetarist case for the importance of the private sector. George Eliot clings to this argument because to relinquish it is to question the very existence of the novel form—a form which assumes that there is a hot-line connecting the individual to history. To doubt the novel is to doubt the optimistic assumptions of liberal humanism which, in George Eliot's intriguing formulation, traces historic influence back to certain overgrown and 'unvisited' graves in Highgate cemetery.

In a fascinating essay, 'The End of the Novel', Mandelstam sets the novel form against the Russian political experience of the first two decades of this century and argues that the novel is no longer viable. He suggests that the flourishing of the novel in the nineteenth century must be viewed as 'directly dependent on the Napoleonic epos' which caused 'the stock value of the individual in history to rise in an extraordinary manner'. Thus the 'typical biography of Bonaparte, the aggressive man of destiny', was scattered throughout Balzac's work in dozens of 'novels of success'. Writing in the mid-1920s, Mandelstam argues that this individualistic confidence is anachronistic:

> It is clear that when we entered the epoch of powerful social movements and organised mass actions, both the stock value of the individual in history and the power and influence of the novel declined, for the generally accepted role of the individual in history serves as a kind of monometer indicating the pressure of the social atmosphere. The measure of the novel is human biography or a system of biographies. Very early on, the new novelist sensed that individual fate did not exist, and he attempted to uproot the social vegetation he needed, its entire root system, radicles and all. Thus the novel always suggests to us a system of phenomena controlled by a biographical connection and measured by a biographical measure.

Prophetically, Mandelstam announces that the future development of the novel will be 'no less than the history of the atomization of biography as a form of personal existence' and he adds that we shall also witness 'the catastrophe of biography'.

131

He concludes:

> Today Europeans are plucked out of their own biographies, like
> balls out of the pockets of billiard tables...A man devoid of
> biography cannot be the thematic pivot of the novel, while the
> novel is meaningless if it lacks interest in an individual, human fate,
> in a plot and all its auxiliary motifs. What is more, the interest in
> psychological motivation (by which the declining novel so skilfully
> sought to escape, already sensing its impending doom) is being
> radically undermined and discredited by the growing impotence of
> psychological motives in the confrontation with the forces of
> reality, forces whose reprisals against psychological motivation
> become more cruel by the hour.

Mandelstam's argument is that history has overwhelmed both
the individual and the novel, and so we can no longer credit the
novelist's assumption of a relation between the finely touched
spirit and the growing good of the world. By implication, this
is the case for documentary writing (Solzhenitsyn's *Gulag
Archipelago*, for example), for super-realist fiction and for the
short story. It also comprehends the last great novel in
English, *Ulysses*, because that epic work is formally very close
to the temporal restrictions of the short story—everything is
concentrated into a single day. And, significantly, *Ulysses*
began life as an idea for a short story about a Dubliner called
Hunter.

The short story writer severs the connections between
individual biography and history, and offers the fictional
equivalent of those moments 'in and out of time' which break
over the 'unmoving' lines of *Four Quartets*. Thus the short story
is a static form which dips out of the historical process and
presents epiphanies, specks of time, or brief complete actions.
A disadvantage here is that a collection of short stories can
offer a surfeit of chill privacies—rather like a gallery full of
Hopper's paintings. Indeed, Bernard Bergonzi has argued in a
discussion of the short story appended to *The Situation of the
Novel* that the form tends to 'filter down experience to the
prime elements of defeat and alienation'. This is an arresting
generalisation but it is based on that confusion of art and life
which vitiates a great deal of literary criticism and which must
bear some responsibility for the current state of literary
studies. Bergonzi writes as a critic of novels when he first
praises the adroit style of a collection of stories by Sally
Bingham and then expresses doubt about how far it is based

on 'direct observation' and how far it relies 'perhaps unconsciously, on established literary models'. "Direct observation", like the term "accurate rendering", presupposes that *within* a fiction there is a distinction between reality and the writer's vision of reality which is his style. Thus the novel is considered to be a deep form which is full of "life", while the short story is a superficial form which is all mere "style" and is therefore very limited in its capacity to 'deepen our understanding of the world, or of one another'. Here the novel critic speaks as a vitalistic moralist who is hostile to pure art: the results of this attitude can be seen in the tedious moral paraphrase which constitutes much literary criticism.

Stylistic self-consciousness and a playful awareness of 'established literary models' are essential to the short story, and many famous short stories declare or imply their relation to certain predecessors. Thus James's 'The Beast in the Jungle' and Joyce's 'A Painful Case' have a common root in Maupassant's 'Regret', which is a story of an old bachelor who has 'never been loved' and who at last sits down under some leafless trees and weeps. Both stories resemble reply-poems in that they alter Maupassant's terms (John Marcher and James Duffy reject the love they are offered). Similarly, Lawrence's 'Samson and Delilah' is in part a tribute to Synge's *The Playboy of the Western World* and 'Odour of Chrysanthemums' is a version of *Riders to the Sea*. Katherine Mansfield's 'Marriage à la Mode' is a reworking of Chekhov's 'The Grasshopper' and Frank O'Connor has a story called 'A Story by Maupassant'.

Maupassant's short stories have what Sean O'Faolain calls a 'whip-crack ending'—they first mobilise and then satisfy an appetency and on re-reading give only a dead or feeble pleasure. Nevertheless Maupassant is one of the great masters of the form and in that ruthlessly brilliant story 'Two Gallants' Joyce set himself the demanding task of bettering Maupassant. In his opening paragraph—crowded streets on a grey warm Sunday evening, lamps like 'illumined pearls'—Joyce designs an impressionist image of Dublin as Paris and this prepares us for a quasi-Parisian story out of Maupassant which involves two seedy *flâneurs* and a girl 'slavey'. Joyce appears not to be concerned to tell a story—the two men, Lenehan and Corley, talk hollowly, and Lenehan appears anxious that his companion should help him in some unspecified manner. Corley boasts of his friendship with a girl who gives him cigarettes and cigars, and pays their tram fares. Corley then meets the girl, Lenehan wanders about the streets and later meets up with his friend. So far the story exists simply as a sketch of fringe lives in Dublin and it's only at the very last moment that it springs a completed plot on the reader. Anxiously, Lenehan asks, '"Can't you tell us?...Did you try her?'" And immediately we are reading the last paragraph:

> Corley halted at the first lamp and stared grimly before him. Then with a grave gesture he extended a hand towards the light and, smiling, opened it slowly to the gaze of his disciple. A small gold coin shone in the palm.

As in a story by Maupassant, there is that snap of recognition— Corley has carried out his unspecified promise to Lenehan by scrounging the coin from the girl, and we can understand this only when we have read the last sentence. However, this ending goes far beyond the cut-and-dried surprise at the end of a story by Maupassant. It is an imagistic, epiphanic conclusion which also glows with a suggestive symbolism—Corley as policeman, Lenehan as paid informer or Judas, the girl as a tawdry emblem of Ireland betrayed. That small gold coin is the vanishing point into which every element in the story rushes, for what at first appeared to be a drifting formless sketch is at the last moment given tense and perfect form. This is what Sean O'Faolain calls 'the eloquence of form' and it is a recognition that is instinct with a sense of joy and aesthetic redemption. This formal pleasure has nothing to do with naive realism or with the 'accurate rendering' of experience.

Poe describes this aesthetic experience best in his famous review of Hawthorne's *Twice-Told Tales* where he argues that in the 'brief tale' an artist is able to carry out 'the fullness of his intention'. He aims at a 'certain unique or *single* effect' and ensures that every word tends to 'the one pre-established design':

> And by such means, with such care and skill, a picture is at length painted which leaves in the mind of him who contemplates it with a kindred art, a sense of the fullest satisfaction. The idea of the tale has been presented unblemished, because undisturbed; and this is an end unattainable by the novel.

Poe's aesthetic argument is close to our experience of 'Two Gallants', and his analogy with painting is inspiring for it suggests that the literary critic must follow the art critic in discussing style, technique, form and tradition, rather than content, the achievement of 'felt life' or imaginative sympathy. In a discussion of the origins of the modern short story with which he opens his study *The Short Story in English*, Walter Allen draws a helpful quotation from Poe's review of Hawthorne and he also remarks interestingly on Flaubert's influence. By his exemplary dedication to his art, Flaubert stressed that treatment is 'almost everything' while subject is 'relatively unimportant'. For him, the 'capital difficulty' was 'style, form, the indefinable beauty, which is the result of the conception itself, and which is the splendour of truth, as Plato used to say'.

Although the characters in many short stories lack the social status which characters in a novel almost invariably possess, those in Lawrence's stories are often redeemed from isolation by their commitment to a relationship. Instead of existing permanently on the fringes of society, they acquire through that commitment the confidence of life we associate with characters in a novel. In such stories as 'The Horse Dealer's Daughter', 'Fanny and Annie' and 'You Touched Me', the characters begin to emerge from that condition of fugitive downtrodden privacy which is the underground world of the short story. And like George Eliot in *Middlemarch*, Lawrence gives to his provincial characters a momentousness of treatment which never admits to any sense of inferiority about their relation to the capital.

Lawrence's stories have received scant critical attention. This is because critics ignore formal questions and fatuously concentrate on intensity and flux and on that doctrine of the dark mysteries of experience which the novels preach. Unfortunately, Walter Allen subscribes to this novelistic view when he states that most of the stories in *The Prussian Officer* are 'products of Lawrence's day-to-day experience in the Nottinghamshire and Derbyshire coalfields'. And Allen's mistaken belief that short stories are paraphrases of experience is responsible for a critical method which does little more than glue moral comment to expansive summaries of numerous stories. However, he quotes aptly, communicates a ripe sense of enjoyment, and discusses a wide range of writers—he pays a deserved tribute to Henry Lawson, though his exclusion of John McGahern is mystifying. In first tracing the beginnings of the modern short story to Scott's 'The Two Drovers' and then arguing for its influence on Mérimée's 'Mateo Falcone' he valuably gives the form a solid historical foundation which future critics must attend to. For it is only by combining formalism with the historical sense that literary studies can survive the deep-seated crisis of confidence which in their different ways Allen's study and the split in the Cambridge English Faculty represent.

Britishmen

Two months after the suspension of Stormont in 1972, Belfast's retiring Lord Mayor, Sir Joseph Cairns, delivered a farewell speech in which he reflected on the political situation. Ulster, he said, had been cynically betrayed by Britain's policies—policies that had relegated it to 'the status of a Fuzzy Wuzzy colony'. The Lord Mayor's parting shot is one of my favourite quotations, for as well as being banal, ridiculous, righteously angry and very dim, it offers a profound insight into the Northern Irish troubles. It has an ironic resonance—a sort of Belfast *ou-boum*—which must haunt and torment anyone who probes the nature of Ulster Loyalism. It's a deeply parochial statement, and like all such statements it issues from an intense love of place, while also containing a definition of nationality and cultural identity.

On his last day as civic chief of Belfast, Sir Joseph Cairns was claiming to be something called a 'Britishman' and asserting an imperial idea that once flourished in many places but which now clings to the Rock of Gibraltar, the Falklands and parts of the north-east counties of Ireland. The Gibraltar equivalent of Sir Joseph Cairns is a politician called Sir Joshua Hassan who believes that the Rock is indissolubly part of the United Kingdom. Both these colonised knights must often dream of the Queen and the Duke of Edinburgh. They must have a special fondness for the Duke of Edinburgh, and like those inhabitants of what were once the New Hebrides they probably believe that it is the Great Duke who has packed cargo ships full of blue passports, welfare benefits, cheap tin trays and signed photographs of himself. It is the Duke of Edinburgh who guarantees that mystic consumer durable called "Britishness".

Although Jack Holland ignores Cairns's rich insight, he does explore the confused nature of Loyalist identity and in a revealing anecdote he describes a train journey towards the

---

Too Long a Sacrifice: Life and Death in Northern Ireland since 1969 by Jack Holland.
A History of Northern Ireland by Patrick Buckland.

Loyalist stronghold of Larne. Three youths were clowning about, throwing cans and bottles out of the window:

> In the middle of the mayhem one of the youths shouted breathlessly, 'No wonder they say the Irish are mad!' There was a short but sudden silence. His two companions looked at him uneasily, and he almost blushed with embarrassment. It was as if a taboo had been broken, and in front of strangers. After a second or so the biggest youth, obviously the leader of the group, shouted with bluff confidence and an aggressive voice, 'Hey, what d'ya mean? We're not Irish—we're British.' They laughed at each other, but rather self-consciously. It was obvious they were discomfited, unsettled, and they flung themselves with increased vigour into another round of furious and distracting activity.

This fascinating, almost parabolic story follows Holland's subtle and intelligent discussion of Loyalist terrorism. That particularly sadistic form of terrorism partly issues from a cultural quality which might be described as a trapped and backward-looking anger—the Protestant working class is unique in Europe 'in that it is the only working class not to have been radicalised by World War I'. And when UVF terrorists were imprisoned in Long Kesh they named their huts after the battlefields of the Great War. Like the Lord Mayor, they believed they were Britishmen and they were prepared to torture and kill in order to remain in their chosen imperial time-warp. As Holland shows, there is a firm connection between the ethic of Britishness and the practice of torture, and the notorious 'five techniques' which were employed during the interrogation of internees followed an established practice that had been employed in all of Britain's colonial wars since 1946. When these interrogation techniques were investigated by an enquiry headed by Lord Parker, two reports were issued. Parker's majority report justified the use of sensory deprivation by claiming that it provided the authorities with 'much-needed information about the terrorists', while Lord Gardiner's minority report dissented.

Gardiner stated that the five techniques 'were and are illegal', and he argued that parliament should not legalise them because 'we should both gravely damage our own reputation and deal a severe blow to the whole world movement to improve human rights'. Yet Gardiner also exculpated the Government of Northern Ireland and the RUC by arguing that the Minister of Home Affairs (Brian Faulkner) 'had no idea' that the techniques were illegal. The fact that someone of Gardiner's legal eminence should employ such an obviously invalid argument demonstrates 'the extent to which Northern Ireland was clouding British thinking'.

This is a most important point and the nub of Holland's argument is that 'British democracy has been poisoned by repressive legislation' which in many ways resembles the kind of laws the Civil Rights Movement set out to change in Northern Ireland. The recent, hasty legislation which prevents convicted terrorists standing for election in Northern Ireland is another example of this sapping of legality, and so, too, is the case of Constable William McCaughey. Along with a police sergeant called Weir, McCaughey was tried and convicted of murdering a Catholic shopkeeper in revenge for an attack by the Provisional IRA. Both policemen were also convicted of kidnapping and threatening to murder a Catholic priest and of bombing a Catholic bar. Holland comments:

> One of the remarkable things about this case was the sentences handed down by Chief Justice Robert Lowry. While McCaughey and Weir were given life sentences, the other policemen involved in the bar bombing were let off with suspended sentences. McCaughey's father, who aided his son in concealing the priest on his farm, was also released with a suspended sentence. In his summing-up Lowry stated that the action of McCaughey in murdering the Catholic was 'understandable' but 'inexcusable'. He described it as 'really an act of retribution, or revenge because of other murders that had been committed'. The victim was a totally innocent man, a father of eight children with no connection to the IRA or the Republican movement. Why it was 'understandable' to murder such a man was not at all made clear by Justice Lowry.

This is an example of the way in which legality is being undermined by its representatives and it is also a compelling illustration of Protestant middle-class sympathy with Loyalist terrorism (Lowry is an ex-Unionist politician, hence his use of that extenuating word 'understandable').

One of the most valuable sections of Holland's study concerns the relationship of the UDA—the chief Loyalist paramilitary organisation—with traditional Unionist politicians. Over the last four years, the UDA has moved towards a policy of an independent Northern Ireland and in a discussion with two American congressmen Glen Barr explained the reasons for his organisation's changed attitude:

On the Loyalist side, the Loyalist politicians have manipulated the Protestant people, who believed the Unionists. And we also believe that on the Catholic side they have been used and manipulated by emotional-type politicians. Because, over the years if you look at politics in Northern Ireland, no one has talked about pure politics. Every election time, all you have is a flag being waved at you repeating threats to your constitutional position... We are not prepared to be used any longer by these manipulating politicians. What we are saying is that we want to formulate a policy that will serve the two sections of the community in Northern Ireland, the Protestant and Catholic people.

Barr also called for 'a complete withdrawal of Britain out of the scene' and his policy was later endorsed by James Callaghan. It is difficult to overestimate the significance of this argument—an argument which shows that one section of Loyalist opinion is breaking out of a backward-looking Britishness and beginning to formulate a truly northern, non-sectarian identity. In a sense, the UDA has begun to move away from the traditions and values of 'Carson's Army' towards the ideals of the United Irishmen, the revolutionary organisation founded by Wolfe Tone and a group of Belfast radicals in 1791. However, Holland also explores the savage nature of Loyalist terrorism and he is sceptical about the change that has taken place in Loyalist attitudes. Some Loyalists have replaced 'a sheep-like willingness to follow their middle-class leaders' with a sort of populist anger and frustration at the way those leaders have misled them. And so the most "advanced" sections of Loyalist opinion are still groping towards a purely political ethic.

Holland also probes the internal politics of the IRA and describes the tensions between Dublin intellectuals like David O'Connell and the Belfast leaders. As in his account of Loyalist terrorism, he analyses the movement's theoretical ideas and also describes some of their murderous acts. His work is not polemical and it is remarkable both for its fidelity to ordinary experience of the troubles and for its open-mindedness. Although he is often critical of the RUC, he also argues sympathetically that that organisation has been damaged by the policy of 'criminalisation': the term given to the removal of Special Category status, which was the first stage in the British policy of 'Ulsterization'. This meant giving the RUC the primary role in dealing with violence, in the hope that doing so would gradually lead to a reduction of British Army commitments. Holland argues shrewdly that this policy is merely 'a compromised form of withdrawal' and that it places dangerous burdens on the police themselves. Although *Too Long A Sacrifice* is repetitious and rather scrappily constructed, it is an intelligent account of the Ulster troubles and one which is unusually sensitive to the experience of the last twelve years.

In his conclusion Holland cites a phrase which A.J.P. Taylor applied to India and Pakistan and suggests that Northern Ireland is a 'non-historical state'. Thus its population exists and suffers in the kind of ahistorical vacuum which Eliot imagines in 'Little Gidding':

> A people without history
> Is not redeemed from time, for history is a pattern
> Of timeless moments.

It must therefore be one of the tasks of the self-conscious historian to seek out those timeless moments and to form them into a pattern. If Northern Ireland were to become a genuinely independent state then it's likely that a historian connected with the UDA would offer an epic account of the formation of that state, but as Northern Ireland is merely an administrative entity like the Borough of Hendon or South Humberside it can only—at least from the Unionist point of view—possess a kind of parish history. For the Official Unionist, who believes that Northern Ireland is permanently part of the United Kingdom, history is static and therefore parochial, while for the republican it is a developing process which aims at the establishment of a full cultural identity.

Unfortunately, Patrick Buckland has not meditated on these questions and his title, *A History of Northern Ireland*, is offered without irony. Although Buckland is more of a memorialist than a serious historian, he has performed a valuable service in such works as *The Factory of Grievances* and *James Craig*, in both of which he cites example after example of Unionist incompetence and mediocrity. He has gathered masses of valuable facts from Cabinet and Civil Service records, old newspapers and various published sources. What he lacks is a vision of his subject and a prose style. Also his present work at times recycles sentences which first saw the light of day in his earlier books: in his biography of Craig (1980) he describes Edward Carson as a 'vain, hatchet-faced, hypochondriacal but talented lawyer with a penchant for histrionics', and in *A History of Northern Ireland* Carson appears again as a 'vain, hatchet-faced, hypochondriacal but talented lawyer with a penchant for histrionics'. The result is a rigidly arid work whose sentences are often distracted by exclamation-marks and which has little empathy with its subject. Even so, Buckland does put his incremental fact-gathering historio-graphical method to some purpose. He writes of the 'political immaturity' of Ulster Loyalists and he remarks on their failure to develop a political philosophy. He opposes the two-nations theory, insists the Ulster Protestants have 'only a very hazy sense of nationality' and explores the complex financial relationship between Northern Ireland and the rest of the United Kingdom. He notices a remark of Brian Faulkner's objecting to Northern Ireland being treated as a 'coconut colony' and he also cites this statement made by a UDA leader in 1973: 'For four hundred years we have known nothing but uprising, murder, destruction and repression. We ourselves have repeatedly come to the support of the British Crown, only to be betrayed within twenty years or so by a fresh government of that Crown... Second-class Englishmen, half-caste Irishmen.' Although Buckland doesn't say so, this is another example of that quality of cultural self-pity from which many Unionists suffer. It also represents a stage in the evolution of Loyalist paramilitary thinking, and Glen Barr's call five years later for complete British withdrawal clearly follows from it.

It is a pity that Buckland has failed to consider the nature of British and Irish identity in any depth because every discussion of the Northern Irish situation must start by asking questions about those identities. Some historians clearly agree with Brian Faulkner and that ex-Lord Mayor of Belfast and base their writing on the premise that Northern Ireland is not a colony. Others take the view that it is a colony. Every historian who writes about Northern Ireland is either a loyalist like J.C. Beckett and A.T.Q. Stewart, or a republican like Michael Farrell, though I suspect that Buckland attempts to occupy the middle-ground which is represented politically by the Alliance Party. His book resembles the minutes of a borough council, but we must be grateful to him for his diligent burrowing in government archives.

James Joyce: A Centenary Celebration

Outside a communal ritual—raising a full glass, say, or a witty chalice—the act of celebrating Joyce's centenary can sound solemnly personal, even a shade tendentious. And the reason must be that although there are many individuals ready to offer homage, there is as yet no society which can give that feeling a ceremonial form. Joyce the artist and many of his readers still wait for the word which will admit them to that 'new Bloomusalem in the Nova Hibernia of the future'.

Oddly, many of Joyce's critics have avoided discussing his social vision—Raymond Williams sidesteps Irish history entirely in his scant remarks on Joyce in *The Country and the City*, while F.R. Leavis passed a long and vinegary critical life in complete aesthetic ignorance of his work. Only Dominic Manganiello, in his excellent pioneering study, *Joyce's Politics*, has explored his historical imagination. (I find Colin McCabe's semi-literate attempt to do so quite unreadable.) For some reason, Joyce is still less highly regarded in England than he is in Europe and America (in Ireland he is revered as a modern Virgil), and it may be that his republican and proudly anti-colonial imagination resists any attempt to co-opt him into the great tradition.

James Joyce was born in Dublin on 2 February 1882, and he grew up in a stagnant colonial Ireland which he symbolises as 'Great Britain Street' in *Dubliners*. He set himself the task of liberating his country by an exemplary dedication to his art, and in the famous Christmas Dinner scene in *A Portrait of the Artist as a Young Man* he designs a Parnellite epiphany which crucially shapes the young Stephen's imagination. The future artist becomes dedicated to an ethic of intransigent pride and freedom, and he assumes a revolutionary temperament. Joyce's ambition was to create a full and complete Irish identity—to forge 'the uncreated conscience of my race', as Stephen Dedalus says—and in a perfect, ideal sense he succeeded, because *Ulysses* stands as an epic monument that faces towards a united, independent Ireland. Joyce had nothing but scorn for what is now termed "the two nations theory" and his wonderfully capacious imagination is the most inclusive of any Irish writer's (in *Finnegans Wake*, especially, everyone is invited to

143

the party).

Curiously, although Joyce's imagination is profoundly catholic in its symbolism, cadencing and rigorous pattern-making, he hated the Pope and the Roman Catholic Church almost as much as Ian Paisley does, and he reserved a particular hatred for one Nicholas Brakespear, who as Pope Adrian IV justified the invasion of Ireland by Henry II. Joyce referred to Catholicism as a 'coherent absurdity' and Protestantism as an 'incoherent absurdity', and his prose style—at least until the leguminous *Wake*—is remarkable for its coherence and strictness. This quality he partly owed to Flaubert, for like many Irish intellectuals he was deeply influenced by French culture and drew on a long tradition of Franco-Irish republicanism.

The absolute selfless dedication which informs Joyce's aesthetic has always reminded me of the complete commitment of a hunger striker, and in Richard Ellmann's magnificent biography there is an episode where these ostensibly separate realities cross. Joyce had a grudge against Sir Horace Rumbold, the British Minister to Berne, and he recalled this in 1920 when Terence MacSwiney, the Lord Mayor of Cork, died on hunger strike. In a moment of reflex bitterness Joyce sent these lines to his long-suffering brother Stanislaus:

> Of spinach and gammon
> Bull's full to the crupper
> White lice and black famine
> Are the Mayor of Cork's supper;
> But the pride of old Ireland
> Must be damnably humbled
> If a Joyce is found cleaning
> The boots of a Rumbold.

Joyce identified his unyielding personal and artistic pride with MacSwiney's idealism, and like Yeats he drew a parallel between the Flaubertian sacrifice of life for art and a revolutionary's absolute commitment to a particular cause. However, where Yeats often mobilises some of the more rabid goblins of nationalist emotion, Joyce scorned consciously *völkisch* ideas. He described himself as a 'socialistic artist' and although he sympathized with the aims of Sinn Féin he criticised that movement for avoiding social questions and 'educating the people of Ireland on the old pap of racial hatred'. In *Ulysses*, therefore, he gives anti-semitic views to Mr Deasy, the Unionist headmaster, and to the Nationalist

Citizen in order to demonstrate their provincial narrowness and sectarian stupidity. Joyce detested any idea of racial purity and his concern was with cultural identity, with substituting the common name of Irishman for the religious racism and colonial bigotry which still divide Ireland sixty years after the publication of *Ulysses*.

In an ironic and fascinating lecture which he gave during his exile in Trieste, the young Joyce argued against the exclusive type of nationalism which his cyclopean Citizen embodies:

> ...to exclude from the present nation all who are descended from foreign families would be impossible, and to deny the name of patriot to all who are not of Irish stock would be to deny it to almost all the heroes of the modern movement—Lord Edward Fitzgerald, Robert Emmet, Theobald Wolfe Tone and Napper Tandy, leaders of the uprising of 1798, Thomas Davis and John Mitchel, leaders of the Young Ireland movement, Isaac Butt, Joseph Biggar, the inventor of parliamentary obstructionism, many of the anticlerical Fenians, and, finally, Charles Stewart Parnell, who was perhaps the most formidable man who ever led the Irish, but in whose veins there was not even a drop of Celtic blood.

The liberators listed here prefigure the heroic stature of 'Stephen Hero', and by naming them Joyce invokes Calliope, the muse of epic. It is a significant moment of imaginative conception which was to result, many years later, in the publication of *Ulysses*. Like Anchises in Dryden's *Aeneid*, he prophetically transforms an anonymous, obscure territory into a famous and civilised place:

> But they, who crowned with oaken wreaths appear,
> Shall Gabian walls and strong Fidenae rear;
> Nomentum, Bola, with Pometia, found;
> And raise Collatian towers on rocky ground.
> All these shall then be towns of mighty fame,
> Though now they lie obscure, and lands without a name.

The 'mighty fame' of Joyce's epic style redeems his Dubliners, assures their identity, and makes their social existence appear permanent and immortal, like the streets they walk. And one small example of this civilising process is the way in which the martello tower at Sandycove is now known as 'Joyce's Tower'—his imagination dominates a colonial watchtower which once dominated him by its reminder of the tragic dispersal of the French invasion of Ireland. Like Matthew Arnold in that neglected essay 'Equality', Joyce regretted Napoleon's failure to reach these islands.

Joyce's departure from Dublin into European exile was analogous to that of many Irish revolutionaries, and this parallel is cunningly developed in *Ulysses* where Stephen recalls meeting the old Fenian, Kevin Egan, in Paris. For Joyce, the Fenian rebellion of 1867 wasn't self-defeating because it 'inculcated into the minds of the future generation the doctrine of separatism'. And that doctrine lies at the very foundations of Joyce's imagination.

It's an imagination so complete that history and the personal life, art and politics, are continually identified. Thus Molly Bloom's girlhood in colonial Gibraltar and her admiration for redcoat soldiers needs to be understood in relation to Bloom's support for the Boers (she is pro-imperial, he is anti-imperial). In a sense, her attraction to the military can be seen in context if we align it with these famous stanzas from Seamus Heaney's 'Punishment':

I who have stood dumb
when your betraying sisters,
cauled in tar,
wept by the railings,

who would connive
in civilised outrage
yet understand the exact
and tribal, intimate revenge.

Molly betrays Bloom with Blazes Boylan but we are not invited to judge her morally—only to make the significant connection between biography and history. Similarly, Bloom's gentle, rather boring civic-mindedness needs to be seen as a version of the Fabian socialism which Joyce took from Wells and the Webbs.

Joyce is both *flâneur* and rebel, aesthete and revolutionary, and his gay, joyous, libertarian vision is remarkable for its ruthlessly ironic intelligence and for a pure delight in style and surface. He is a deeply European figure dreaming of an impossible country, and one of his Parisian friends tells the intriguing story of how Joyce waited for the first government of the Irish Free State to summon him back to Dublin and put bay leaves in his hair. To his intense disappointment, the summons never came, though perhaps in Bloom's Nova Hibernia February 2nd will be known as 'Joyce's Day', just as January 25th is Burns' Day in Scotland. It could be a national holiday dedicated to full glasses, song, and conversation. Perhaps before the bicentenary comes round there will be a ceremony where his exiled ghost returns to receive that crown of bays?

English Now

Many academic teachers of English are at the moment united in the dismayed recognition that their subject is in a state of acute crisis. Some nourish the suspicion that English literature isn't properly an academic subject, while others believe that its study can be revitalised by adopting structuralist procedures and developing a 'materialist criticism'. Partly, the crisis which now afflicts English studies is a reflection of a more general cultural atmosphere—for example, that futureless and pastless sense of blankness which distinguishes the present generation of students. It could also be seen as a response to the period of critical exhaustion which followed the puritan revolution that Leavis and his disciples led many years ago. And it could be interpreted as a reaction against the failure of traditional scholarly procedures to recognise that they were addressing an audience which increasingly believed in 'relevance'. On the other hand, it could be argued that English studies ought to be in as confidently healthy a state as American studies. Like American studies it is about everything and nothing, and so is endlessly plastic, endlessly receptive to new texts, modish theories and infinite exchanges of opinion. Even so, English studies—and, by implication, American studies within Great Britain—is currently experiencing a major crisis of confidence and it is to this unhealthy condition that *Re-Reading English* is addressed.

The contributors are collectively of the opinion that English literature is a dying subject and they argue that it can be revived by adopting a 'socialist pedagogy' and introducing onto the syllabus 'other forms of writing and cultural production than the canon of Literature'. Where Christopher Ricks believes that it is the teacher's job to uphold that canon, his opponents assert that it is now time to challenge various 'hierarchical' and 'elitist' conceptions of literature and to demolish the bourgeois ideology which has been 'naturalised' as literary value. It is essential, they argue, to demystify this

Re-Reading English, edited by Peter Widdowson.
Against Criticism by Iain McGilchrist.

myth of literary value 'as a universal and immanent category'. They wish to develop 'a politics of reading' and to redefine the term 'text' in order to admit newspaper reports, songs, and even mass demonstrations as subjects for tutorial discussion. Texts no longer have to be books; indeed, 'it may be more democratic to study *Coronation St.* than *Middlemarch*'. That verb 'may' is a quaint survivor from the world of tentative liberal open-mindedness, rather like the ghost of John Bayley infiltrating a branch of Militant Tendency.

Before considering the terminal ironies of this rejection of printed texts, it is essential to examine the history of English as an academic subject. As Brian Doyle shows in the only valuable essay in this collection, the earliest instruction in English language and literature was provided at University College, London, from the 1820s. As a subject it resembled eighteenth-century Scottish Rhetoric and Belles Lettres, though it laid a novel emphasis on literature as a vehicle for moral instruction and aimed to offset the utilitarian principles on which the new London foundation was based. And English was given a crucial role in many schools, training colleges and other institutions of female instruction which were founded in the latter half of the nineteenth century. Charles Kingsley, in his inaugural lecture as Professor of English at Queen's College, London, argued that the reading of English would help towards an understanding of the 'English spirit' and would therefore counteract the notion that 'the minds of young women are becoming unEnglish'. At Oxford there was little support for English studies, but in 1873 English was included in the examinations for a Pass Degree. After a public campaign during the 1880s, a final Honours School of English Language and Literature was founded in 1893. For a long time this remained largely a women's course and in *The Women at Oxford* Vera Brittain noted that English was commonly dismissed as 'pink sunsets'. In the 1920s English freed itself from its dependent status as an element in the study of 'the national culture' and became an autonomous academic subject whose prestige was closely bound to the Cambridge English Faculty. Obsessively, the contributors to this collection return to the figure of F.R. Leavis, and although they would like to make that sour puritan redundant they concede that radical theory cannot bypass something called 'Left-Leavism'—i.e. an embattled and doubly puritan hostility to 'the critical establishment.'

Here, we must notice that there is no such thing as a critical establishment in the United Kingdom. Instead, there is in every generation a conspiracy of taste among a number of gifted reviewers who publish their critical judgements in various newspapers and journals (the line of influential poetry reviewing stretches from Edward Thomas to Ian Hamilton). Sooner or later, the taste which innovating literary journalists shape and enforce seeps through to institutions of higher education which then disseminate it to their students, many of whom transmit it to the next generation of schoolchildren. Thus today's rave review of *Jake's Thing* is tomorrow's 'Discuss foregrounding and *différance* with reference to the novels of Kingsley Amis and/or *Coronation Street*.' Leavis, who was fond of denouncing 'Amis and the age of Tottenham Hotspur', believed that cultural life ought to be purer than this. He led an essentially moralistic campaign against what he saw as the establishment (Oxford, London journalism, the British Council), but because his influential critical enterprise shirked actual politics he remained a Cromwell fulminating in a college garden. Nevertheless he helped to discredit formal academic procedures—textual scholarship, the compilation of reference works, footnotes, indexes, bibliographies and the writing of scholarly articles and "standard" works. His championing of Lawrence and dismissal of Joyce was particularly destructive because it encouraged the rejection of classical ideas of form, the espousal of merely adversarial attitudes, and a romantic belief in original inspiration and experience. It was Leavis who succeeded in transforming "life" into a critical term, a touchstone of aesthetic value. He adopted a self-consciously awkward prose style and it may be due to his influence that good critical prose is now dismissed as 'belle-lettrism' (see, for example, Stephen Trombley's dismally representative approach in his study of Virginia Woolf).

For many years, the Cambridge stress on the private spirit—practical criticism is an example—helped to energise the study of literature and most critics would admit to having learnt from this informal procedure. Its weakness, however, lay in the assumption that students brought an informed knowledge of history, the classics and the Bible to their reading of a short, isolated text. The teacher addressed an audience which was in possession of its own cultural history and which had a developed sense of memory to draw on and add to. Unfortunately, the emphasis given to the isolated text's autonomous nature—its freedom from a historical context—implicitly argued the inferiority of history, and as a result successive generations of students became increasingly indifferent to memory, the past, and traditional forms. They learnt to scorn reference works and that detailed historical knowledge which the practitioners of close reading termed 'extrinsic irrelevance'. When a Lawrentian ethic of experience became fashionable in the 1960s, the idea of culture as the pursuit of perfection was subverted by a kind of earnest vitalism which preferred paraphrasing the moral content of novels to discussing the formal properties of literary texts. The result is a blank generation of students who are eager to repair their ignorance, but who are often confronted in lectures by a sophisticated gobbledygook in which terms like 'foregrounding' and 'backgrounding' jostle with sonorous phrases like 'the unceasing present of enunciation'. The result is a nightmare of subsidised nonsense, an arid wilderness of combative attitudes, deconstructed texts, abolished authors and demonic critical technicians intent on laying down what they fondly believe is a 'barrage of finely-honed theoretical work'.

In what is perhaps the dimmest essay in this collection, Antony Easthope argues that traditional literary criticism encourages the reader to identify with the poet and that this is a 'narcissistic and élitist identification (you too can *be* Sir Philip Sidney)'. Readers who surrender to their 'misrecognition of themselves in the Poet' deny themselves as readers:

> In contrast, literary science will discuss the poem as construction, acknowledging it as labour; and in so doing, it poses the reader as active and productive in reading the poem.

Like many of his fellow contributors, Easthope has a Stalinist preference for mechanistic metaphor and he is able to make the experience of reading a sonnet by Sidney sound like a spell in a forced labour camp.

Easthope shares with most contributors an attitude of mind which appears to have emerged in England during the last few years and which Charles Kingsley would have termed 'unEnglish'. This new attitude is interested in ideas and issues, committed to revolution, self-consciously critical of sexual

151

tokenism, sympathetic to structuralism, and hostile to 'bour-geois poetry', liberalism and the concept of sensibility. It accuses much Marxist criticism of creeping liberalism and admonishes it for paying 'undue and unexamined deference to the privileged, discrete text'. It has broken with patriarchal repression by replacing the formal third person pronoun with 's/he', and in Yeats's terms it is ferociously opinionated and 'fanatic'. Academic study, it argues, should cease to be 'text-centred' and instead concentrate on 'problems' and 'topics'. For the academic who possesses this particular cast of mind, Colin McCabe is a liberating figure while Christopher Ricks is a tyrannical élitist who upholds what Terence Hawkes glumly terms 'the prestigious realms of Culture'.

This new way of thinking—or, perhaps more accurately, of feeling—is a phenomenon which anyone acquainted with less peaceful cultures than the English is bound to recognise. For me it represents the rare possibility of actually envisaging a Turgenevian novel set in England, and it is probably a tiny indication of the massive social crisis which economic decline and mass unemployment may soon bring about. Although the contributors to *Re-Reading English* are employed in institutions funded by the state, and although they are published by a capitalist publisher, they have at least the aura of belonging to an underground movement. They appear to be members of a dissident intelligentsia which is preparing the theoretical ground from which an English National Liberation Army may one day emerge. The embattled, anonymous prose-style they share speaks for a dissenting population within an entity which used to be confidently referred to as "Great Britain" but whose imminent fragmentation is prophesied by Tom Nairn and others. Unfortunately, Peter Widdowson and most of the other contributors appear to share a deep hatred of art and to be united in a desire to abolish texts and authors. They are frustrated sociologists who believe that sonnets and beer mats ought to be treated in an egalitarian manner and examined as interesting 'cultural artefacts' (this stupidly philistine term is favoured by David Lodge and other members of the new critical generation). They also wish to abolish value judgements and inaugurate a new era of scientific criticism which will overthrow the hegemony of canonical texts. Some find that hegemony so oppressive that they appear to believe in a parallel world of different texts, or in a random world of any and every text, or a black hole of absent texts which resembles a kind of Mallarmean mass demo. Collectively, they wish to 'puncture English's pretensions to cultural centrality' by turning it into something even woollier called 'Cultural Studies'. They recommend the Centre for Contemporary Cultural Studies at Birmingham University as a model for the future, though prospective applicants who read Michael Green's vulnerable and tedious account of the Centre's procedures are likely to think again. One contributor—the hapless Easthope—prefers oral poetry to 'official written poetry, high cultural poetry', another wants critical discussions of Shakespeare to *foreground* such matters as patronage, the social composition of audiences' etc. Others speak of 'the production side of the literary process' and sound the death-knell of 'the subterfuge text within the text, the ideal text of bourgeois criticism'.

Every member of this critical collective stops well short of the fundamental innovating idea and treatment which their diagnosis would seem to require. The result is a series of essays which with the exception of Brian Doyle's 'The Hidden History of English Studies' deserves to be regarded as a symptom of a morbid condition rather than an analytic account of a crisis. Many of the contributions remind me of Edward Thomas's remark about 'a self-conscious civilisation turning in disgust upon itself': culture must be in a terminal condition when teachers of English preach the destruction of their discipline and offer only a few simplistic gestures in its place.

Another morbid symptom is Iain McGilchrist's meandering and infinitely tedious non-argument that 'the only genuine critical theory is that of no theory'. McGilchrist is a fellow of All Souls and an upholder of that elitist culture which so angers Widdowson's contributors. He appears to be highly cultured—he talks confidently of 'the ornate, yet simple splendour of Vierzehnheiligen', notes the resemblances between Lu Chi and Alexander Pope, and sprinkles his text with impressive bits of Greek, Latin, Italian and German. He is, alas, fatally dull: 'One could say of art what Lewis said of the *Faerie Queene*, that it is life itself in another mode.' One could indeed, but one could, on the other hand, feel that those who want to re-read English are justified in their angry alienation from the vacuous and unintelligent attitudes which McGilchrist holds. His harmless Sitwellian waffle makes me wonder whether English studies will go the way of phrenology. Indeed, one could argue that it has always been phrenology in another mode.

Paisley's Progress

In 1969, while he was serving a prison sentence for unlawful assembly, Ian Paisley sent this message to his congregation:

> I rejoice with you in the rich blessings of last weekend. I knew that our faithful God would pour out His bounty. In prayer in this cell I touched the Eternal Throne and had the gracious assurance of answered prayer. What a joy to hear from Mr Beggs of a £1000 gift for the pulpit. Hallelujah! May that pulpit be the storm centre of the great hurricane of revival. Oh for a tempest of power, a veritable cyclone of blessing. Lord, let it come!

Eight years later, the preacher rose up in that enormous pulpit and waved a copy of a historical study which had just been published. 'Brethren and sisters in Christ,' he shouted, 'here is a great book that tells the Truth about Ulster. Go home, friend, and read it.'

The book was *The Narrow Ground* by A.T.Q. Stewart and until I heard of that Sabbath review I'd believed that historians were a type of Brahmin – pure vegetarians who existed at a level of consciousness far above that of politicians and other carnivores. I'd believed in their disinterestedness, their objectivity, their lack of axes to grind. Now I began to understand what F.H. Bradley meant when he said that we reflect 'in general not to find the facts, but to prove our theories at the expense of them'. In that moment of discovery historiography appeared like an ascent towards the Supreme Fiction, and among the mountaineers were Daniel Defoe, Wallace Stevens, Edward Gibbon and A.T.Q. Stewart – all imaginative writers with a style and vision of their own, but none with a style that was any "truer" than another's.

Historians may be disinterested – some of them certainly like to congratulate each other on their disinterestedness – but they are doomed to be read by an *interested* audience. And many people must recall the comic sequel to the two televised accounts of Irish history in which an earnest Ludovic Kennedy asked Paisley what he'd learnt from the programmes and a group of Irish historians back in the studio held their noses at the whole enterprise. Inevitably, historians are drawn into politics – E.P. Thompson, for example, has an audience which supports both the Campaign for Nuclear Disarmament and the Labour Party, while historians in the North of Ireland have power-bases or followings on the Republican side or in the Democratic Unionist Party. How far historians are able to free themselves from the simplifications which their readers visit on them is problematic, but as far as the writing of Irish history is concerned I'm convinced that it is now, and will be for the foreseeable future, inescapably *political*. Those historians who are bored or embarrassed by the version of history offered in the schools and elsewhere in the Irish Republic may believe that it is possible to escape from that version into a sophisticated objectivity, but as far as I can see they simply become trapped in a rival simplification – the Unionist version of history. In either case, the embarrassment of, in that well-worn phrase, "legitimising" a particular cause is bound to result.

The question that concerns me initially is this – where does the imaginative inspiration for a historical argument come from? Did *The Narrow Ground* inspire Paisley, or did the voice of Old Ravenhill inspire *The Narrow Ground*? Accompanying this question is the problem of the relation of middle-class Unionism to working-class Unionism, or – to put it in cultural terms – the relation of establishment and anti-establishment ideas within Unionism. As Unionism cracks and splinters a form of class politics begins to emerge – a populism in the case of Paisleyism and a form of socialism in the Ulster Defence Association.

For the UDA the problem is essentially one of identity: 'The Prods have been brainwashed into believing that they were strictly a British Community, have no Irish or Ulster traditions and therefore didn't need to learn Irish dancing, Gaelic, or folk music.' Thus Andy Tyrie, the leader of the UDA. Tyrie supports this view with a historical argument to the effect that there was an ancient British people ("British" in the non-imperial sense) who were called the Cruthin and who existed in Ulster long before the seventeenth-century settlement. He also emphasizes his Ulsterness by having a photograph of the statue of Cuchulain in the GPO above his desk. Cuchulain is therefore an authentically *Ulster* hero in a way that Carson – a Dubliner who privately despised the province – can never be. Where James Joyce offers a definition of Irish identity which is non-sectarian and truly republican, and which exists somewhere in the future, the UDA looks back to a dreamtime occupied by aboriginal ancestors in order to affirm an identity which is both epic and provincial. At the moment the UDA has stepped aside from the conflict and is insisting that it is a socialist and non-sectarian organisation composed of forward-looking people who are 'tired of being classed as Neanderthal bigots'. They may draw their inspiration from a form of atavistic energy, but they are also modern in their outlook and they are opposed to the link with Britain. They have parted company with what is now termed 'Official Unionism'.

Although the UDA has now distanced itself from Ian Paisley, he more than any other Unionist politician appears to belong to a dreamtime of Presbyterian aborigines – giant preachers who strode the Antrim coast long before the birth of Christ. He is a complex and protean personality who imagines cyclones of blessings, compares himself to the diminutive figure of a famous Brahmin called Mahatma Gandhi, and probably nurses a secret admiration for Parnell on whose parliamentary tactics some of his own appear to be modelled.

Ian Paisley was born in Armagh in 1926. His father, James Paisley, came of a Church of Ireland family who had lived in Co. Tyrone for many generations. In 1908 his father was 'saved' by an evangelical preacher and became a Baptist. In a memorial sermon, the son describes how his father went down to a frozen River Strule one Easter Sunday morning with a pastor who first broke the ice and then put him under the water:

> My father tells when he went under the waters of that river he identified himself with his Lord in death, in burial and in resurrection. When he came out that day he had lost many of his friends, he had lost many of the people that once associated themselves with him in the gospel. He realised that there was a reproach with the gospel. My father as I told you, was uncompromising in his character. He did not care. The more he was opposed the more he preached and the more he was persecuted the more he excelled in evangelism. God blessed him and eventually he went to Armagh to business.

This is a characteristically Protestant piece of writing: there is the assertion of uncompromising principle, a strong self-justifying theme which runs throughout the sermon, an affirmation of the work ethic (that brutal verb 'to business'

157

echoing the anti-Home Rule slogan, 'Ulster Means Business'), and finally there is the idea of being born again. In a very fundamental sense it is a description of revolutionary commitment because this is, imaginatively, a seventeenth-century world where religion and politics are synonymous. And so on Easter Sunday 1908 the puritan revolutionary rises out of the deep, having rejected friends, family, leisure and the private life. The old life of compromise, scepticism and individual personality is set aside in the moment of commitment. And that commitment is made out in the open air, as compared with, say, T.S. Eliot's Anglican and institutional commitment which is a 'moment in a draughty church at smokefall'.

Paisley senior later broke with the Baptists because of their ecumenism and set up his own Independent Fundamentalist Church. The son has inherited this characteristic of breaking with established institutions and he has a Cromwellian scorn of formalism, an instinctive libertarianism which conceals, or creates, a monumentally dictatorial personality. It appears that the alternative to compromised institutions could be a series of pyramids dedicated to his version of the egotistical sublime, to his relentless monomania.

One of the strongest features of puritanism is its autobiographical tendency, its passionate self-regard. Paisley likes talking about himself and in one of his published sermons he describes his 'apprenticeship in preaching in the open air'. During the Second World War he was a student at the Barry School of Evangelism in South Wales and his tutor in open-air preaching was an ex-boxer:

> He had his prize gold belt always at the gospel meetings. He used to swing that great gold belt, which he won as the welter-weight for the South of England, around his head and shout as only Ted Sherwood could shout. He had a voice like a trumpet. People had to heed and listen to him. When he got tired and husky, he used to say, 'Go on Ian, you have a go.' So he drew the crowd, and so I served my apprenticeship, preaching when his voice was gone, his throat husky and his powerful frame exhausted.

It's like a scene from Ben Jonson: a fairground world where that ex-boxer swinging his gold belt is a Herculean showman with a voice so powerful it might bring walls crashing down. The charismatic mountebank – or sincere preacher – must draw and play the crowd, amuse it, hector it and put down hecklers. He is like a politician on a platform as well as being a flashy Autolycus-figure. That ex-boxer with the greenwood name stands as an archetype of inspiration, an entertainer and fighter, a displaced version of Cuchulain.

In 1949 Paisley began a mission in Belfast's dockland and he also joined the anti-Roman Catholic National Union of Protestants. Somewhere about this time there is a moment outside the printed record where he appears to have been snubbed by a member of the Unionist establishment. That establishment regarded him as a working-class rabble-rouser and his outspoken unrestrained bigotry threatened and parodied its defter sectarianism. The rebuff demanded vengeance and Paisley began the long march which was to bring him to the walls of the Unionist establishment, to the barrier around the demesne.

The Paisley of this period is partly modelled on the Reverend Henry Cooke, a reactionary and highly influential nineteenth-century preacher who did much to counter Presbyterian radicalism. This Paisley is an autochthonous bigot who once organised a mock-mass on the platform of the Ulster Hall. Patrick Marrinan, his biographer, describes the sinister shabbiness of this occasion, the nervous fascination of the audience laughing at a renegade Spanish priest reciting unfamiliar Latin words, the canny showmanship, the plastic buckets brimming with money.

Paisley's particular kind of puritan egotism is voracious in its subjectivity and for all its insistence on sincerity is in practice highly theatrical. He is a compulsive role-player and is fond of dressing up in other people's personalities. After the Almighty, after St Paul – for whom he confesses 'a strange liking' – his most influential model, or imaginative ikon, is John Bunyan, whose life and work obsess him. He calls Bunyan a 'poor unschooled tinker' who became 'the most prominent man of letters as far as English literature is concerned'. Bunyan is this 'dreamer and penman' who had 'the tinker's power of reaching the heart' – there is a hint of rural superstition and natural magic here. He admires Bunyan for his 'strong doctrinal preaching', his opposition to the civil and ecclesiastical authorities, the enormous crowds he drew, and for his prose-style. Bunyan's appeal is theological, social and aesthetic – he *is* culture and tradition. It's here that we enter a time-warp and see that world of Ranters, Fifth Monarchy Men, Levellers and millenarian preachers which E. P. Thompson and

Christopher Hill describe in their work. For Thompson, *Pilgrim's Progress* is one of the two 'founding texts of the English working-class movement' (the other is Paine's *Rights of Man*). And so to admire Bunyan is by definition to be a dissenting radical, a nonconformist and a republican – Bunyan was a soldier in the Parliamentary Army.

Bunyan was also imprisoned for twelve years for preaching without a licence, and in 1966 Paisley was imprisoned for three months for demonstrating outside the General Assembly of the Presbyterian Church. In a statement he said, 'it will take more than Captain O'Neill's nasal twang to defy us' – the class grudge is clear, even though class politics was an impossible concept then. O'Neill warned of the dangers of alienating 'our British friends' and with an unconscious dismissiveness referred to Northern Ireland as 'this small corner of the British Commonwealth'. Angered by this diminution, Paisley retorted: 'To Our Lord, puppet politicians are but grasshoppers with portfolios.' Like any republican he refused, in one of his favourite phrases, to 'bow the knee' to the colonial authority and its deputies. And so, in a small corner of the British Commonwealth, Ulster's Bunyan was imprisoned by a grasshopper with a portfolio.

While he was in prison Paisley wrote the most substantial of his four books. It is an exposition of Paul's Epistle to the Romans cast in the form of a puritan journal. Each section is dated and the *Exposition* ends with this dramatic, deadpan postscript: 'This section completed in the dawn of the eighty-third day of imprisonment: Tuesday, 11 October 1966.' It is the dawn of righteousness, conviction and inspiration, and it looks forward to Paisley's second prison term, three years later, when he sent this letter to his congregation:

Beloved in the Lord,
   The day which we have prayed for and longed for has dawned. Captain O'Neill the tyrant is no longer the ruler of our country. We, who have suffered under his tyranny and wrath can surely sing Psalm 124. The Lord has wrought for us a great deliverance, and to His great Name we ascribe the glory. Let us be careful to return our heartfelt thanks.
   I heard the news here in my cell, No.20 (B2), as prisoner 636, at approximately 4.30 on Monday afternoon. Immediately I sang the doxology and fell upon my knees to give God thanks. We have had a long and bitter struggle. As a people we have suffered. As your

minister I have been maligned and persecuted, and you have all shared the maligning and persecuting. We have been in the depths together. Every effort has been made to smash the testimony of the Church and the credibility of me, the minister of the church. THEY HAVE FAILED, FOR GOD WAS OUR HELPER. We are just a lot of nobodies, and the enemy thought he could trample us out, BUT GOD DELIVERED US.

Like some Luddite pamphlet, this message rises up from the very depths of popular culture, and that phrase 'We are just a lot of nobodies' concentrates much of the emotion which Paisleyism draws on and expresses. The plain, strenuous, autodidactic atmosphere that clings to Paisley's published works – a combination of earnest assertive pride and a deep lack of confidence – tells of a disadvantaged population which feeds its persecution complex by reading the Psalms and which dreams of emerging from the underground status of subculture into the light of power and society.

It is impossible to nourish such an ambitious dream and to see yourself as a grateful inhabitant of a small corner of the British Commonwealth, and Paisley's rejection of that dependent status is formulated in a theological argument. Commenting on Romans 1. 1 – 'Paul, a servant of Jesus Christ, called to be an apostle, separated unto the gospel of God' – Paisley notes, 'Paul was a separatist'. This idea of separation is one of his major themes and in his commentary on Romans he is forming an idea of Ulster nationalism which entails separation from both the United Kingdom and the Republic of Ireland.

He is also fascinated by the phrase 'for a little season' which occurs in Revelations 6. 11, and he cites a similar phrase from Hebrews: 'By faith Moses, when he was come to years, refused to be called the son of Pharaoh's daughter; choosing rather to suffer affliction with the people of God, than to enjoy the pleasures of sin for a season (11. 25-6). For Paisley, Ulster under O'Neill is like Egypt under Pharoah, a sinful bondage which is to be endured for a season. He draws this analogy in his commentary and it appears to be a puritan favourite. In Richardson's *Pamela*, for example, Pamela confides to her journal:

I think I was loth to leave the house. Can you believe it? – what could be the matter with me, I wonder?...Surely I cannot be like the old murmuring Israelites, to long after the onions and garlic of Egypt, when they had suffered there such heavy bondage?

In its restless search for liberty the puritan spirit sometimes welcomes suffering, sometimes looks back over its shoulder to a warm and muddied slavery, to the old temporising life of compromise and subjection.

There is an epic moment in one of Paisley's published sermons where he insists obsessively that *'the sea speaks of separation'*:

> I stand at the edge of the sea. I look over its waves, and my loved ones are across in another continent. Between me and them stretches the waves of the briny depths. I know what it is to be separated from them. Nothing separates like the sea. What a barrier the sea makes. What a terrible barrier the sea makes. Separation.

The word obsesses him and in a cassette recording entitled *Separation*, which was released in 1980, he explains that Moses 'chose the affliction of the people of God' and rejected 'the beggarly elements of Egypt'. Here, Egypt is the United Kingdom – Ulster under Direct Rule from Westminster – and Paisley is offering a Pauline separatist argument: 'May God make us a separated people.' By 'us' he means the Protestants – there is a tribal exclusiveness central to this definition – and he sees himself as Moses leading his people out of bondage to the Promised Land. This parallel is employed more elaborately by Joyce in *Ulysses* where Bloom is Moses the precursor of Christ, the liberator; Parnell is both Moses and Christ, and Stephen is Christ the Hero. However, Joyce's idea of the Irish nation is inclusive rather than exclusive – it is a definition beyond tribalism, beyond religious creed. And those Irish historians who congratulate themselves on their freedom from tribal simplicities might reflect on whom exactly they mean by 'we' – what audience do they speak for and address? A long time ago Yeats asked himself this question in 'The Fisherman' and answered it by praying for an ideal reader, a 'man who is but a dream'.

Paisley's political ambition and his motivating fire – a fire he has stolen from the Unionist establishment – are sometimes transparently evident in his scriptural exegesis. Commenting on the phrase, 'for it is the power of God' (Romans 1. 16), he remarks:

> Gospel preaching is charged with the dynamic of heaven. Dynamite to be displayed in all its mighty potency must have the fuse and the

fire. When the fuse of true prayer is set alight with the fire of the Holy Ghost and thus the gospel dynamite is exploded, what tremendous results occur. Then do the strongholds of Satan topple. Then do the bulwarks of idolatry collapse. Then do the towering walls of sin suddenly fall. Then is the enemy dislodged. Then is all opposition blasted and the power of truth is proved to be more than a conqueror. Oh for a day of real gospel preaching and gospel power! Lord let me witness such a day.

This prayer for power was offered in the prison cell in 1966 and three years later, in April 1969, there were a series of explosions which were blamed on the IRA, and which helped to bring about O'Neill's resignation. Though no one had accused them, the Ulster Volunteer Force denied responsibility for the explosions and it's generally accepted that they, or freelance Protestant terrorists, were responsible. Puritan metaphor is a form of irony which has a habit of becoming literal: a dynamic millenarian rhetoric can inspire men to place actual dynamite under the status quo.

Paisley's theological argument is that 'righteousness without the law' must be received by Faith and he explains that the seed of Abraham are not heirs of the law but heirs by the righteousness of faith without the law. According to the Anglican *New Commentary on Holy Scripture* Paul argues that an 'act of faith' procured Abraham's acquittal and by 'faith' Paul means 'the whole act, or attitude, of surrender to Christ, intellectual, moral, and emotional'.

This idea of an act of faith is fundamental to Paisley's thought, and from time to time it is given calculated existential expression – as, for example, his demonstration in the House of Commons after the assassination of the Reverend Robert Bradford and his subsequent call for a campaign of passive disobedience to force the British out. Of necessity, the leap of faith is intensely subjective and assertive, and it is informed or sustained by an idea of martyrdom. Paisley comments that Christ makes frequent references to his death as 'the culminating act of his ministry on earth', and this inspires his projection of himself as an exemplary figure, ready to stake all and do or die for his faith and his people ('sell our lives dearly,' as he put it outside the House of Commons).

Although Paisley resembles De Valera in the theological cast of his mind, the religion he subscribes to is an apparently unstructured, intensely emotional experience. 'Justification,' he argues, 'is heart work as opposed to head work.' This assertion of emotion over intellect is both authoritarian and romantic, and Paisley finds its dogmatic justification in Romans 10. 10: 'For with the heart man believeth unto righteousness; and with the mouth confession is made unto salvation.' This is what he terms 'heart belief', though according to the meek and wily Anglican commentary 'heart' is a word which designates 'the inner self, with special reference to the intellect'. Essentially, this is a version of that dull old eighteenth-century dichotomy between the heart and the head: the Anglican hegemony is for Reason, the puritan evangelical opposition is for Feeling. Reason is a form of social control, Feeling a type of subversion – as Henry Fielding implies in his criticisms of Whitefield.

Paisley's argument in his *Exposition* is that when 'the Spirit comes, the curse of the law is removed and its hideous tyranny broken and he [Paul] is freed from the law of sin and death'. Although this does appear to have connections with anti-nomianism, Paisley rejects 'the pernicious doctrines of the antinomians' in his introduction to chapter seven where he discusses the concepts of 'law' and 'grace'. Although he later states that a Christian 'must also give due and proper respect to those above him in society', it's impossible not to perceive that 'law' and 'grace' are essentially irreconcilable.

In his commentary on Romans, C.K. Barrett remarks:

> Jesus had been condemned by the law. He had been tried and found guilty of blasphemy (Mark 14. 64) by the supreme court of his people; moreover, he had died a death which exposed him to the curse declared in the law (Deuteronomy 21. 23; Galatians 3. 13). Yet God had not cursed him; on the contrary, he had ratified his claims and declared his approval of him by raising him from the dead. On this crucial issue, therefore, the law – or, at least, Israel's understanding of the law – had been wrong. This did not mean that the law was to be rejected out of hand. Jesus himself had reaffirmed its validity as the word of God, and, rightly understood, it bore witness to him. But it must be rightly understood, and not understood in the old way. It could no longer be regarded as the mediator between God and man; this function had been assumed by Jesus Christ.

Barrett further states that Paul's theological development consists 'in the adjustment of old convictions based upon the Old Testament and formulated within Judaism to the new

Christian conviction that Jesus is Lord'. Ironically and paradoxically, therefore, Paisley here appears to be on the side of what
is new, rather than being a simple Mosaic fundamentalist.
Inevitably, his *Exposition* is both political and theological, and
his assertion that 'Election' is an act of God 'governed only and
solely by His good pleasure' looks forward to his two election
victories in 1970.

At this pitch of imaginative extremity, metaphor and
irony take on a superreal brightness and the conventional line
between fact and fiction melts in a manner that is characteristic of puritan journalism. This is apparent in one of Paisley's
prison messages:

> We are not the servants of men, nor the servants of the rulers of
> men. We are the servants of the Lord. This, of course, does not
> appear to the world. They think of us as devils, as troublemakers,
> as servants of hell, and as disturbers of the peace. *They do not recognise*
> *our imperial royalty* as they did not recognise the imperial royalty of
> our Master. For if the princes of this world had known they would
> not have crucified the Lord of Glory. Some day, however, our
> imperial royalty will be manifested before heaven, earth and hell.

He was in prison for abusing the Governor of Northern
Ireland who was the representative of 'imperial royalty'.
However, the royal glow which it was his function to impart
appears not to have warmed the unofficial side of Unionism,
and Paisley's statement is an assertion of his and his followers'
sense of their own worth, their own 'imperial royalty'. It is a
gesture of defiance and independence, and if the attitude
which informs it is characteristically raw, edgy, brutal, dangerous, it is at least the beginning of an idea and so is far in advance
of official Unionism. That dismal political philosophy has
never shown any talent for, or interest in, forming ideas.

Terence O'Neill dismissed Ian Paisley's chiliastic rhetoric
and his political demonstrations as 'mindless', and the establishment view of him is expressed in two later remarks of Brian
Faulkner's. When the British Government suspended Stormont, Faulkner accused it of reducing Northern Ireland to 'a
coconut colony'. Later, when the power-sharing Executive
fell, Faulkner called Paisley 'this demon doctor'. This habit of
drawing analogies – whether with Hungary or Algeria – is a
deep-seated Irish characteristic and the parallel here must be
familiar to anyone who has read the novels of V.S. Naipaul. It

invites us to imagine a West Indian island, drums beating, the governor's mansion, a messianic revolutionary leader, riots, carnival and independence. Indeed, Paisleyism is curiously similar to reggae music – both are assertions of post-colonial identity, though reggae is much more advanced, sophisticated and culturally eclectic.

In 1970 Paisley became a Stormont MP, then a Westminster MP. In the following year Brian Faulkner introduced internment, and towards the end of 1971 Paisley emerged as a kind of republican statesman. With the SDLP, he opposed the introduction of internment 'in principle', though he had favoured it at first. At the end of November he suggested that if the constitution of the Irish Republic were amended then 'good neighbourliness in the highest possible sense' might prevail between the Republic and Northern Ireland. He said:

> I would like to see anything done that would be for the good of all the people of Northern Ireland and all the people of Ireland. I believe it could deal with the cancer and the cancer is not the 1920 Act and not the partitition of the country but the cancer is the 1937 Constitution and the domination of the Catholic Church through it. I would like to see the whole thing thrown out.

When asked if he would favour a united Ireland if the Republic were to remove Protestant fears by amending its Constitution, he replied:

> If you ask me whether I can see at some time some way, somewhere in the future a united Ireland, that is a question I cannot answer because I cannot now say what will happen in the future and, anyway, I cannot answer the question because I am too much of a realist and such a question is really not even worthy of consideration now.

The establishment Unionists were quick to exploit this apparent rejection of the old anti-Home Rule slogan, 'We won't have it', and they accused Paisley of being prepared to sell out to Republicanism. He quickly drew back and claimed he'd been misquoted.

Three months later he emerged as a total integrationist in a pamphlet called *The Ulster Problem, Spring 1972: A Discussion of the True Situation in Northern Ireland*. This pamphlet contains a section called 'A brief history of Ireland' which is an interesting example of Unionist historiography. All mention of the 1798 rebellion is carefully avoided and we are moved briskly from the plantation of Ulster to the year 1800:

> ...the Irish Parliament decided for legislative union or parliamentary union with Great Britain; and there was passed the Act of Union. The Irish Parliament was abolished, and from 1800 the members of Parliament from Ireland had their seats in the mother of Parliaments – the British House of Commons at Westminster.

Later in the pamphlet Paisley insists on the necessity of 'the complete union of Northern Ireland and the United Kingdom'. He wants 'full legislative union'. This appears straightforward – it was for a long time the policy of Enoch Powell and the Official Unionists – except that that favourite word 'separated' appears three times in his brief history of Ireland. He describes Daniel O'Connell and Parnell as separatist leaders, and the wish to equal them in stature is not beyond his ambition – he is a natural overreacher who has no regard for the ideas of balance, decorum and limitation which are such strong features of English culture.

In order to 'separate' he has had to appear to be leading his people back into Egypt, and it is now clear that Britain has absolutely no intention of granting Northern Ireland full, permanent legislative union. Paisley therefore understands Austen Chamberlain's remark that Northern Ireland is 'an illogical and indefensible compromise', and his policy can be interpreted as an ironic double bluff which invites both Britain and the Republic to lay their cards on the table. British policy may now be defined as 'get out' – the phrase hurled at Paisley, McQuade and Robinson by angry Westminster MPs – while the policy of the Irish Republic has recently become clear in the New Ireland Forum Report.

If total integration is a dead duck (and everyone recognises that it is), and if a united Ireland is an impossibility, then the only alternative is for Northern Ireland to secede and go independent – to 'separate'. Ultimately – and tragically – there never is any choice between this, that, and a something else which is neither this nor that. However, the idea of Ulster independence does express a conflict which is other than the Unionist/Republican conflict. Southerners appear to regard Northerners as incomprehensible savages, while Northerners look South and see, in the words of Henry Joy McCracken, 'a set of gasconaders'. At a deep level there is a shared perception, a common bond, between the minority and majority populations in the North, and this bond is altogether other than the sentimental concept of 'ould dacency' purveyed by writers like Benedict Kiely.

It emerges, for example, in a speech which Paisley made in 1973, the year the House of Commons approved a White Paper for a Northern Ireland Assembly. During the Commons debate, Paisley said this:

> For too long the representatives of Northern Ireland have been asked: 'Who do you speak for?' It is important at this juncture that the people be given the opportunity to speak by the ballot box. In many senses we have been caught up in a struggle that goes far beyond the basic differences between two sections of the community. There are other elements in the situation that do not want a settlement of any kind, that are purely and utterly destructive, that want to see the destruction of Northern Ireland not merely as an entity in the UK, but as part of the Western democratic system. This House must face up to the fact that these forces in Northern Ireland care not about any Government White Paper or the democratic vote. They believe that violence in the end shall pay. It is sad but in many degrees violence has paid off in Ulster. Throughout this debate there has been the dangerous suggestion that if the elections throw up a group in Northern Ireland which this House does not like, then, with a stroke of the pen, they can say on 31 March next year: 'fare thee well'. When we say this makes us feel like second-class citizens, we are telling the truth. I would not like to see Northern Ireland ever going outside the Union, but there is a section there who are feeling restless with the attitudes of the members of this House and the Government.

Perhaps this was the first time that a Unionist stated in public that he felt like a 'second-class citizen'. It marks a significant movement of the spirit and helps to define the difference between official and unofficial Unionism. The majority of the constituents of Fermanagh and South Tyrone will hardly have needed to recall the phrase when the House of Commons simply ignored their wishes in a dangerous display of near-unanimity, or 'me-tooism' as one dissenting Labour MP courageously defined it.

Here we arrive at something hard and fast – a principle which unites Paisleyism with Republicanism. We come up against the collision between that principle and the sort of eyes-averted Burkean shuffle which characterizes British policy towards Ireland. The principle of one-man-one-vote is a great leveller and it has even prompted one Burkean commentator to suggest that Fermanagh-South Tyrone should become United Nations territory.

The complication in Paisley's attitude to this principle lies in his perception of himself as British. It is an intermittent and fluctuating perception (for the *Sunday Times* he is a 'defiler of the British way of life'), and it was expressed forcibly during a meeting Paisley had with Bernadette Devlin in 1968. She suggested that the Unionist state had been unjust and unfair, and although he conceded that there might have been injustices Paisley insisted, 'I would rather be British than fair'. In Ulster, the condition of being British is that you somehow believe in one-man-one-vote but are selective about its implementation. And so it is possible to have a situation where a group of demonstrators waves a placard saying ONE MAN ONE VOTE and a rival group waves either the Union Jack or a placard saying BETTER BRITISH THAN FAIR.

Paisley would appear to have discarded the idea of Britishness now, though his response to Bernadette Devlin's question shows his wish to reduce every question to fundamental principles. And here, John Hume's remark the day after Bloody Sunday – 'it's a united Ireland now or nothing' – defined another fundamental principle for the first time.

Because he possesses a theological temperament, Paisley is as opposed to liberalism as any Marxist. In one sermon, for example, he attacks the 'sinking sands of an easy believism' – he means ecumenism, liberal theology and politics. In another sermon he begins by stating, 'Ours is a Laodicean age,' and in another he says, 'make sure of this, there will be no neutrals in this service. There will not be a man or a woman go down the stairs today, out onto the streets of Ballymena who will not have made a vital and a terrible decision.' This is the Baptist doctrine of total immersion or complete commitment, and anyone familiar with the ideological temperament will recognise it here in an earlier, theological form. It's a temperament dipped in icy, not lukewarm, water, an urgent single-minded attitude which says that the 'only minute you can be sure of is this minute' and which states that it's 'now or never'.

This tremendous leap of faith is directed both at personal political power and at an idea of God, and Paisley's God resembles a cross between Judge Jeffreys and Albert Pierrepoint. This 'God of inflexible justice' is described in a sermon called 'After This Judgment' in which Paisley gives a relished description of a court 'in the old days' where the chaplain comes and gives the judge 'the black cap'. He then states, 'Some day Jesus will put on the black cap', and this idea of God as a hanging judge is developed in his study of George Whitefield where he quotes a contemporary witness:

> 'I have known him...avail himself of the formality of the judge putting on his black cap to pronounce sentence. With his eyes full of tears, and his heart almost too big to admit of speech, he would say after a momentary pause, 'I am now going to put on my condemning cap. Sinner, I MUST do it! I MUST do it. I MUST pronounce sentence.' Then in a burst of tremendous eloquence he would repeat our Lord's words, 'Depart ye cursed!' and not without a powerful description of the nature of that curse.'

Paisley admires this obscene, righteous and murderous egotism – an egotism which violently overthrows formalities and social bonds. Somewhere deep in his personality there lies a fascination with judicial murder which involves a contradictory identification with both the victim and his executioner.

In a published sermon, 'Richard Cameron: The Lion of the Covenant', there is a stark and savoured quotation from the sentence of hanging and disembowelling which the 'Council of Blood' passed on one of the Covenanters. Here Paisley appears as a Scottish Nationalist laying the 'tribute wreath' of his sermon on the memorial to a Protestant martyr (his mother was 'born into a Scots Covenanting home' and he makes much of his Scottish inheritance). This is apparent in two cassette sermons on the Covenanters which are awash with cries of 'blood' and whose delivery at times resembles the intonation necessary to a reading of the closing lines of Yeats's 'Easter 1916'. Although Paisley doesn't write the sacred names out in a verse, he does recite them in a rolling, drawn-out, ululating intonation which elevates the 'Covenanting martyrs' and affirms their holiness. These almost forgotten historical figures are invested with a vocal halo by the preacher and so are changed into transcendent heroes. This is a Protestantism which is pushing deep into the territory of mystery and mythology; it is a celebration of chthonic forces and a rejection of secular and utilitarian values.

In particular, Paisley singles out one young Covenanter,

Hugh McKail, who was 'only 27 years old' when he was led to the scaffold. His description of McKail's execution is ironically similar to Patrick Pearse's account of Robert Emmet's execution where the body of the 'comely' young man is desecrated on the scaffold. Paisley thanks God that there is 'in my heart a wonderful affinity with Richard Cameron', and here he again identifies with the martyred victim rather than the hanging judge. The Covenanters, he states, were 'bold, courageous, strong men...these were not the putty paper men of the twentieth century – these were the rugged men of the Reformation'. Quoting a 'great master of English literature' – someone he calls 'Jupiter Carlyle' – he terms them 'real heroes', and he refers to this passage from *Heroes and Hero Worship*:

> ...many men in the van do always, like Russian soldiers, march into the ditch at Schweidnitz, and fill it up with their dead bodies, that the rear may pass-over them dry shod, and gain the honour...How many earnest rugged Cromwells, Knoxes, poor Peasant Covenanters, wrestling, battling for very life, in rough miry places, have to struggle, and suffer, and fall, greatly censured, *bemired*, – before a beautiful Revolution of Eight-eight can step over them in official pumps and silk-stockings, with universal three-times-three!

This is a burning and rebarbative evocation of that buried unrecorded level of anonymous historical experience from which Paisley draws much of his inspiration, and it could be that other Irish historians are also fired by this subterranean energy.

When heaven was opened, Paisley says, the Covenanters hoped to see Christ 'on his white horse coming forth to put every enemy underneath his feet'. Here, Christ and William of Orange, the Second Coming and the Glorious Revolution, melt into each other. The Day of Judgement is a gable-end in Sandy Row and the white horse becomes the pale horse of Revelations. Paisley is an amateur and obsessive numerologist and he has a particular fascination for the apocalyptic vision of Revelations. In another Covenanting sermon he explains the symbolism of the fifth seal in terms which echo his discussion of grace and law in the *Exposition*. Five is the 'number of grace' and this is the 'mighty sovereign free grace of God' which enabled the Covenanters to 'stand true and uncompromisingly'.

In this sermon, metaphor and substance become confused:

blood is both symbol and reality. The preacher shouts out:

> ...all the attributes of God flow in the bloodstream of Calvary...
> we're under the blood-stained banner of the Cross...must sail
> through bloody seas...blood...blood...blood...

The sermon lurches towards a Churchillian rhetoric – 'there's a
storm coming that will try all our foundations' – and it also has
moments of bloody and paranoid dementia. At times it sounds
a note of bitter failure, at others it is fired with a notion of
glorious martyrdom. It looks beyond this world to the
resurrection, yet it is also directed towards this world in its
imagination of a radically new, radically changed society. It is
part Protestant triumphalism careering off into heaven, part
an attempt to heal the puritan split in consciousness by
summoning a millenarian vision of a new heaven and a new
earth. This sermon offers an essentially Lawrentian ethic –
blood consciousness and the healing rainbow at the end.

This apocalyptic vision is given an antiquarian treatment in
Paisley's book, *The 'Fifty Nine' Revival*, which is an account of
the revolutionary 'flood time of revival' which swept parts of
Ulster in 1859. F.S.L. Lyons discusses this movement briefly in
Culture and Anarchy in Ireland, though he sees it – wrongly I think
– as an almost exclusively emotional and psychological phenomenon. His understanding of Presbyterianism is limited and
inadequate, and this is because historiography – at least in the
North – is still at the polemical stage. Future historians will
have a mass of pamphlets, tracts, sermons and journalism to
draw on. Lyons has failed to commence this excavation and
this may explain why his discussion of northern culture is so
unsatisfactory.

In his conclusion, Lyons states that between the fall of
Parnell and the death of Yeats there was an anarchy

> ...in the mind and in the heart, an anarchy which forbade not just
> unity of territories, but also 'unity of being', an anarchy that sprang
> from the collision within a small and intimate island of seemingly
> irreconcilable cultures, unable to live together or to live apart,
> caught inextricably in the web of their tragic history.

Despite the counterbalancing quotation from Yeats with
which he caps this, Lyons's Arnoldian terminology is unhelpful,
and it could be argued – indeed it *was* argued long ago by
George Birmingham in *The Red Hand of Ulster* – that Irish
culture is really unified at its extremes. An example of this can

172

be found in Paisley's historical study, *The Massacre of St Bartholomew*, where he explores the doctrine of martyrdom. He believes that 'true faith is a martyred faith' and argues that the blood of the martyrs is the 'seed' of the Church. This is close to the phrase 'elect seed' which he employs in his *Exposition* and it resembles Pearse's notion of martyrdom.

Does this mean, then, that it is Paisley's ambition to take over the GPO in Belfast and give his life for Ulster? Will there be a generation of Democratic Unionist hunger-strikers? Will there be a civil war of the kind Paisley describes in his history of the Huguenots? Will a shrunken, independent Northern Ireland barricade itself against an enlarged Republic? And will an ambitious group of Ulster Nationalists demand the return of Cavan, Monaghan and Donegal, as well as the counties lost from the six? Or will there be negotiation, argument, compromise, a new constitution, a parliament in Armagh and the beginnings of a way of writing history that is neither Orange nor Green, but is instead as white as the middle band of the Irish tricolour?

History, by its very nature, has no answers.

A New England

In Roman mythology the god Terminus presides over walls and boundaries. He expresses the ancient doctrine that human nature is limited and life irredeemably imperfect. Terminus agrees with Robert Frost in saying 'good fences make good neighbors' and he also takes a classical view of artistic creation by insisting on formal constraints and closed symmetry. Although Terminus inhabits hedges and drystone walls, he is not a property of pastoral verse and this is because pastoral writing, like fantasy writing, is a convention which licenses an imaginative freedom from reality. In fantasy literature the result is the ennui of utopia, a luminous envelope that absorbs the world.

In *The Passion of New Eve*, a fantasy of late-seventies America, Angela Carter's androgynous protagonist describes a room like this:

> Soft clouds of dust rose from the yellowed pelts of polar bears flung on the floor and their mummified heads roared mutely at us in balked fury. The walls of this long, low, serpentine room were made of glass tiles, so we could see the undersides of more furniture upstairs, and here and there the back of another rug—all dim and subtly distorted.

Reading this passage of descriptive narrative, I asked myself how the walls of a fantasy room could possibly be distorted? The problem is ontological: fantasy by its very nature is a distortion of reality, therefore a distorted effect within a distortion must be something which appears incontrovertibly and recalcitrantly real—a positivist with a half-brick, for example. The easy fluency and soft stylishness of Angela Carter's fictions is won at the expense of form and mimesis, and the result is an expansive territory without boundaries or horizons, a kind of permanent and infinite vanishing.

Carter's journalism, however, is remarkable for a style which arches brilliantly between sociological observation and self-delighting irony. This introductory paragraph is emblematic of her technique:

Nothing Sacred: Selected Writings by Angela Carter.

Getting a buzz off the stones of Bath, occupying a conspicuous site not fifty yards from the mysterious, chthonic aperture from which the hot springs bubble out of the inner earth, there is usually a local alcoholic or two on the wooden benches outside the Abbey. On warm summer afternoons they come out in great numbers, as if to inform the tourists this city is a trove of other national treasures besides architectural ones. Some of them are quite young, one or two very young, maybe not booze but acid burned their brain cells away, you can't tell the difference, now.

Bath is a Roman city and that adjective "chthonic" derives from the Greek word for "earth". Carter has a pre-Christian concern for the spirit of place and the springs of particular cultures. Characteristically, she seeks to locate the folk imagination and its congenial ethnicity within those clean well-lighted spaces we call "reality". She enters an antiseptic world called Arndale Centre and then discovers the yeastiness of real culture: curd tarts, balm-cakes, live pigeons, and local cheeses wrapped in 'authentic mired bandages'.

In Bath, Carter discovers 'a lot of fine-boned, blue-eyed English madness' which forces her to insist on her Scottish extraction and see the city wryly as 'an icon of sensibility'. Her sophisticated primitivism designs this vividly intelligent image:

> That golden light, the light of pure nostalgia, gives the young boys in their bright jerseys playing football after tea in front of Royal Crescent the look of Rousseau's football players caught in the amber of the perpetual Sunday afternoon of the painter.

Douannier Rousseau was loved by all his friends for his saintly and peaceable personality, and his extraordinary marriage of quotidian reality with fantasy is particularly current at the moment. In 'A Whole School of Bourgeois Primitives', for example, Christopher Reid designs another version of England caught in a moment of buzzy stasis:

> Our lawn in stripes, the cat's pyjamas,
> rain on a sultry afternoon
>
> and the drenching, mnemonic smell this brings us
> surging out of the heart of the garden:
>
> these are the sacraments and luxuries
> we could not do without.
>
> Welcome to our peaceable kingdom,
> where baby lies down with the tiger-rug

and bumblebees roll over like puppies
inside foxglove-bells...

Carter, like Reid, is busily and wittily designing a new form of
the English sensibility—an ironic, ludic, cultivated imagination
which is free from class-guilt, bored by the old-fashioned idea
of Great Britain, peace-loving, and generously multi-racial.
Carter sees England as a crowded and shabbily decent third-
world country, and she shares with Reid and Craig Raine a
splendidly Mediterranean sense of joy. Where Larkin and
Motion are the troubled elegists of a vanished world power,
these writers inhabit the liberated atmosphere of light-filled
studios. They are flâneurs in an English market that resembles
'the peasant markets of Europe'.

Carter has a special affection for Yorkshire and in this
description of Bradford she creates that sense of the marvellous
which is so essential to the folk imagination:

> Like monstrous *genii loci*, petrifications of stern industrialists pose
> in squares and on road islands, clasping technological devices or
> depicted in the act of raising a weeping orphan. There is something
> inherently risible in a monumental statue showing a man in full
> mid-Victorian rig, watch-chain and all, shoving one hand in his
> waistcoat *à la* Napoleon and, with the other, exhorting the masses
> to, presumably, greater and yet greater productiveness.

This is the new post-imperial sensibility singing its delighted
sense of being free from all that pompous gruffness which goes
with a concept of progress and national destiny. Carter is the
laureate of de-industrialised England and the hedonistic egali-
tarianism of her prose—like Ashbery with stringency—makes
her the most advanced stylist in the country. With a bemused
delight, she creates an England of 'disparate ethnic elements'—
black puddings, signs in Urdu, bottles of Polish vodka next to
'the British sherry, brown ale and dandelion-and-burdock'.
Although she draws on Orwell's essays in popular culture,
Carter's prose style lacks his strenuous puritanism—the weather
of her style is warmly catholic and familial, where Orwell's
style often seems solitary, private and rather chilly.

Like Christopher Reid, Carter has a particular fascination
for Japan and her accounts of Japanese culture have a quality
reminiscent of the "charm" which nuclear physicists attribute
to certain atomic particles. Carter is "quarky" rather than
"quirky", and she possesses a rare ability to write about the
unusual and ridiculous without disdain:

One stall sells cocks made of bright pink sugar at 75 p a time. In the course of the afternoon, they sell 300 of the things—their entire stock. One other stall, and one other stall only, sells cookies in all manner of phallic and vulvic shapes, as well as lollipops on sticks with a coy little striped candy cock nestling in a bed of pink sugar.

Where V.S. Naipaul would have drained his disgust into bad prose, Carter lets the images happen in a manner that has a direct, super-real intelligence and grace. Her account of samurai comics issues from her prefatory statement, 'In Japan, I learned what it is to be a woman and became radicalised':

> Tanaka perpetrates lyrically bizarre holocausts, in décors simplified to the point of abstraction. His emphasis on decorative elements— the pattern on a screen; on a kimono; that of the complications of combs in a girl's hair—and his marked distortion of human form, create an effect something between Gustav Klimt and Walt Disney. His baby-faced heroines typify Woman as a masochistic object, her usual function in the strips.

That image of Klimt crossed with Disney is one of the most perfect moments in Carter's prose and her essays are distinguished by a fineness of visual imagination and an ability to make abrupt and exact transitions which create a sense of relatedness among apparently disparate things. As a result, the world becomes a gregariously coloured fiction that issues perpetually from an ironic and chthonic intelligence.

Carter's radical feminism offers startling portraits of Japanese sexuality and she also battles sporadically with D.H. Lawrence: 'Lawrence, the great, guilty chronicler of English social mobility, the classic, seedy Brit full of queasy, self-justificatory class shame and that is why they identify with him so much in British universities, I tell you.' Unfortunately, prose-rhapsody cannot properly cope with the phenomenon of Lawrentianism, its canonisation by Leavis and enduringly unexamined presence on courses in English literature. Carter ought, urgently, to write a companion to *The Sadeian Woman* and explore not just the assumptions on which Lawrence's fictions are based, but the often-hilarious attitudes which his benighted critics reveal when they discuss his work. She is a very distinguished stylist in her discursive prose but her fictions suffer from the absence of what Keats termed 'disagreeables'. It could be that her cerulean imagination would benefit from the constraints of the documentary novel.

A New Look at the Language Question

The history of a language is often a story of possession and dispossession, territorial struggle and the establishment or imposition of a culture. Arguments about the "evolution" or the "purity" of a language can be based on a simplistic notion of progress or on a doctrine of racial stereotypes. Thus a Spenserian phrase which Samuel Johnson employs in the famous preface to his dictionary—'the wells of English undefiled'—is instinct with a mystic and exclusive idea of nationhood. It defines a language and a culture in terms of a chimerical idea of racial purity. But Johnson doesn't profess this idea either visibly or aggressively, and in the less well-known essay which follows his preface he comments on the historical sources of the English language. Reflecting on the extinction of the ancient British language, he remarks:

> ...it is scarcely possible that a nation, however depressed, should have been mixed in considerable numbers with the Saxons without some communication of their tongue, and therefore it may, with great reason, be imagined, that those, who were not sheltered in the mountains, perished by the sword.

Anglo-Saxon society was among the very first European societies to establish a tradition of vernacular prose. However, for several centuries after the Norman conquest English was regarded as a rude and uncultivated tongue. At the beginning of the fourteenth century, the chronicler Robert of Gloucester notes with concern that English is spoken only by 'lowe men'. He remarks that England is the only country in the world that doesn't 'hold' to its own speech, and implies that such a situation is unnatural. Here he is clearly influenced by the English nationalism which developed after the crown lost Normandy early in the thirteenth century. French, however, continued to be the official language of England until a parliamentary statute of 1362 stated that all law suits must be conducted in English. French was displaced and the English language returned from a form of internal exile.

The English language was first brought to Ireland by the followers of Strongbow's Norman invaders in the twelfth century. Norman French and English became established as vernacular languages, though their speakers gradually crossed over to Irish. Attempts were made to resist this process—for example in the statutes of Kilkenny (1366)—but the Irishing of the settlers was completed by the Reformation which united the "Old English" with the native Irish against the Protestant "New English". And as Alan Bliss has shown, the Cromwellian Settlement of the 1650s was to be crucial to the history of the English language in Ireland. With the exception of Ulster, the English spoken in most parts of Ireland today is descended from the language of Cromwell's planters. The result, according to Diarmaid Ó Muirithe, is 'a distinctive Irish speech—Anglo-Irish or Hiberno-English, call it what you will'.

In England, the English language reached a peak of creative power during the Elizabethan and Jacobean periods when writers formed sentences by instinct or guesswork rather than by stated rule. In time it was felt that the language was overseeded and in need of more careful cultivation. Writers began to argue that the absence of a standard of "correct" English created an ugly and uncivilised linguistic climate, and Dryden remarked that he sometimes had to translate an idea into Latin before he could decide on the proper way of expressing it in English. In a *Discourse Concerning Satire* he noted, 'we have yet no prosodia, not so much as a tolerable dictionary, or a grammar, so that our language is in a manner barbarous'. Dryden's neoclassicism had an epic scope and power and like Virgil's Aeneas he wished to found a new *civitas* in a country damaged by violence and conflict. He argued that in order to properly regulate and refine the language England must have an academy modelled on the Académie Française. His criticism of the state of the language was developed by Swift in *A Proposal for Correcting, Improving, and Ascertaining the English Tongue*, which was addressed to Robert Harley, the Lord High Treasurer of England, and published in 1712. Although Swift strategically avoided mentioning the idea of an academy, it is clear that he intended his readers to make that deduction. Only an academy would be capable of 'ascertaining and fixing our language for ever, after such alterations are made in it as shall be thought requisite'.

Swift's proposal appears to be innocent of political interest, but a Whig paper, the *Medley*, detected Jacobitism in his preference for the Romance languages over the Saxon on the grounds that he was opposed to any 'new addition of Saxon words by bringing over the Hanover family'. According to his Whig critic, Swift wished to hasten 'a new invasion by the Pretender and the French, because that language has more Latin words than the Saxon'. Partly as a result, the idea of an academy came to be regarded as essentially unpatriotic, and it was on these grounds that Johnson took issue with Swift's 'petty treatise'. In the preface to his dictionary he remarks that he does not wish 'to see dependence multiplied' and hopes that 'the spirit of English liberty' will hinder or destroy any attempt to set up an academy in England. Although Matthew Arnold revived Swift's proposal in a provocative essay entitled 'The Literary Influence of Academies', the idea of an academic legislature for the language was effectively extinguished by Johnson's preface.

Johnson's argument is insular, aggressive and somewhat sentimental, yet there can be no doubt that he is expressing an ingrained cultural hostility to state intervention in the language. Johnson believed that a dictionary could perform the function of correcting English better than an academy could, and he argued that the organic nature of language ought to be respected. It was both misguided and tyrannical to attempt to freeze the English language artificially as Swift had suggested.

Johnson's English patriotism and his anarchistic conservatism inform his view of the language, and in accordance with his libertarian principles he avoids imposing any guide to pronunciation in his dictionary. Swift, however, advocated a standard English pronunciation and in an essay 'On Barbarous Denominations in Ireland' he criticised the Scottish accent and most English regional accents as 'offensive'. He also observed that an Irish accent made 'the deliverer...ridiculous and despised', and remarked that 'from such a mouth, an Englishman expects nothing but bulls, blunders, and follies'. For Swift, a standard English accent is a platonic ideal which will give dignity and self-respect to anyone who acquires it. He is therefore rejecting a concept of "Hiberno-English" or "Anglo-Irish" and is advocating a unified culture which embraces both Britain and Ireland. This ideal of complete integration still has its supporters, but it must now be apparent that a Unionist who retains a marked Irish accent is either an unconscious contradiction or a subversive ironist.

Dictionaries generally do legislate for pronunciation and towards the end of the eighteenth century a 'war of the dictionaries' took place in England. The argument was between supporters of Thomas Sheridan's 'pronouncing dictionary' and those who preferred John Walker's rival dictionary. Sheridan had what Johnson termed 'the disadvantage of being an Irishman' and so was not allowed to fix the pronunciation of English. On patriotic grounds the controversy was therefore decided in Walker's favour.

If sentiments about the English language can at times be informed by an idea of ethnicity, attempts to refine and ascertain the language almost instinctively relate it to the Houses of Parliament, to those institutions where speech exercises power. In his *Dictionary of Modern English Usage* H.W. Fowler frequently draws examples from parliamentary debates, and in this entry he reveals the simple patriotism which fires his concept of correct usage:

> *England, English(man).* The incorrect use of these words as equivalents of *Great Britain* or *The United Kingdom*, *British*, *Briton*, is often resented by other nationals of the U.K., like the book-reviewer who writes of Lord Cherwell's 'dedication to the service of Britain, which, in the annoying way foreigners have, he persisted in calling "England"'. Their susceptibilities are natural, but are not necessarily always to be deferred to. For many purposes the wider words are the natural ones. We speak of the *British Commonwealth*, the *British Navy*, *Army*, and *Air Force* and *British trade*; we boast that *Britons* never never never shall be slaves; we know that Sir John Moore sleeps in a grave where a *Briton* has laid him, and there is no alternative to *British* English if we want to distinguish our idiom from the American. But it must be remembered that no Englishman, or perhaps no Scotsman even, calls himself a Briton without a sneaking sense of the ludicrous, or hears himself referred to as a BRITISHER without squirming. How should an Englishman utter the words *Great Britain* with the glow of emotion that for him goes with *England*? His sovereign may be Her *Britannic* Majesty to outsiders, but to him is Queen of *England*; he talks the *English* language; he has been taught *English* history as one continuous tale from Alfred to his own day; he has heard of the word of an *Englishman* and aspires to be an *English* gentleman; and he knows that *England* expects every man to do his duty. 'Speak for *England*' was the challenge flung across the floor of the House of Commons by Leo Amery to the Leader of the Opposition on 2 September 1939. In the word *England*, not in *Britain* all those things are implicit. It is unreasonable to ask forty millions of people to refrain from the use of the only names that are in tune with patriotic emotion, or to make them stop and think whether they mean their country in a narrower or wider sense each time they name it.

More recently, a Conservative MP praised Michael Foot for 'speaking for England' during the comic and hysterical debate which followed Argentina's invasion of the Malvinas Islands. It would appear that at moments of crisis in the United Kingdom a ruling Englishness overcomes the less satisfying concept, British.

Englishness is an instinctual, ethnic identification, while the relatively recent concept, British, lacks its inspirational power. Indeed, as Fowler demonstrates, some English people feel a form of cultural cringe in relation to the imperial label, and in the 1980s terms like "British car", "British justice" or "British industry" have increasingly either a less confident or a downright pejorative usage within England. In many ways this new usage is connected with a movement of consciousness which Tom Nairn has termed 'the break-up of Britain'. On the other hand, Great Britain is a society composed of many different ethnic cultures and those who identify with it would argue that the term "British" can be seen as inclusive, positive and multi-racial, where "English" may be construed in an exclusive and negative manner. Again, many West Indians and Asians would reject this idea and argue that racist attitudes are on the increase in Britain.

Fundamentally, the language question is a question about nationhood and government, and some lexicographers perceive an occult connection between the English language and the English constitution. Johnson appears to have initiated the analogy when he concluded his attack on the idea of an academy by saying, 'we have long preserved our constitution, let us make some struggles for our language'. James Murray, the editor-in-chief of the *New English Dictionary*, developed this analogy when he observed that 'the English Dictionary, like the English Constitution, is the creation of no one man, and of no one age; it is a growth that has slowly developed itself down the ages'. Murray also compared Johnson's work to a 'lexicographic cairn' and so added a sense of primitive magic to the idea of anonymous tradition which he was asserting. Murray's twin comparisons to cairn and constitution help to infuse a magisterial, legislative authority with a form of natural piety that is partly the expression of his Scottishness. For Swift's platonic or rational ideal of complete integration and classic standardisation, Murray substitutes a slightly lichened idea of the dictionary as the equivalent of Wordsworth's leech-gatherer. It is both book and sacred natural object, one of the guardians of the nation's soul. And because the *New English Dictionary* was dedicated to Queen Victoria the imaginative power of the crown was joined to the natural magic of the cairn and the reverential power of the unwritten constitution. Thus the *NED*, or *Oxford English Dictionary* as it became, stands as one of the cornerstones of the culture which created it. It is a monumental work of scholarship and possesses a quasi-divine authority.

The *Oxford English Dictionary* is the chief lexicon of a language which can be more accurately described as "British English". In a sense, its compilers worked in the shadow of Noah Webster's *An American Dictionary of the English Language**. Something of the rivalry which Murray's team felt with American culture is reflected in the single example of a "typical" reader's quotation-slip which is given in the preface to the *NED*:

Britisher
1883 Freeman Impressions U.S. iv. 29
I always told my American friends that I
had rather be called a Britisher than an
Englishman, if by calling me an Englishman they meant to imply that they were
not Englishmen themselves.

The disinterested scholar, laboriously and often thanklessly at work on a dictionary, cannot fail to have first asked himself this fundamental question: for what nation am I compiling this lexicon? Murray's identification with Victorian Britain and his sense of the importance of the Scottish scholarly tradition to that cultural hegemony clearly inspired his labours.

The career of Noah Webster, like that of James Murray, was partly fired by an inherited Calvinism, but it was a career dedicated to overthrowing, not consolidating, an imperial hegemony. Webster had to challenge the dominating force of Johnson's dictionary and personality. And the challenge he mounted was so effective that Webster's *Dictionary of American English* became a great originating work, the scholarly equivalent of an epic poem or a prose epic like *Ulysses*.

*Published in 1828. The change in title from *A Dictionary of the American Language* (1800) reflects Webster's growing conservatism.

Webster was born in 1758 and served briefly in the American Revolution. While working as a schoolteacher he became dissatisfied with textbooks which ignored American culture. He was convinced that America needed a uniform language, its own school books and its own intellectual life. In 1783 he published his famous 'Blue-Backed Speller' or *American Spelling Book* and this initiated his concept of linguistic separation. The social and political totality of that concept is expressed in an influential pamphlet of 1778 in which he advocated the adoption of the Federal Constitution. Two years later, in his *Dissertations on the English Language*, Webster offered a powerful argument for linguistic and cultural independence.

In the *Dissertations* Webster attacks Johnson's lumpy neo-classicism, criticising him for the 'intolerable' Latinity of his style and for a pedantry which has 'corrupted the purity of our language'. He argues that it is essential for America to grow away from the concept of language and nationality which Johnson's dictionary enforces:

> As an independent nation, our honor requires us to have a system of our own, in language as well as government. Great Britain, whose children we are, and whose language we speak, should no longer be *our* standard; for the taste of her writers is already corrupted, and her language is on the decline.

Webster argues that 'uniformity of speech' helps to form 'national attachments', while local accents hinder a sense of national identity. Here his argument resembles Dante's in *De Vulgari Eloquentia*, for like Dante he is advocating a language that is common to every region without being tied to any particular locality.

In a concluding appeal, Webster states:

> Let us then seize the present moment, and establish a *national language*, as well as a national government. Let us remember that there is a certain respect due to the opinions of other nations. As an independent people, our reputation abroad demands that, in all things, we should be federal; be *national*; for if we do not respect *ourselves*, we may be assured that *other nations* will not respect us. In short, let it be impressed upon the mind of every American, that to neglect the means of commanding respect abroad, is treason against the character and dignity of a brave independent people.

Like Swift, whose Gulliver he echoes,* Webster argues for linguistic self-respect, but he does so as a separatist, not an integrationist. His classicism is national and federal, and does not aspire to a platonic norm which transcends the nationalities inhabiting different countries. This separatist idea has been influential and there now exist a *Scottish National Dictionary*, a *Dictionary of Canadianisms on Historical Principles*, and a *Dictionary of Jamaican English*.

Webster's dictionary and the concept of American English which it embodies succeeded in making that language appear to be a native growth. In Ireland, the English language has traditionally been regarded as an imposed colonial tongue, and Irish as the autochthonous language of the island. British policy was hostile to Irish and in 1904, for example, a Commissioner of National Education wrote to Douglas Hyde: 'I will use all my influence, as in the past, to ensure that Irish as a spoken language shall die out as quickly as possible.' However, as Sean De Fréine has argued, the movement away from Irish in the nineteenth century was not the product of 'any law or official regulation'. Instead it was the result of a 'social self-generated movement of collective behaviour among the people themselves'. English was the language of power, commerce and social acceptance, and the Irish people largely accepted Daniel O'Connell's view that Gaelic monolingualism was an obstacle to freedom. Particularly after the Famine, parents encouraged their children to learn English as this would help them make new lives in America.

Although the conflict between English and Irish can be compared to the struggle between Anglo-Saxon and Old British, such an analogy conceals the ironies and complexities of the problem. This is because the English language in Ireland, like English in America, became so naturalised that it appeared to be indigenous. The Irish language, however, was not completely suppressed or rejected, and it became central to the new national consciousness which formed late in the nineteenth century. As a result of the struggle for independence it was reinstated as the national language of a country which comprised three provinces and three counties of the four ancient provinces of Ireland. It forms an important part

*In 'A Voyage to Lilliput' Gulliver protests that he 'would never be an instrument of bringing a free and brave people into slavery'.

of the school syllabus in the Irish Republic, is on the syllabus of schools administered by the Roman Catholic Church in Northern Ireland, and is absent from the curricula of Northern Irish state schools.

Traditionally, a majority of Unionist Protestants have regarded the Irish language as belonging exclusively to Irish Catholic culture. Although this is a misapprehension, it helps to confirm the essentially racist ethic which influences some sections of Unionist opinion and which is also present in the old-fashioned nationalist concept of the "pure Gael". As a result, Unionist schools are monolingual while non-Unionist schools offer some counterbalance to English monolingualism. Put another way, state education in Northern Ireland is based on a pragmatic view of the English language and a short-sighted assumption of colonial status, while education in the Irish Republic is based on an idealistic view of Irish which aims to conserve the language and assert the cultural difference of the country.

Although there are scholarly studies of "Hiberno English" and "Ulster English",* the language appears at present to be in a state of near anarchy. Spoken Irish English exists in a number of provincial and local forms, but because no scholar has as yet compiled a *Dictionary of Irish English* many words are literally homeless. They live in the careless richness of speech, but they rarely appear in print. When they do, many readers are unable to understand them and have no dictionary where they can discover their meaning. The language therefore lives freely and spontaneously as speech, but it lacks any institutional existence and so is impoverished as a literary medium. It is a language without a lexicon, a language without form. Like some strange creature of the open air, it exists simply as *Geist* or spirit.

Here, a fundamental problem is the absence of a classic style of discursive prose. Although Yeats argues for a tradition of cold, sinewy and passionate Anglo-Irish prose, this style is almost defunct now. Where it still exists it appears both bottled and self-conscious, and no distinctive new style has

---

*Notably by Alan Bliss and John Braidwood. Professor Braidwood is at present compiling an Ulster Dialect Dictionary. A dictionary of Hiberno-English, which was begun under the auspices of the Royal Irish Academy, has been abandoned due to lack of funds.

replaced it. Contributors to the *Irish Times*—Owen Dudley Edwards, for example—tend to write in a slack and blathery manner, while the *Belfast Newsletter* offers only a form of rasping businessman's prose. The *Irish Press* differs from the *Irish Times* in having an exemplary literary editor, but its copy-editing is not of a high standard.* And although Irish historians often like to congratulate themselves on their disinterested purity, a glance at the prose of F.S.L. Lyons reveals a style drawn from the claggy fringes of local journalism. †

Perhaps the alternative to a style based on assorted Deasyisms ‡ is a form of ideal, international English? Samuel Beckett's prose is a repudiation of the provincial nature of Hiberno-English in favour of a stateless language which is an English passed through the Cartesian rigours of the French language. In its purity, elegance and simplicity, Beckett's language is a version of the platonic standard which Swift recommended nearly three centuries ago in his *Proposal*. Paradoxically, though, Beckett's language is both purer than Swift's and yet inhabited by faint, wistful presences which emanate from Hiberno-English.

Most people, however, demand that the language which they speak have a much closer contact with their native or habitual climate. Here, dialect is notable for its intimacy and for the bonds which it creates among speakers. Standard speech frequently gives way to dialect when people soothe or talk to small children, and sexual love, too, is often expressed through dialect words. Such words are local and "warm", while their standard alternatives can be regarded as coldly public and extra-familial. Often a clash is felt between the intimacy of

*E.g. 'Born in Rathdrum, Co. Wicklow, where her father was a flour miller, she was educated privately and later at a convent school but, when her father died, when she was 14, she was told that she would have to learn to earn her own living.' Obituary of Maire Comerford in the *Irish Press*, 16 December 1982.

† E.g. 'Nevertheless, the university remained the objective and as Charles settled into harness his work and even, apparently, his manners, improved and we learn of village cricket (he was that valuable commodity, a good wicket-keeper-batsman) and of frequent invitations to dances. And at last Cambridge materialized.' *Charles Stewart Parnell*, Chapter 1.

‡ See Mr Deasy's letter about foot-and-mouth disease in the Nestor section of *Ulysses*.

dialect—from which a non-standard accent is inseparable—
and the demands of a wider professional world where standard
speech and accent are the norm. For English people such
tensions are invariably a product of the class system, but in
Ireland they spring from more complex loyalties (listeners to
the 1982 Reith lectures will have noticed how Denis Donoghue's accent oscillates between educated southern speech
and a slight Ulster ululation).

If Donoghue speaks for a partitioned island, G.B. Thompson speaks for a divided culture:

> As to the content of the book I must confess to being ill-equipped
> to comment on it. I am not a serious student of dialect, and any
> knowledge I have of the subject comes from the fact that as a native
> of County Antrim my first "language" was the Ulster-Scots dialect
> of the area, described elsewhere in this book by G.B. Adams and by
> my fellow townsman Robert Gregg. Eventually, like so many
> others before and since, I was "educated" to the point where I
> looked upon dialect as merely a low-class, ungrammatical way of
> speaking. The essays in this book, therefore, have been a revelation
> to me, and I find myself hoping that my experience will be shared
> by others who have not as yet come to realise the full significance
> of Ulster dialect, but who may still see it as merely a source of
> humour and the language of Ulster's folk plays—the kitchen
> comedies. That it can be, and often is, incomparably humorous is
> undeniable, but it also makes for eloquence of power and beauty,
> and if this book were to do no more than help raise the popular
> conception of our dialect above the level of the after-dinner story
> it would serve a useful purpose.*

This statement was made in 1964 and with hindsight we can
see in it a slight movement of consciousness towards the
separatist idea which is now held by a significant section of
"loyalist" opinion. Nearly twenty later, Ian Adamson has
offered an account of language which is wholly separatist in
intention. It is a response to the homeless or displaced feeling
which is now such a significant part of the loyalist imagination,
and its historical teleology points to an independent Ulster
where socialist politics have replaced the sectarian divisions of
the past.

Adamson is in some ways the most interesting of recent
loyalist historians because he writes from the dangerous and
intelligent edges of that consciousness. In 'The Language of

*Preface to *Ulster Dialects: An Introductory Symposium.*

Ulster' Adamson argues that the province's indigenous language—Old British—was displaced by Irish, just as Irish was later displaced by English. In this way he denies an absolute territorial claim to either community in Northern Ireland and this allows him to argue for a concept of 'our homeland' which includes both communities. His account of an ancient British, or Cruthin, people is a significant influence on the UDA's Ulster nationalism and has helped shape that organisation's hostility to the British state.

Where the IRA seeks to make a nation out of four provinces, the UDA aspires to make six counties of one province into an independent nation. Official Unionism, on the other hand, tries to conserve what remains of the Act of Union and clings to a concept of nationality which no longer satisfies many of the British people whom the Unionists wish to identify with. This can now be observed in England where the movement of opinion against Cruise missiles and the continuing demonstration at Greenham Common exemplify that alternative English nationalism which is expressed in Blake's vision of Albion and reflected in the writings of E.P. Thompson. Despite the recent election, this visionary commitment is still a powerful force within English society and it is connected with the shift in public opinion in favour of withdrawal from Northern Ireland.

Adamson's historical myth necessarily involves the concept of a national language, and he is deeply conscious of the need to prove that he speaks a language which is as indigenous—or as nearly indigenous—as Irish. He argues:

> Neither Ulster Lallans nor Ulster English are "foreign" since the original dialects were modified in the mouths of the local Gaelic speakers who acquired them and eventually, after a bilingual period, lost their native tongue. These modified dialects were then gradually adopted by the Scottish and English settlers themselves, since the Irish constituted the majority population. The dialect of Belfast is a variety of Ulster English, so that the people of the Shankill Road speak English which is almost a literal translation of Gaelic.

Adamson's argument is obviously vulnerable and yet it forms part of a worthwhile attempt to offer a historical vision which goes beyond traditional barriers. The inclusive and egalitarian nature of his vision also ensures that it lacks the viciousness of the historical myth which was purveyed by the notorious Tara organisation, blessed by the Reverend Martin Smyth and other leading Unionists, and which figured so prominently in the still unresolved Kincora scandal.*

In *The Identity of Ulster* Adamson reveals that the loyalist community he speaks for is conscious of itself as a 'minority people'. Like the Irish language, Lallans—or Ulster Scots—is threatened by the English language and Adamson calls for the preservation of both languages within an Independent Ulster. However, a hostile critic would argue that Adamson's work springs from a sentimental and evasive concept of 'ould dacency'. Although the leaders of the main political parties in the Irish Republic have paid at least lip service to the idea of a "pluralist" state with safeguards for minorities, it is clear that most loyalists distrust them almost as much as they distrust British politicians. Adamson therefore offers an alternative to both the Irish Republic and the United Kingdom. But one of the weaknesses in his argument is an uncertainty about the status and the nature of the English language in Ireland. He sees Ulster Scots as oppressed by educated "Ulster English"—

---

*'On 28 June 1970 Ireland's Heritage Orange Lodge was founded. This was largely a reflection of McGrath's ideas although the Lodge had originally been associated with St Mary's Church of Ireland on Belfast's Crumlin Road and many members shared an obscure sense of Irish identity. It seems to me that many Ulster Protestants have an identity crisis. They don't really like to think of themselves as British, and the Irish Republic has become a foreign nation, with strange ways, to most Protestants. The Lodge did however seem to awaken in many a sense of Irishness which was not uncomfortable. It seems that the objective in having an "Irish" Orange Lodge was to provide a legitimate means of promoting McGrath's ideas.

'Rev. Martin Smyth and Rev. John Bryans, who was also known as a British Israelite though a non-militant one and was Grand Master of the Orange Order at the time, took part in the inauguration of the Lodge. We sang a hymn from McGrath's hymn book, "Let me carry your cross for Ireland Lord" which had been written by Thomas Ashe, an IRA hunger-striker who died in a Dublin jail in 1917. Dr Hillery, the Irish Minister for External Affairs at the time, corresponded with the Lodge soon after it was founded and two Irish Government Bulletins were produced depicting the Lodge Banner and carrying the correspondence. McGrath earlier proposed that the flags of the four Irish provinces be carried but rejected any suggestion that the six county Ulster flag be carried.' Roy Garland in the *Irish Times*, 15 April 1982.

the provincial language of Official Unionism, for example—but he lacks a concept of Irish English. This is because Adamson, like G.B. Thompson, is unwilling to contemplate the all-Ireland context which a federal concept of Irish English would necessarily express. Such a concept would redeem many words from that too-exclusive, too-local usage which amounts to a kind of introverted neglect. Many words which now appear simply gnarled, or which 'make strange' or seem opaque to most readers, would be released into the shaped flow of a new public language. Thus in Ireland there would exist three fully-fledged languages—Irish, Ulster Scots and Irish English. Irish and Ulster Scots would be preserved and nourished, while Irish English would be a form of modern English which draws on Irish, the Yola and Fingallian dialects, Ulster Scots, Elizabethan English, Hiberno-English, British English and American English. A confident concept of Irish English would substantially increase the vocabulary and this would invigorate the written language. A language that lives lithely on the tongue ought to be capable of becoming the flexible written instrument of a complete cultural idea.

Until recently, few Irish writers appear to have felt frustrated by the absence of a dictionary which might define those words which are in common usage in Ireland, but which do not appear in the *OED*. This is probably because most writers have instinctively moulded their language to the expectations of the larger audience outside Ireland. The result is a language which lives a type of romantic, unfettered existence—no dictionary accommodates it, no academy regulates it, no common legislative body speaks it, and no national newspaper guards it. Thus the writer who professes this language must either explain dialect words tediously in a glossary or restrict his audience at each particular "dialectical" moment. A writer who employs a word like "geg" or "gulder" or Kavanagh's lovely "gobshite", will create a form of closed, secret communication with readers who come from the same region. This will express something very near to a familial relationship because every family has its hoard of relished words which express its members' sense of kinship. These words act as a kind of secret sign and serve to exclude the outside world. They constitute a dialect of endearment within the wider dialect.

In the case of some northern Irish writers—John Morrow,

for example—dialect words can be over-used, while southern Irish writers sometimes appear to have been infected by Frank Delaney's saccharine gabbiness. However, the Irish writer who excludes dialect words altogether runs the risk of wilfully impoverishing a rich linguistic resource. Although there might be, somewhere, a platonic Unionist author who believes that good prose should always be as close as possible to Standard British English, such an aspiration must always be impossible for any Irish writer. This is because the platonic standard has an actual location—it isn't simply free and transcendental—and that location is the British House of Commons. There, in moments of profound crisis, people speak exclusively 'for England'. On such occasions, all dialect words are the subject of an invisible exclusion-order and archaic Anglo-Norman words like "treason" and "vouch" are suddenly dunted into a kind of life.

There may exist, however, a type of modern English which offers an alternative to Webster's patriotic argument (Imagist poetry, for example, is written in a form of minimal international English). Beckett's language is obviously a form of this cosmopolitan English and some Irish writers would argue that this is the best available language. By such an argument, it is perfectly possible to draw on, say, French and Irish without being aligned with a particular concept of society. For creative writers this can adumbrate a pure civility which should not be pressed into the service of history or politics.

This is not the case with discursive writers who must start from a concept of civil duty and a definite cultural affiliation. Discursive prose is always committed in some sense or other and it is dishonest to pretend that it isn't. Historiography and literary criticism are related to journalism, however much historians of the new brahmin school resist such an "impure" relation. Indeed, a language can live both gracefully and intensely in its literary and political journalism. Unfortunately, the establishment of a tradition of good critical prose, like the publication of *A Dictionary of Irish English* or the rewriting of the Irish Constitution, appear to be impossible in the present climate of confused opinions and violent politics. One of the results of this enormous cultural impoverishment is a living, but fragmented speech, untold numbers of homeless words, and an uncertain or a derelict prose.

BIBLIOGRAPHY

G.B. Adams, ed.	*Ulster Dialects: An Introductory Symposium* (1964)
Ian Adamson	'The Language of Ulster' in *The Identity of Ulster* (1982)
A.C. Baugh	*A History of the English Language* (1965)
Alan Bliss	*Spoken English in Ireland: 1600-1740* (1979)
John Braidwood	'Ulster and Elizabethan English' in *Ulster Dialects* *The Ulster Dialect Lexicon* (1969)
H.W. Fowler	*A Dictionary of Modern English Usage* (1965)
James Root Hulbert	*Dictionaries British and American* (1955)
Samuel Johnson	Preface to *A Dictionary of the English Language* (1755)
	'The History of the English Language' in *A Dictionary of the English Language*
H.L. Mencken	*The American Language* (1937)
James Milroy	*Regional Accents of English: Belfast* (1981)
James A.H. Murray	*The Evolution of English Lexicography* (1900)
K.M. Elisabeth Murray	*Caught in the Web of Words: James Murray and the Oxford English Dictionary* (1977)
Diarmaid Ó Miurithe, ed.	*The English Language in Ireland* (1977)
John Pepper	*What a Thing to Say* (1977)
Jonathan Swift	*A Proposal for Correcting, Improving, and Ascertaining the English Tongue* (1712)
G.B. Thompson	Preface to *Ulster Dialects*
Noah Webster	*The American Spelling Book* (1783)
	Dissertations on the English Language (1789)

The Aesthetic Fenian: Oscar Wilde

In the spring of 1882, Oscar Wilde travelled to a huge mining town in the Rocky Mountains called Leadville where he lectured the miners on the 'secret of Botticelli'. A fortnight later, he gave a lecture at the state university of Nebraska and afterwards the undergraduates took him out to the state penitentiary where he saw:

> Poor odd types of humanity in hideous striped dresses making bricks in the sun, and all mean-looking, which consoled me, for I should hate to see a criminal with a noble face. Little whitewashed cells, so tragically tidy, but with books in them. In one I found a translation of Dante, and a Shelley. Strange and beautiful it seemed to me that the sorrow of a single Florentine in exile should, hundreds of years afterwards, lighten the sorrow of some common prisoner in a modern gaol, and one murderer with melancholy eyes—to be hung they told me in three weeks—spending that interval in reading novels, a bad preparation for facing either God or Nothing.

With hindsight, it is easy to regard this flip moment from a letter to Helena Sickert as one of those luminous recognitions in which a writer discovers both a subject and a proleptic image that fits him to his biography. Wilde was to become a 'common prisoner', wear convict dress, read Dante in Reading Gaol and write a great and scarifying ballad about a murderer's execution. However, what fascinated him in 1882 was the image of that tidy, white, utilitarian building with books of poems inside it. What relation could Dante and Shelley possibly have to its state architecture? What relation had his lecture on Botticelli to the society of Leadville? What was his own relation to late Victorian society?

Joyce's answer to the last question was that Wilde made the mistake of becoming 'court jester to the English'. Although Joyce praised Wilde for his distinctive qualities of 'keenness, generosity, and a sexless intellect', he aligned him with

---

The Last Testament of Oscar Wilde: A Novel by Peter Ackroyd.
The Importance of Being Constance: A Biography of Oscar Wilde's Wife by Joyce Bentley.
Mrs Oscar Wilde: A Woman of Some Importance by Anne Clark Amor.

Sheridan, Goldsmith and Shaw in seeing him as a clown figure. The implied parallel is with Tom Moore, that paradigm of the Irish artist as *entryiste*, entertainer and harmless fool. But the comparison cannot explain the tragically symbolic pattern of Wilde's life: that story of 'my Neronian hours, rich, profligate, cynical, materialistic', followed by his trials, conviction, imprisonment, exile and death.

Before Wilde's self-destructive vanity and narcissistic love for Lord Alfred Douglas impelled him to prosecute the Marquis of Queensberry, his position had been that of an ironic dandy in a brutalised and hypocritical society. Wilde defined dandyism as 'the assertion of the absolute modernity of Beauty' and by this definition the dandy lives at the very forefront of the spirit of the age. Nowadays the ethic of dandyism—living at the sharpest, the most advanced, pitch of consciousness—is represented by punk rockers whose heroic nihilism reflects and mocks certain dominant social values. There is a strong self-punishing, sometimes suicidal, element in dandyism and as a result its apparent superficiality can become a form of extreme and exemplary integrity. Describing himself and his fellow convicts in *De Profundis*, Wilde exclaims: 'Our very dress makes us grotesques. We are the zanies of sorrow. We are clowns whose hearts are broken. We are specially designed to appeal to the sense of humour.' Like punks, the convicts reflect back through their dress their victimisation by an ugly and unjust society, And Wilde moves immediately from this to describe how he stood for half an hour handcuffed on the centre platform at Clapham Junction, 'in the grey November rain surrounded by a jeering mob'.

At the height of his fame and social success, Wilde's position was similar to that of an artist in a totalitarian society. There is a terse prose-poem, 'Pan Cogito's Thoughts on Hell', in which the Polish poet Zbigniew Herbert gives a parabolic account of such an artist's position:

> Contrary to popular belief, the lowest circle of hell is not inhabited either by despots, matricides or those who are seekers after the flesh. It is a refuge for artists, full of mirrors, pictures and instruments.
>
> [*trans. Adam Czerniawski*]

Here, Beelzebub guarantees his artists 'peace, good food and total isolation from infernal life'. Wilde's dedication to luxurious consumption ('the clear turtle soup, the luscious ortolans

195

…wonderful *pâtés*, marvellous *fine champagne*') resembles Herbert's parable translated into capitalist terms. Had Wilde not made an essentially moral repudiation of prudential moderation and caution, he could have remained a gourmandising entertainer in the lowest circle of hell. But as he nurtured a deep hatred of his society and was drawn to attitudes which derive from anarchism, socialism and republicanism, he took the ironic and subversive temper of his dissidence to the logical extreme of martyrdom and humiliation.

Such an assertion depends crucially on how we interpret certain moments that blip in and out of Wilde's biography. Did he make an active decision not to flee the country after the failure of his case against Queensberry? Or did he simply dither until the detectives knocked on the door of Douglas's suite in the Cadogan Hotel? The legal authorities hoped that he would flee and his friends repeatedly urged him to catch the Dover train. He kept saying 'It is too late' and 'The train has gone', and he remained in the hotel all afternoon until the detectives arrived either at 6.30, according to H. Montgomery Hyde, or 'between 7 and 8 o'clock', according to Hesketh Pearson. Hyde argues that Wilde 'could not make up his mind what to do, until it was made up for him by the force of events'. Pearson evasively maintains that Wilde was 'partially paralysed by the shock' and 'half-hypnotised by the picture of himself as one predestined to suffer'.

The jury at Wilde's first trial disagreed and was discharged. Wilde was released on bail and a gang of Queensberry's toughs hunted him from hotel to hotel. Shortly before 1 a.m. he arrived at his mother's house in Chelsea, his elder brother opened the door and Wilde said 'Give me shelter, Willie. Let me lie on the floor or I shall die on the streets.' Yeats, hearing of this, asked various Irish writers to give him letters of sympathy for Wilde and called at the house. Willie Wilde told Yeats he supposed they wanted his brother to run away and Yeats replied that he did not advise this and nor did the others. Willie then said that Oscar could escape but 'he has resolved to stay, to face it out, to stand the music like Christ'. And Willie also said that although he and Oscar were on bad terms 'he came to me like a wounded stag, and I took him in'.

Lady Wilde appears to have exerted a strong influence at this crisis: she imagined Wilde in the dock, defying the authorities rather like Robert Emmet, and she said she would never speak to him again if he fled the country. Lady Wilde was a famous patriotic poet (she published under the name 'Speranza') and was closely associated with the Fenian Movement. In 1882, Wilde told a lecture audience in San Francisco that Smith O'Brien, one of the leaders of the abortive uprising of 1848, was the 'earliest hero of my childhood', and he said that he had been trained by his mother to love and reverence the Fenians 'as a Catholic child is the saints of the calendar'.

Although this statement might appear to have been tailored for an Irish-American audience, Wilde was to express a similar conviction seven years later in a bitter review which he published in the *Pall Mall Gazette*. Discussing J.A. Froude's novel, *The Two Chiefs of Dunboy: An Irish Romance of the Last Century*, Wilde attacks Froude's patronising ignorance and then states:

> If in the last century she [England] tried to govern Ireland with an insolence that was intensified by race hatred and religious prejudice, she has sought to rule her in this century with a stupidity that is aggravated by good intentions.

By current standards, this is an unusually extreme statement for an expatriate Irish writer to make, and one result of the more moderate and ambivalent contemporary attitude is that critics nowadays believe that Irish writers have always been similarly moderate. Thus the influence of the Fenians on Wilde, Yeats and Joyce has been overlooked or minimised, and their work has been distorted in order to make it more easily assimilable. It would appear that such a misreading will only be rectified when Irish Studies is established as an academic discipline which is similar to, but distinct from, American Studies and English Studies.

The iconography of Wilde's downfall—wounded stag and Christ—which Yeats designs in *Autobiographies* links him to Parnell and to a potent combination of Paterian aestheticism, homoeroticism and Christianity. Yeats is using that metaphor of the hunted animal which Richard Ellmann has shown to be a traditional image that was 'applied to Parnell in his last phase' and adopted by Yeats and Joyce. In *Ulysses*, Joyce designs an analogy between Parnell and 'our saviour', while the aesthetic identification with Christ can be seen in this passage from a sermon which Pater's ex-pupil, Gerard Manley Hopkins, delivered in 1879:

There met in Jesus Christ all things that can make man lovely and loveable. In his body he was most beautiful...They tell us that he was moderately tall, well built and slender in frame, his features straight and beautiful, his hair inclining to auburn, parted in the midst, curling and clustering about the ears and neck as the leaves of a filbert, so they speak, upon the nut.

In *De Profundis*, Wilde insists rather too self-consciously on his imitation of Christ and it would appear that both he and Hopkins saw Christ as the perfect aesthete. Thus Wilde had to make a conscious decision to 'stand the music', because had he fled he would have betrayed both his art and his maimed nationhood.

Like Hopkins, Joyce and Yeats, Wilde possessed a temperament that was fundamentally hardline, theological, extreme, and incapable of moderation or compromise. Wilde directed his intellectual 'keenness' against the philistine complacency of the Victorian middle class, and in *The Importance of Being Earnest* he turns a nihilistic upper-class English irony against the stodgy certainties of Victorian Britain:

> 'Really, if the lower orders don't set us a good example, what on earth is the use of them? They seem, as a class, to have absolutely no sense of moral responsibility.'

It seems that the ironic artist admires the sort of people who might, say, shelter Lord Lucan and regard the police as comic and tasteless vulgarians. Yet at the same time Wilde is asking his audience how they can belong to such a class-ridden and hypocritically moralistic society? Why does the middle class—a class that preaches hard work to the working class it exploits—not realise that the upper class regards its values with derision? This point is made by a stage direction in act three: *'Enter Jack followed by Algernon. They whistle some dreadful popular air from a British Opera.'* It would seem that Wilde is playing a set of Sloane Rangers against the imperial sentiments of those who like Gilbert and Sullivan and read the *Daily Express*.

Wilde's essential disaffection from the values of his society is the real subject of some hostile verses which were published in *Punch* two weeks before his first trial:

Is *this* your 'Culture', to asphyxiate
   With upas-perfume sons of English race,
With manhood-blighting cant-of-art to prate,
   The jargon of an epicene disgrace?

For *Punch*, Wilde and the aesthetic movement are part of a conspiracy to corrupt 'our boys', and its anonymous versifier concludes his prejudicial attack by exclaiming:

> If such be 'Artists', then may Philistines
> Arise, plain sturdy Britons as of yore,
> And sweep them off and purge away the signs
> That England e'er such noxious offspring bore!*

This is the obverse of Wilde's threat, after the banning of *Salomé*, to take out French citizenship. *Punch* is suggesting that artists are foreign subversives who ought to be forcibly repatriated.

It would be a mistake to enforce a simple polarity between 'plain sturdy Britons' and decadent aesthetes, because there is an interesting passage in *De Profundis* where Wilde anticipates that particular form of English sensibility which belongs to Edward Thomas, the Georgian poets and the early Lawrence:

> We call ourselves a utilitarian age, and we do not know the uses of any single thing. We have forgotten that Water can cleanse, and Fire purify, and that the Earth is mother to us all. As a consequence our Art is of the Moon and plays with shadows, while Greek art is of the Sun and deals directly with things. I feel sure that in elemental forces there is purification, and I want to go back to them and live in their presence...I tremble with pleasure when I think that on the very day of my leaving prison both the laburnum and the lilac will be blooming in the gardens, and that I shall see the wind stir into restless beauty the swaying gold of the one, and make the other toss the pale purple of its plumes so that all the air shall be Arabia for me.

Wilde's Paterian prose has the texture of some cheap alloy and is unable to grasp the natural authenticity it invokes. Nevertheless, in this anticipation of Thomas's aesthetic ruralism and Lawrence's evangelical prose, Wilde's idea of freedom ceases to be urbane and becomes temporarily romantic and Wordsworthian.

Peter Ackroyd is aware of Wilde's relation to the Young Ireland movement and in his fictional account of Wilde's last months in Paris he makes a courageous attempt to align his subject with the Irish libertarian tradition. Wilde's enemies

---

*Quoted by R.K.R. Thornton in his recent and helpful study, *The Decadent Dilemma* (1983).

...mocked me also because my utter want of seriousness represented a terrible threat to all their values. I was a Nihilist of the imagination, in revolt against my period—although I could hardly be accused of shedding blood, I used the weapons which were closest to hand, for they were those which my own class had fashioned for me.

Unfortunately, Ackroyd adds to his imitation of Wilde's prose a certain explicatory earnestness which leaves nothing to the imagination:

I am Solomon and Job, both the most fortunate and the least fortunate of men. I have known the emptiness of pleasure and the reality of sorrow.

Ackroyd's Wilde tends to spell things out for the reader and to present himself as the victim of several melodramatic situations. He is the illegitimate son of Smith O'Brien and he is also the victim of an establishment cover-up designed to placate Queensberry by enforcing Wilde's prosecution. (Lord Drumlanrigg, Queensberry's eldest son, was Lord Rosebery's private secretary and in the novel Queensberry threatens to reveal evidence of a homosexual relationship between them.) This is a clever idea—Rosebery was Prime Minister from March 1894 to June 1895 and Drumlanrig was killed when his gun exploded in October 1894. In Ackroyd's version Drumlanrig believes he has betrayed Rosebery and commits suicide. Sadly, Ackroyd wastes this provocative narrative opportunity by devoting only a few sentences to the possible scandal which he has so tantalizingly aired.

Although it is pointless to accuse a novelist of getting his facts wrong, it is hard to see why A.2.11, the Reading convict named Prince about whom Wilde wrote angrily to the *Daily Chronicle*, should appear as 'King' in this story. Wilde's account of this prisoner's treatment is so horrific that it would have been an act of piety and compassion to get his name right. There are other moments which are similarly inauthentic and the result is another exercise in Victorian pastiche, a fictional genre which deserves to be neglected for a century or two.

In a keenly symbolic image Ackroyd's Wilde states: 'I was the Juggernaut, heaped with flowers, which crushes all those who come near it.' This image belongs to a mode of existential feminist biography which could give an account of Constance Mary Lloyd's experience. As the ground of a biographer's attitude to subject and personality, it might help to detach

Constance from her subordinate biographical role and centre the major narrative on her. Although it is possible to intuit the terrible personal tragedy which she suffered, neither of her biographers is able to create an autonomous personality, an integrity of experience, or equivalent centre of self, which was uniquely her own.

Joyce Bentley offers this account of the Wildes' honeymoon:

> Constance, looking radiant and wearing an exquisite creation which set every head turning, was enjoying herself immensely. Accompanied by the impeccably dressed Oscar, swinging a silver-topped cane, she presented herself to the public at large. The Eiffel Tower, the Bois de Boulogne, the Sacré Coeur: Constance was familiar with them all, but, heightened by the consciousness of love, they achieved another dimension of splendour.

Anne Clark Amor's prose is less pestered with clichés, but she too must see Constance through Oscar, instead of establishing her as a separate personality. Thus Amor says at one point, 'The name of Mrs Oscar Wilde really counted for something now in women's political circles', and like Bentley she appears to find Oscar more fascinating than Constance.

This is partly because this type of biography is so much more difficult to write than that of an established literary figure—it demands a semi-fictional, semi-*annaliste* treatment which can compensate for the absence of immediate source material and documentation. Constance Wilde did publish some journalism, but her life and opinions are much less accessible than her husband's and she is accordingly more difficult to establish in print. I suspect that Lady Windermere is a version of Constance and wish that her biographers could have brought her to life. Both write in a breezy manner which conceals the suffering of someone whom Wilde broke on the wheel of his enormous egotism. Oscar's tragedy has attracted much attention, but Constance's deeper tragic experience still waits a chronicler who has a more complete feminist vision. Feminist biography is a new and inspiring literary mode which aims to alter current perceptions and create permanent aesthetic forms. By rigorously respecting the autonomy of its subject it can create an absolutely modern style, an innovating beauty. Meanwhile, Bentley and Amor help us to recognise something of the suffering Wilde caused when he unleashed 'the tiger, Life' on his family.

Shadow of the Gunmen

Towards the end of his life Yeats was asked whether he regretted the partition of Ireland? No, the national poet replied, he did not. The Northern Irish were 'such unpleasant people' that he hoped the country would never be reunited. Thus Yeats's obsessive invocations to 'unity of being'—i.e. a sinewy nonchalance or *sprezzatura*—did not apply to the country whose partial independence he had done so much to inspire. Now that Irish unity is again being discussed, it's essential to consider the paradoxical, even lop-sided nature of Yeats's nationalism.

Yeats sang, he insisted, 'to sweeten Ireland's wrong', and his lyrics depend crucially on symbolic ideas of mystery and power: 'that most ancient race', a 'great wind of love and hate', the aggressively sexual Cuchulain. He imagined Dark Rosaleen nailed to the 'rood of time' and by his careful choice of that Anglo-Saxon word 'rood' he suggested that Ireland was impaled upon English history, a coarse cross that was all hard, sharp angles, geometrically regular and punitive.

The problem is that in adopting this tendentious manner Yeats nourished his imagination on 'the old pap of racial hatred', as Joyce said of Patrick Pearse's Gaelic classes. He drew freely, therefore, on savage ideas of blood, earth, race, myth. And so there falls across Yeats's imagination always that 'shadow of a gunman' which Sean O'Casey so subversively observed. And like Donal Davoren in O'Casey's comedy, Yeats is at times a foolishly sentimental nationalist, 'poet and poltroon, poltroon and poet'.

Often there is a "poltroonery" in Yeats's diction: he cements his lines 'silver-proud' and then pesters them with ramparts, towers, helmets, swords and 'fiery blood'. In offering this phallocentric vision, he imagines an Ireland which appears to be entirely surrounded by semen. He is in the various current senses of the word a "producer" of images and his libertarian paganism is always fiercely and heroically chill: 'Cold as the March wind his eyes'. As a result, his work reeks of

---

W.B. Yeats: The Poems, a new edition edited by Richard J. Finneran. *Editing Yeats's Poems* by Richard J. Finneran.

strange salts which aim to rouse the torpid reader and set sparks flying in our blood and speech.

And yet both the Irish Free State and its successor, the Irish Republic, were hostile to libertarian ideas—divorce was forbidden and censorship introduced. Yeats protested on behalf of 'his people'—i.e. the Anglo-Irish whom he fatuously termed 'one of the great stocks of Europe'—but as an Irish nationalist he acquiesced in confused bitterness. Like the very old man in that marvellous, self-lacerating play *The Death of Cuchulain*, he shouted at reality: 'sciolists all, pickpockets and opinionated bitches...I spit! I spit! I spit!' Instead of attacking specific targets and injustices, he substituted a formless mystic rage for that secular alternative which, as a Freemason, had always been open to him.

Yeats the canny, unacknowledged mason is present at the funeral of his uncle, George Pollexfen, 'the astrologer':

> And Masons drove from miles away
> To scatter the Acacia spray
> Upon a melancholy man
> Who had ended where his breath began.

Rather like Raleigh and his fellow poets throwing sonnets into Spenser's grave, the ritual farewell appeals to Yeats, and yet he spent his life denouncing those secular, egalitarian, rational ideas which are, at least historically, at the basis of Freemasonry. He was self-consciously old-fashioned and unlike O'Casey was quite incapable of identifying with socialism, feminism or any movement which depended upon what he scorned as 'Whiggish' notions of progress. This means that if Yeats were able to read the New Ireland Forum Report's most important recommendation that a 'unitary state' be established which 'would seek to unite in agreement the two major identities and traditions in Ireland' he might wonder if his long fight had not been a complete 'folly'. The great theocratic gazebo he had helped to tack together must give way to something constructed on more level, and more 'unpleasant' foundations.

It remains to be seen whether the noble, inspiring, secular language of the Forum Report will be enabled to take root in Ireland or whether it will wither like those Acacia sprays. Yeats's readers, however, must be gladdened by Richard Finneran's scrupulous new edition of the poems. He has added more than 120 that were not in the *Collected Poems* which this edition supersedes, and he has striven always to be true to Yeats's final intentions.

Inevitably, the 'new' poems which Finneran includes are a mixed bag: 'Cuchulain has killed kings' (a song from the play *On Baile's Strand*) is superb, and although the Parnell-elegy 'Mourn—And Then Onward!' is flaccid rhetoric it is essential to our appreciation of Yeats. Again, though there are sound editorial reasons for ending Yeats's lyric poems with 'Politics' rather than with 'Under Ben Bulben', the effect is rather like finding a molehill where you expected a mountain.

Finneran is an exemplary scholar and his arguments in his crisp apologia, *Editing Yeats's Poems*, are always convincing. Nevertheless, we have grown accustomed to watching lust and rage 'dance attention' on the poet's old age ('The Spur'). Finneran prefers 'dance attendance', though to my hyperborean ear there is a certain nougatine softness and medieval falseness in that word 'attendance', and it also backs up an unhelpful internal rhyme on 'dance'. The word 'attention' is altogether tougher, terser, sprightlier, and it is quite free from the ersatz feudalism Yeats often affects.

Of course, Yeats *is* the greatest poet in English this century—he is magnificent and magniloquent—but we must learn to cast a cold eye on his imaginative extremism. The Yeats who supported 'the gunmen on both sides' during the Irish Civil War is a figure whom a hypothetical new Ireland may come to regard with a certain wry and wary coolness.

In the Beginning was the Aeneid: On Translation

Perhaps all verse translation must begin and end with a version of the *Aeneid*, or with an essentially Virgilian concept of art's relation to society? In these islands, the first translator of Virgil was Gavin Douglas whose *Eneados* was completed in 1513. Although my *Concise Oxford Dictionary of English Literature* appropriates Douglas as the earliest translator of the classics 'into English', his version was of course written in Scots and is an ennobling monument to Scotland's separate cultural identity.

Douglas addresses Virgil as:

> Thou peirles perle, patroun of poetry,
> Roys, regester, palm, lawrer, and glory,
> Chosyn charbukkil, cheif flour, and cedyr tre,
> Lantarn, laid stern, myrrour, and A per se.

For Douglas, Virgil is a holy, original and perfect figure, a divine law-giver who inspires his readers with the pure form and essence of culture. He is end and beginning, both cedar tree and 'A per se'. And as James Kinsley suggests, Virgil's best translators acquire something of his luminous stature: 'the ancient author becomes culturally effective, and the translator a "noble collateral" with him'.

Henry Howard, Earl of Surrey, relied heavily on Douglas's *Eneados* when he translated books two and four of Virgil's epic into English. Surrey rejected Douglas's use of rhyming couplets and drew on Italian *verso sciolto* to create the earliest form of blank verse in English. His lines are often supple and beautiful, and his translation is a remarkable pioneering work, a rich seed which has produced a sacred wood. However, it wasn't until Dryden's translation of 1697 that the *Aeneid* became naturalised as a major English poem. Like Gavin Douglas, Dryden writes out of pride in his nation and native language, and he aims to

---

Poetry and Metamorphosis by Charles Tomlinson.
Conversation with the Prince and Other Poems by Tadeusz Różewicz, translated by Adam Czerniawski.
An Empty Room by Leopold Staff, translated by Adam Czerniawski.

create a consolidating, monumental work. In a long, dedicatory preface he states that his expressed confidence in his own translation may appear arrogant 'yet is intended for the honour of my country'. He attacks the 'affected purity' of the French language and asserts that the self-conscious perfectionism of French writers has 'unsinewed' their heroic verse.

Although Dryden is a much more cautious prose writer than Yeats, he translates the *Aeneid* in a masterful, dominating style which is even more confident than Yeats's mature verse. Its firm, architectonic power can be felt in these lines:

An age is ripening in revolving fate,
When Troy shall overturn the Grecian state,
And sweet revenge her conquering sons shall call,
To crush the people that conspired her fall.
Then Caesar from the Julian stock shall rise,
Whose empire ocean, and whose fame the skies
Alone shall bound; whom, fraught with eastern spoils,
Our heaven, the just reward of human toils,
Securely shall repay with rights divine;
And incense shall ascend before his sacred shrine.
Then dire debate, and impious war, shall cease,
And the stern age be softened into peace:
Then banished faith shall once again return,
And Vestal fires in hallowed temples burn.

Virgil identifies Aeneas's founding of Rome with Augustus's long stable rule, and Dryden's version is informed by his experience of civil war, restoration, rebellion and the Williamite revolution. Dryden had a fundamentally Hobbesian love of law and order, and his career was a slippery mixture of principled conviction and clever accommodation to the ruling powers. Although he lacked Milton's heroism, his position after the Glorious Revolution resembled Milton's after the Restoration, and in a postscript to his translation he sighs shrewdly, ''Tis enough for me, if the government will let me pass unquestioned.' However, there is a curious moment in his preface where he goes out of his way to assert that Virgil was 'still of republican principles in his heart'. He then contrives to make Augustus sound like a constitutional monarch and so edges a step closer to the new Whig establishment which had stripped him of the laureateship and given it to his old enemy, Shadwell. This covert effort at rapprochement is made overt by the plates of Aeneas in the first edition which make him resemble William III, and the initiative is emphasized by the other plates which carry dedications to members of the royal family. Like Virgil, Douglas and Surrey, Dryden identifies with the establishment and so must see his translation as a central pillar of the state and not as a dissident's challenge to it.

A hostile critic would call Dryden an opportunist, but it would be more accurate to say that he is attempting to heal old wounds and soften his 'stern age' into peace. Similarly, C. Day Lewis's translation of the *Aeneid* (1952) might be regarded as a shrewd strategy by an establishment operator who hoped one day to succeed Masefield as poet laureate. More charitably, it could be argued that Day Lewis's translation had patriotic inspirations in the movement of consciousness that led to the Festival of Britain. Also, Day Lewis was writing for radio and his version therefore has significant connections with the democratic idea of "court" poetry and drama which MacNeice and other members of the thirties generation brought to the BBC.

In his translation, Day Lewis rejects Dryden's impetuous, often Homeric, style in favour of a six-stress metre which allows him to protract a line to seventeen syllables or shorten it to twelve. This, he explains, is the range between 'a full Latin-hexameter line and an alexandrine'. The result is a fresh and relaxed translation which has affinities with Whitman's free verse and with the egalitarian ideas that inform it:

I tell about war and the hero who first from Troy's frontier,
Displaced by destiny, came to the Lavinian shores,
To Italy—a man much travailed on sea and land
By the powers above, because of the brooding anger of Juno,
Suffering much in war until he could found a city
And march his gods into Latium, whence rose the Latin race,
The royal line of Alba and the high walls of Rome.

Although his democratic principles sometimes make him seem dreary, Day Lewis's version was appropriate to post-1945 Britain and to the great achievements of Attlee's government.

The central theme of the *Aeneid* is the establishment of national identity, and Dryden's translations of Virgil, Ovid, Juvenal, Horace and other classical authors were intended as weighty contributions to the neoclassical cultural ideal which he initiated. His intention was to turn the classical poets into living Englishmen and make them speak a noble and refined language. As Rossetti said, the only true motive for translating poetry into 'a fresh language' must be to endow 'a fresh nation...with one more possession of beauty'. The translator, therefore, can resemble a Washington or Jefferson as much as a traditional monarch, for like Aeneas he plants the old gods in a new place and a new language.

The Virgilian theme and language question are subtly explored in Brian Friel's *Translations*, a play that was first performed in the Guildhall, Derry, in 1980, and published the following year. It is set in an Irish hedge-school and although all the characters, with the exception of two British soldiers, are Gaelic speakers, the play exists as a "translation" of their speech into Irish English. Towards the end, the schoolmaster addresses his sleeping friend:

> Take care, Owen. To remember everything is a form of madness. (*He looks around the room, carefully, as if he were about to leave it forever. Then he looks at* JIMMY, *asleep again.*)
> The road to Sligo. A spring morning. 1798. Going into battle. Do you remember, James? Two young gallants with pikes across their shoulders and the *Aeneid* in their pockets. Everything seemed to find definition that spring—a congruence, a miraculous matching of hope and past and present and possibility. Striding across the fresh, green land. The rhythms of perception heightened. The whole enterprise of consciousness accelerated. We were gods that morning, James; and I had recently married *my* goddess, Caitlin Dubh Nic Reactainn, may she rest in peace. And to leave her and my infant son in his cradle—that was heroic, too. By God, sir, we were magnificent. We marched as far as—where was it?—Glenties! All of twenty-three miles in one day. And it was there, in Phelan's pub, that we got homesick for Athens, just like Ulysses. The *desiderium nostrorum*—the need for our own. Our *pietas*, James, was for older, quieter things. And that was the longest twenty-three miles back I ever made. (*Toasts* JIMMY.) My friend, confusion is not an ignoble condition.

This inspiring speech fuses memories of Nisus and Euryalus with a civilised, mock-heroic rejection of epic action. And the link Friel establishes with Homer serves to remind his audience of Joyce's epic, *Ulysses*, which was published in 1922, the year when civil war broke out in Ireland. Just as Dryden translates Virgil in a Homeric manner, so Joyce's "imitation" of the *Odyssey* has fundamental affinities with the *Aeneid*. Joyce is law-giver, cedar tree and 'A per se'. He founds a capital city and affirms a sophisticated, highly civilised, pluralistic identity which is entirely free from ethnic rancour and chauvinist aggression.

Not all translators, however, have followed Dryden and Joyce in seeing their task as a contribution to the formation of a national 'conscience' (Joyce's special definition of the word is not in the *OED*). When Ezra Pound set out to purify the English language in his *Cathay* volume of translations from the Chinese he created a pellucid international English rather than a species of American or British English. This stateless language is an enlightened and idealistic concept, and it informs the Clark Lectures which Charles Tomlinson delivered in Dryden's old college, Trinity, Cambridge, in 1982. Tomlinson is an enthusiastic admirer of Dryden whom he terms 'the Poundian figure of his age', and he also speaks inspiringly of the 'unity of European culture'. His cosmopolitan range, command of languages, knowledge of music and highly civilised idea of 'our literary heritage' impressively insist on that unity. Unfortunately, they are powerless to prevent these lectures from being often confused and sometimes deeply silly. There is a Pooterish tone in Tomlinson's acknowledgement of the 'gracious kindness' he received at Trinity, and his piercing use of 'one' has an agonized and desperate shrillness.

Speaking of several European masterpieces, Tomlinson observes:

> Sooner or later, if one hasn't already done so, one is going to encounter these works, and if one looks on Eliot as an exemplary creator, one is bound to notice what he did in reactivating passages from them.

This prissy sentence is part of an otherwise interesting discussion of Eliot's literary and musical sources which soon disappears into an assertion of Tomlinson's single idea—metamorphosis. This idea so obsesses him that he must find it everywhere. Everything turns into everything else and Eliot's idea of tradition becomes 'a conception, one might add, of the entire history of art as one vast process of metamorphosis'. Contemplating this process, Tomlinson asks: 'Wouldn't one sooner, in certain circumstances, be a tree than human?' Elsewhere he refers to something called 'the merely human' which may refer to liberal humanists, the unemployed or other unfortunates.

At times, Tomlinson appears to believe that he has been

translated into T.S. Eliot, and his puzzling reference to 'the tortures of the self-enclosed ego' suggests that he is trapped in some uncomfortably private obsession which he is unable to communicate. Elsewhere a brusquely Leavisian tone—'Canto II, of course, is an exemplary work of the utmost literary tact'—cuts across the protean Eliotese and foists an unexamined assertion on the audience. Like Leavis, Tomlinson appears to believe that bad prose is a sign of virtue:

> Thus the political Dryden—and it is a besetting sin of commentators to thrust the political references to the forefront of an imagination which digests political 'innovation' and 'act' to its own purposes— the political Dryden brings to the realisation of Ovid in English (Ovid translated) the power of his own hard-won wisdom, a wisdom then reaching, with Ovid, beyond politics towards (one is tempted to say) the origin of species.

Tomlinson's critical failure, like Iain McGilchrist's, issues from his inability to perceive that English society is at the moment deeply divided and in need of the kind of healing initiatives which Dryden's neoclassicism offered his generation. His comparison of Pound to Dryden is superficial and misleading because it ignores the question of language and national culture. Dryden writes a lovely sinewy English for the 'honour' of his country, while Pound refuses to tie his language to any particular nation. It is partly for this reason that Dryden's Virgil is much more important than his translations from Ovid, but Tomlinson's blindness to the present cultural chaos prevents him from understanding this. The new breed of semiotician would dismiss Tomlinson as a reactionary and influential élitist, though he is in fact a marginal and self-regarding critic with some resemblance to Peter Conrad. Although he is often linked with Donald Davie, Tomlinson lacks Davie's passionate critical intelligence and his observations are usually platitudinous.

Towards the end of the final lecture, 'Metamorphosis as Translation', Tomlinson recycles parts of his crisp and helpful introduction to *The Oxford Book of Verse in English Translation*. In doing so, he leaves his audience with a conclusion that should properly have been a starting-point: the relation of Douglas's *Eneados* to 'the tensions and energies of an age'. It is a lost opportunity which leaves behind a waste of splintered waffle and hollow exquisiteness.

Dryden distinguished three separate kinds of translation:

'metaphrase' or 'word by word' translation, 'paraphrase' or 'translation with latitude', and 'imitation', which is a form of free translation. Although he rejected both metaphrase and imitation, there must always be a practical need for metaphrastic prose translation (Sinclair's *Divine Comedy*, for example). And the case for imitation is made forcibly by Johnson's 'Vanity of Human Wishes' where Johnson collaborates with Juvenal to create a poem which is modern and therefore original, as well as being part of classical tradition.

Nowadays, some poets feel a slight resentment towards translations, and in his clever 'Poem Waiting to be Translated', Peter Porter asks:

Why not remember the heroes
of hard situations,
those who answered inquisitors
in fresh parables,
whose lyrical rejoinders
are assembled here
in memorial Penguins?

Porter is glancing at the work of Zbigniew Herbert and Tadeusz Różewicz, and with a slight sourness he remarks: 'I have seen with my own eyes/ a dissident poet eating whitebait/ and joking from the corner of his mouth.' The basis of his complaint is that in England the poet can be neither dissident nor dignified laureate, and is therefore condemned to be a harmless and neglected figure.

Adam Czerniawski, who has translated both Herbert and Różewicz, is one the most distinguished verse translators now writing in English. He has the rare gift of being able to translate from his native language—Polish—into a beautiful English plain style. His versions of Różewicz have a quartz-like integrity and transparency, and in 'The Survivor' the idea of a divine, Virgilian poet is invoked by this bare litany:

I seek a teacher and a master
may he restore my sight hearing and speech
may he again name objects and ideas
may he separate darkness from light.

I am twenty-four
led to slaughter
I survived.

This form of anti-poetry is born out of the Polish historical experience and its hard, pure style aims to express the inexpressible. Commenting on Czerniawski's sympathetic artistry, Michael Irwin has noted that while Miłosz's translations of Różewicz appear 'irreducible' Czerniawski improves on them by his daring elisions and sharp intelligence. The result is a poetry of 'absolute transparency' and some Polish reviewers have claimed that some of Różewicz's poems improve in Czerniawski's English.

In Poland writers are regarded as the embodiments and custodians of the national conscience, and this necessarily means that they must face or try to elude the censor (some years ago a Polish poet and translator informed me that censors have to attend regular practical criticism classes in order to spot symbolism, ambiguity, subversive irony, etc). In 'Poem of Pathos' Różewicz images the censored poet:

A poet buried alive
is like a subterranean river
he preserves within
faces names
hope
and homeland

The poet is mnemonist, oral historian, underground river, dissident—he is Virgil condemned to the underworld rather than a public figure who is acknowledged by the authorities. He is 'a teacher and a master' who can restore sight and set the alphabet to work, naming things. The Polish literary world, however, contains a number of neo-Stalinist laureates and it must be to one of them that Różewicz is referring in his conclusion:

... a poet's lie
is multilingual
as monumental
as the Tower of Babel

it is monstrous
and does not die.

It is fascinating to notice that when the Congress for Cultural Freedom despatched Robert Lowell to South America he refused to tell lies and play the part of CIA Virgil. Instead he freaked, sent telegrams to the Pope on the theme of 'America as the Roman Empire', insulted every general he met, tried to climb all the equestrian statues in Buenos Aires, and eventually proclaimed himself 'Caesar of Argentina'. He was flown back to the States in a straitjacket, his madness a form of extreme integrity.

For the Polish poet, translation is an essential part of the struggle to achieve 'conscience'. Czerniawski is therefore advancing his country's honour and self-respect by writing in the English language. At the same time he is making a notable contribution to English poetic style and it is unfortunate that D.M. Thomas's shoddy translations of Pushkin and Akhmatova should have received more attention than Czerniawski's compelling work.

Leopold Staff, who died in 1957, was one of the founding fathers of modern Polish literature and his sophisticated simplicity won the admiration of Milosz, Rozewicz, and other leading poets. In Czerniawski's translation of 'Ars' there is a Horatian terseness and a wise, unillusioned, colloquial gravity:

Look sharply ahead
But don't prophesy,
Leave that to quacks.
Difficult enough to portray what is.
I write poems slowly,
I labour like an ox.
I am patient
Like a trembling raindrop.
Time always has time.
The world's as old as the world.
Seeking novelty
You will create nothing new.

Although Staff appears consistently to reject public poetry in favour of a stoic privacy ('I hum a song by the fence/ Where they're digging spuds/ And will be planting beans'), there is a concealed social criticism in the last stanza of 'Portrait'. Staff comments on sculptural images of the male form—a powerful athlete, Donatello's knight in armour—and he concludes:

Finally Michelangelo scored
Crushing with a hammer
A marble lump of dead flesh
Which the sorrowing mother
Supports by the arms
When her son can no longer bear
His own inhuman saintliness.

The reference is obviously to the Pietas, but that phrase

'inhuman saintliness' refers to the *'terribilità'* which Michelangelo acknowledged his works possessed. This cruel pagan humanism can be seen in his statue of David and it is impossible to read Staff's lines without remembering it. Michelangelo's David, like Marlowe's Tamburlaine, is an inhuman, terrifying, Stalinist killer, and the citizens of Florence were so disturbed by their first sight of the statue that they called the figure *'il gigante'* and threw stones at it. By contrast, the Pietàs are tragic works which reject a confident human magnificence (Staff's allusion to Michelangelo's smashing of the Florentine Pietà introduces a paradoxical perfectionism). In settling for what Tomlinson would term 'the merely human', Staff offers a vision which resembles the suffering Christian humanism in the last three lines of 'The Windhover'. Like Hopkins, he rejects the vicious *sprezzatura* of military heroism and in doing so comments on his society.

During the last ten years, many Irish poets have been translated into Polish and this is partly because Poles see an analogy between their country's fate and Ireland's. Although this analogy is vulnerable at certain points (Britain, unlike the Soviet Union, seems fairly eager to make an exit from occupied territory), it means that a translation of any Irish poem into Polish has an invisible reference to the idea of being dominated by a foreign power. To translate and publish an Irish poem in Poland is therefore to make a statement which is both political and aesthetic. Ironically, this means that Irish poets who are either apolitical or mildly sympathetic to Unionism find themselves being given a radically different identity in translation.

As Seamus Deane has pointed out, the translator has been of extraordinary importance in Irish writing. There is a long tradition of translation from Gaelic into Irish English and the result is 'a kind of interstitial literature which responds to the genius of both tongues' and so effects a form of reconciliation that is far in advance of political reality. Thus the translations of Frank O'Connor, John Montague and Thomas Kinsella point towards a national identity which is as yet not fully ratified by law and international treaty. This strong and enduring autochthonous tradition of translation is complemented by a more recent interest in translating classical and European poetry into Irish English. To translate Tibullus, Dante, Nerval and Apollinaire is to offer glimpses of a new landscape, a fresh cultural initiative which may in time be embodied formally and institutionally. Translation is therefore an ambitious type of neoclassicism which helps to form conscience.

The neoclassical ideal and the theme of national identity can be traced in the most brilliant imitation to appear in these islands for many years—Paul Muldoon's 'Immram'. This long, free floating, tightly organised poem is a version of an eighth-century Irish legend, 'The Voyage of Maildun', and is cunningly relocated on the West Coast of the United States. Tennyson read the story in P. W. Joyce's *Old Celtic Romances* and versified it in 1880. He aimed to represent 'the Celtic genius' and grafted some Cromwellian battle scenes onto the much gentler original, as well as adding symbolic references to contemporary arguments between Irish nationalists and unionists.

Alluding a century later to this version, Muldoon puts Tennyson ahead of him in the revolving doors of a Hilton hotel which is a contemporary equivalent of the palace of art (in Poland this would be a piece of Stalinist cheesecake called the Palace of Culture). Translating into a language which combines American and Irish English, Muldoon designs a marvellous voyage which sets the poet's imaginative privacy inside a hallucinated cityscape of high, privatised American capitalism. This "trip" becomes a subtle exploration of the theme of identity which refuses the defining shade of green offered by an Irish American cop:

'My father, God rest him, he held this theory
That the Irish, the American Irish,
Were really the thirteenth tribe,
The Israelites of Europe.
All along, my father believed in fairies
But he might as well have been Jewish.'
His laugh was a slight hiccup.
I guessed that Lieutenant Brendan O'Leary's
Grandmother's pee was green,
And that was why she had to leave old Skibbereen.

If Muldoon is rejecting a sentimental and exclusive form of ethnic Irish nationalism, he is also concerned to examine the symbolist rejection of all forms of patriotism. He does so by transforming 'the hermit of the sea-rock' in the original legend into a derelict figure who resembles Howard Hughes:

He was huddled on an old orthopaedic mattress,
The makings of a skeleton,
Naked but for a pair of draw-string shorts.
His hair was waistlength, as was his beard.
He was covered in bedsores.
He raised one talon.
'I forgive you,' he croaked. 'And I forget.
On your way out, you tell that bastard
To bring me a dish of ice-cream.
I want Baskin-Robbins banana-nut ice-cream.'

The ultimate private billionaire issues a Stevensish request for ice-cream and this suggests that an analogy can be drawn between the autonomy of art and an absolutely self-enclosed hedonism founded on grotesque riches. Like Marvell in 'Upon Appleton House', Muldoon writes with a phantasmagoric civility which is constantly aware of the uncivil processes of history. His work shows that the enterprise of translation and imitation need not necessarily involve a Dryden-like commitment to a masterful national identity. But it does demonstrate that the translator must always be aware of the possible identities which his activity implies.

Muldoon's fluid verse line is Ovidian in its refusal of inflexible definitions, though its 'discandying' qualities and melting hallucinations owe much to the sinuous essence of Gaelic culture. By making the Gaelic original accessible to readers who are ignorant of the language Muldoon significantly aligns his highly assured use of modern English with an ancient tradition. And because the original legend concludes with a feast of reconciliation which follows Maeldun's refusal to kill his father's murderer, we make a contemporary application of the traditional story. The reader of 'Immram' perceives the modern Muldoon's very civilised rejection of those atavistic and vindictive attitudes which inform Irish history. Obliquely and gently, this extraordinary translation aims to heal and salve, just as Dryden did in his *Aeneid*.

Brief Lives

Edward Carson (1854-1935). Irish lawyer and Unionist politician who successfully led northern Irish resistance to the British government's attempts to introduce Home Rule for the whole of Ireland.

Roger Casement (1864-1916). Irish nationalist leader executed for treason in London in 1916.

Austen Chamberlain (1863-1937). British Conservative politician and statesman who was leader of the Conservative Party during the Anglo-Irish negotiations of 1921. He privately criticised the creation of the State of Northern Ireland.

Michael Collins (1890-1922). Irish revolutionary leader who played a vital part in the Anglo-Irish negotiations of 1921 and led the Free State forces against the anti-Treaty republicans during the Irish Civil War. He was killed in an ambush during the Civil War.

Robert Emmet (1778-1803). Irish republican leader who inspired the abortive uprising of 1803. Executed in Dublin after a trial during which he made a famous speech from the dock.

Lord Edward Fitzgerald (1763-1798). Irish republican leader killed while resisting arrest shortly before the 1798 rebellion.

Maude Gonne (1866-1953). Irish revolutionary with whom Yeats was in love. She married the revolutionary leader, John MacBride, in 1903.

Henry Joy McCracken (1767-1798). Northern Irish republican leader executed after the failure of the 1798 rebellion.

Constance Markiewicz, *née* Gore-Booth (1868-1927). Irish revolutionary. Minister of Labour in *Dail Eireann*. Celebrated and criticised by Yeats in 'In Memory of Eva Gore-Booth and Con Markiewicz'; also the subject of his poem 'On a Political Prisoner'.

Conor Cruise O'Brien (born 1917). Irish intellectual, writer, United Nations diplomat and politician.

William Smith O'Brien (1803-1864). A leader of the literary-political Young Ireland movement. He led a futile uprising in 1848 and was exiled to Tasmania for six years.

Daniel O'Connell (1775-1847). Known in Ireland as The Liberator, O'Connell founded the Catholic Association in 1823 and became the first of the great nineteenth-century Irish leaders in the House of Commons.

David O'Connell (born 1926). Provisional IRA leader who helped to negotiate a short-lived ceasefire with William Whitelaw in 1972.

Charles Stewart Parnell (1846-1891). A Wicklow landowner who led the struggle for Irish Home Rule in the late nineteenth century. Known as the 'uncrowned King of Ireland', he came close to securing Home Rule but lost his position as leader of the Irish parliamentary party after a divorce case in 1889.

Patrick Pearse (1879-1916). Irish revolutionary leader who delivered the proclamation of the Irish Republic from the steps of the Dublin General Post Office on Easter Monday 1916. Executed with James Connolly and other rebel leaders.

Wolfe Tone (1763-1798). A Dublin barrister who helped to found the Society of United Irishmen in 1791. He aimed to 'break the connection with England' and to unite 'Protestant, Catholic and Dissenter'. He persuaded the French Directory to launch an invasion of Ireland in 1796, but the expedition was unsuccessful and during the 1798 rebellion Tone again arranged for French help. He was captured and sentenced to death. He committed suicide.

Index

This index only covers people. Books are indexed as authors only. Where a person is the subject of an essay, or the author of a book under review, the page reference is in italics.

Some Other Bloodaxe Books

HART CRANE
Complete Poems
One of America's most important poets. Lowell called Crane
'the Shelley of my age' and 'the great poet of that generation'.
This new *Complete Poems*, based on Brom Weber's definitive
1966 edition, has 22 additional poems.

JENI COUZYN (editor)
Bloodaxe Book of Contemporary Women Poets*
Large selections—with essays on their work—by eleven leading
British poets: Sylvia Plath, Stevie Smith, Kathleen Raine, Fleur
Adcock, Anne Stevenson, Elaine Feinstein, Elizabeth Jennings,
Jenny Joseph, Denise Levertov, Ruth Fainlight and Jeni Couzyn.

FRANCES HOROVITZ
Collected Poems*
'Frances Horovitz inherits the mantle of Kathleen Raine and of
Frances Bellerby. She speaks with a woman's voice, but she
speaks of all experience. It is an honour to be able to say that
her voice is not that of the "age" but of the earth'
– Anne Stevenson.

JENNY JOSEPH
Persephone*
When Persephone returns from the underworld, winter releases
its grip on the earth. But only for a while. Entwining this timeless
story of good and evil with the modern reality, Jenny Joseph
brings Persephone alive in a haunting, hopeful and highly
original book—a novel-length story in poetry and prose.

MIROSLAV HOLUB
On the Contrary and Other Poems*
Translated by Ewald Osers
Miroslav Holub is one of the leading writers of our time. He was
first introduced to English readers with a *Selected Poems* (1967)
in the Penguin Modern European Poets series. This edition
presents a decade of new work, with a foreword by A. Alvarez.
'Miroslav Holub is one of the half dozen most important poets
writing anywhere' – Ted Hughes.

ANGELA CARTER
Come unto these Yellow Sands*
Four radio plays, one to pictures by the mad painter Richard
Dadd. People and animals (or *both*) are never what they seem:
the lady is a vampire, the bridegroom a werewolf, and Puss in
Boots is out on the tiles. Includes *The Company of Wolves*.

B.S. JOHNSON
House Mother Normal

B.S. Johnson (1933-73) was praised by Anthony Burgess as 'the only British author with the guts to reassess the novel form, extend its scope and still work in a recognisable fictional tradition'. *House Mother Normal* was his fifth and finest novel.

KEN SMITH
The Poet Reclining*

The *Selected Poems* of a major British poet: 'A poet of formidable range and strength' – *Chicago Sun-Times*. 'With Ken Smith we expect excellence...his achievement is remarkable' – *Scotsman*. 'Brilliant...impressive' – *Times Literary Supplement*.

SEAN O'BRIEN
The Indoor Park

Sean O'Brien won a Somerset Maugham Award and a Poetry Book Society Recommendation for *The Indoor Park*, his first collection of poems. 'I would back Sean O'Brien as one of our brightest poetic hopes for the Eighties' – Peter Porter, *Observer*.

DAVID CONSTANTINE
Watching for Dolphins

Constantine's second book won him the Alice Hunt Bartlett Prize, and with it the judges' praise for 'a generous, self-aware sensuality which he can express in a dazzling variety of tones on a wide range of themes'.

FLEUR ADCOCK
The Virgin & the Nightingale*

Medieval Latin poems in verse translations with facing Latin text. 'Buoyantly accurate and great fun to read' – Peter Porter. 'lively, rude and eminently readable' – Adrian Henri. 'A very high achievement' – Gavin Ewart.

EDITH SÖDERGRAN
Complete Poems*
Translated by David McDuff

When she died in poverty at 31, Edith Södergran had been dismissed as a mad, megalomaniac aristocrat by most of her Finnish contemporaries. Today she is regarded as Finland's greatest modern poet. The driving force of her visionary poetry (written in Swedish) was her struggle against TB, from which she eventually died in 1923.

*Asterisked titles are available in hardback and paperback. Other books are in paperback only.

For a complete list of Bloodaxe publications write to:
**Bloodaxe Books Ltd, P.O. Box 1SN,
Newcastle upon Tyne NE99 1SN.**